ACTIVATE

A LEADER'S GUIDE TO

PEOPLE | PRACTICES | PROCESSES

ACTIVATE

A LEADER'S GUIDE TO
PEOPLE | PRACTICES | PROCESSES

Elle Allison | Janet Clinton | John Hattie | Connie Kamm | Cathy Lassiter
Brian A. McNulty | Douglas B. Reeves | Ainsley Rose | Jay Trujillo
Stephen Ventura | Mike Wasta | Stephen White

LEAD+
LEARN
PRESS

ENGLEWOOD, COLORADO

The Leadership and Learning Center
317 Inverness Way South, Suite 150
Englewood, Colorado 80112
Phone 1.866.399.6019 | Fax 303.504.9417
www.LeadandLearn.com

Published by Lead + Learn Press, a division of Advanced Learning Centers, Inc.

Library of Congress Cataloging-in-Publication Data

Activate : A leader's guide to people, practices, and processes / Elle Allison ... [et al.].
    p. cm.
  Includes bibliographical references and index.
  ISBN 978-1-935588-11-5 (alk. paper)
1. Educational leadership. 2. School improvement programs. 3. Academic
achievement. I. Allison, Elle, 1960-
  LB2805.L3393 2011
  371.2'011--dc22

                                                                    2011015411

ISBN 978-1-935588-11-5
Printed in the United States of America

15 14 13 12 11   02 03 04 05 06 07

Contents

List of Exhibits

About the Authors

Elle Allison is cofounder and president of Renewal Coaching LLC and founder of Wisdom Out. Along with Douglas Reeves, she is author of the three-book series *Renewal Coaching: Sustainable Change for Individuals and Organizations* (2009, 2010, 2011). Elle's experience in education comes from serving as a teacher, an assistant principal, a principal, a director of school improvement, and an assistant superintendent. Elle is a graduate of the seventh National Staff Development (Learning Forward) Academy and is a member of the National Speakers Association. She earned her doctorate in organizational learning from the University of New Mexico, where she focused on issues related to coaching, consulting, wisdom, leadership, and personal and organizational change. Elle's research, writings, and keynotes addresses illuminate the nature of wisdom and develop a foundation for life strategies that assist individuals and organizations in achieving a greater good. Elle designs and leads seminars and keynotes for leaders who coach and coaches who lead. Elle can be reached at eallison@renewalcoaching.com.

Janet Clinton is an associate professor and a senior evaluator at the Centre for Program Evaluation, University of Melbourne, Victoria, Australia. Janet has considerable experience as an evaluator, psychologist, and educator, and has an extensive publication record. She has worked in Australia, New Zealand, and the USA and has been a principal investigator on many large, complex evaluations and research projects.

John Hattie is currently a professor of education and the Director of the Melbourne Education Research Institute at the University of Melbourne in Australia. One of Australia's most internationally acclaimed academics, John is the author of many articles and publications, including *Visible Learning: A Synthesis of over 800 Meta-analyses Relating to Achievement*.

Connie Kamm is a Senior Professional Development Associate with The Leadership and Learning Center. She is also the president of The KAMM Group, a company that focuses on organizational effectiveness and alignment in both education and industry. With extensive experience at the university, public school, and corporate levels, Connie brings a unique blend of real-world experience and international research to her publications and presentations. She has been active in school reform for more than 25 years and has developed keen insights into the spirit of building positive school cultures. She is noted for her dynamic process for educational change and facilitates system-wide, comprehensive accountability frameworks at the state and district levels.

Cathy J. Lassiter is a Professional Development Associate with The Leadership and Learning Center. She brings a sense of passion and energy to her work on school leadership, accountability, data, curriculum, instruction, and standards. She has worked with superintendents, state departments of education, principals, and teachers to improve leadership and instructional practices. Over the course of her 28 years in public education, Cathy was a successful middle and high school teacher working primarily with urban students. She also served in numerous leadership positions including middle school principal, project manager for federal programs, director of curriculum, instruction and staff development, and executive director of nine middle schools. Cathy has also taught courses in educational leadership at George Washington University.

Brian A. McNulty is the Vice President of Leadership Development for The Leadership and Learning Center. He has previously served as the Vice President for Field Services at Mid-continent Research for Education and Learning (McREL) and was an assistant superintendent for Colorado's Adams County School District 14 and the Assistant Commissioner of Education for the Colorado Department of Education. Brian's work and writing have been featured in books, scholarly journals, and periodicals throughout the world. An author of more than 40 publications, Brian's book *School Leadership That Works: From Research* *to Results* was a best-selling ASCD publication and was coauthored with Robert Marzano and Tim Waters. His most recent book, *Leaders Make it Happen!—An Administrator's Guide to Data Teams*, published by Lead + Learn Press and coauthored with Laura Besser, was chosen as an AASA (American Association of School Administrators) member book.

Douglas Reeves is the founder of The Leadership and Learning Center. As part of Houghton Mifflin Harcourt, a global educational leader, The Center serves school systems around the world. The author of 30 books and many articles on leadership and organizational effectiveness, Doug has twice been named to the Harvard University Distinguished Authors Series. Doug was named the Brock International Laureate for his contributions to education. He also received the Distinguished Service Award from the National Association of Secondary School Principals and the Parents Choice Award for his writing for children and parents. He is the 2010 recipient of the National Staff Development Council's Contribution to the Field Award. In the foreword to Doug's most recent book, Michael Fullan wrote, "Reeves doesn't just tell us what not to do. His research is so carefully documented and so clearly argued that we see precisely what should be our focus. . . . Reeves takes us further and deeper into the critical territory of whole system reform. He does it with such elegance and relentless insistence that we are drawn—indeed, compelled—to want to take action."

Ainsley Rose is a Professional Development Associate with The Leadership and Learning Center. He brings over 39 years in education as a teacher and as an elementary and secondary principal. As the former director of education and curriculum for the Western Quebec School Board, Ainsley was responsible for initiating many systemic changes that continue to impact teaching and learning today. Throughout his career, Ainsley has incorporated his expertise within a wide range of principles, practices, and concepts, all of which have significantly improved schools. Ainsley was recognized for his exemplary leadership in education when he was chosen to receive the Outstanding Achievement Award by the Administrators of English Schools of Quebec. With experience as an elementary and secondary classroom teacher and principal, as well as an instructor of graduate-level courses for administrators and pre-service teachers, Ainsley shares perspectives that resonate with all educators. Ainsley has presented across Canada, Bermuda, and Lusaka, Zambia, as well as the United States on a range of educational topics. Ainsley is a contributing author for many publications, including *The Teacher as Assessment Leader*, *The Principal as Assessment Leader*, *The Collaborative Teacher*, *Data Teams: The Big Picture*, and *Learning for the Future*.

Jay Trujillo is a Professional Development Associate with The Leadership and Learning Center, as well as a currently sitting high school principal. Jay has 16 years of administrative experience, including 13 years as a secondary principal at both the middle and high school levels. Jay's leadership success has earned him two-time *Principal of the Year* honors, as well as numerous accolades at the local, state, and national levels. His professional background and experience include positions as a curriculum and instruction coordinator, as Bilingual Teacher Training Program (BTTP) regional director, and multiple roles as a high school teacher (including student government leader, athletic coach, union leader, and mentor teacher). Jay works with school leaders across the country as both a leadership performance coach and trainer in effective school and leadership practices.

Stephen Ventura is a Professional Development Associate for The Leadership and Learning Center. He is a highly motivational and knowledgeable speaker who approaches high-stakes data collection and decision making armed with practical, research-based strategies. Steve is a former elementary, middle school, and high school teacher. His administrative experiences encompass those of assistant principal, principal, director, and superintendent. Through his own reality-based experiences, Steve has inspired teachers and leaders across the nation to pursue higher levels of implementation with greater focus, rigor, and clarity. In addition to his professional development work with teachers and administrators, Steve is also a frequent speaker at local and state conferences, and has contributed to several books focused on teaching, learning, and leadership. He has a strong moral aspect, intelligence, easy way with people, and saving sense of humor that support him in his life and work.

Mike Wasta is a Professional Development Associate with The Leadership and Learning Center. He served as superintendent of Bristol (Conn.) Public Schools and is currently an external consultant for the Connecticut State Department of Education. Mike led the Bristol Public Schools in adopting many of the programs and initiatives designed by The Leadership and Learning Center, including Data-Driven Decision Making, Data Teams, Holistic Accountability, Making Standards Work, Effective Teaching Strategies, and Common Formative Assessments. By instituting these practices district-wide in a comprehensive and integrated fashion, Mike has ushered in dramatic improvements in student achievement. Mike is a former classroom teacher, special education teacher, director of Pupil Personnel, and assistant superintendent. He earned his Ph.D. in special education from the University of Connecticut.

Stephen White is a nationally recognized educational consultant with proven expertise in data analysis, systems, leadership assessment, program evaluation, and school improvement that is helping to change the way educators view themselves and manage data in an era of high-stakes accountability and testing. His deep experience as a public school administrator includes 19 years of service as a superintendent, an assistant superintendent, an executive director, the CEO of a K–20 board of cooperative educational services, a high school principal, and a coordinator of special education. He is the author of several books, including *Leadership Maps, Beyond the Numbers,* and *Show Me the Proof!* and coauthor of *School Improvement for the Next Generation.* Stephen is the primary author of the PIM™ school improvement framework and the Leadership Maps, a self-assessment instrument, and has reviewed more than 2,300 school improvement plans since 2005.

Introduction

CATHY J. LASSITER

THE CORE AND SUPPORTING FUNCTIONS of any school or district must be learning and achievement for both students and adults. Given that learning is a never-ending process, school leaders will always be involved in leading change to achieve better results. But somehow leaders have come to believe that once they get a change initiative in place and working well, the work is done. In reality, they have just readied themselves for the next change coming down the line. Change can be exhausting for those who cannot accept that it is a way of life, especially in the world of education.

As we examine the changes headed for public schools today, leaders at all levels must be prepared to activate new leadership skills and focus on what will matter most in meeting new demands. According to the Alliance for Excellent Education (2011), nearly 90 percent of American students reside in states that have adopted the Common Core State Standards. The federal government, via Race to the Top grants, insists that teacher and principal evaluation processes be strengthened and tied to student results. It further insists that the lowest-performing schools be turned around. The economic crisis continues to ravage public-sector budgets, and schools are expected to do much more with much less. Indeed, change is upon us, and leading change for success under these circumstances can be daunting for even the most experienced leaders.

In this book, the authors have taken into account the challenges and demands being made on school leaders now. They offer personal success stories, compelling research, and interesting comparisons to empower the reader to embrace change and activate strategies to successfully lead change in their organizations. The book is presented in three sections, which allows the reader to understand how a simultaneous focus on developing people, implementing a few but effective practices, and consistently monitoring processes will lead to the desired results of change leaders. Each of these foci is essential to successful change leaders.

In Section 1 the authors recognize the undeniable human element at the heart of any organization, but most especially in school organizations. Change cannot occur without ongoing, focused, and planned development of the people being asked to make the change. We have no hope of conquering the challenges ahead if we do not nurture, develop, and motivate the people who work in our schools. According to Peter Drucker (1990, p. 145), "People decisions are the ultimate—perhaps the only—control of an organization. People determine the capacity of the organization." Drucker, like the researchers from Gallup, advocates a strengths-based approach to developing people into jobs that are fulfilling and satisfying to them personally and professionally. Developing our teachers and school leaders will require what Liz Wiseman calls watching native genius. In Wiseman's book *Multipliers: How the Best Leaders Make Everyone Smarter*, she asserts that leaders should become people watchers to identify those native strengths that team members exhibit and then put them to work in positions that allow them to maximize their native genius.

Building the capacity of people to enable change also involves moving them beyond work for compliance and into work from a commitment. Research shows that this can be accomplished through a mission and vision that are purpose driven (Pink, 2009). People have a genuine desire to be part of work bigger than themselves. They want to contribute to the greater good of their communities. Being clear about what their work entails, with strong connections to a shared vision, and providing feedback for growth and deliberate practice have been proven to be effective in motivating people toward a collective goal. In fact, Allison and Reeves (2009) argue that through coaching, performance is drawn out not with short-term rewards but with bone-deep conviction that our work matters far beyond quarterly objectives. The coaching approach develops the individual and the organization in service of the greater good.

Section 1 of the book, Leaders Focusing on People, shines a light on the human side of school improvement and provides strategies, insights, and real-world examples of administrators activating leadership practices which result in a more engaged and committed workforce. The first chapter begins with an inspiring story about how one principal turned a chronically low-performing high school into one of California's most improved and best-performing schools by overcoming the fear of change, creating a compelling shared vision, and recognizing and rewarding team members for their work. Chapter 2 discusses the research and powerful results of renewal coaching. With concrete tools and action plans, the author makes a strong case for coaching people to achieve greater organizational results. In Chapter 3, the author explains mindset as it relates to school leaders and describes how a growth, as opposed to a fixed, mindset is a leader's key to developing people to their full potential. Using the research of Carol Dweck, respected psychology professor and researcher at Stanford University, combined with the research by Jim Collins on Level 5 leadership featured in his book *Good to Great*, the author provides an insightful approach to leading change for all leaders. The last chapter in Section 1 provides a compelling argument about what really motivates people and how to use this intrinsic motivation to create a culture that is high performing. In a high-performance culture, change is anticipated, welcomed, and planned for. Based on research from business, education, human motivation, and execution, the five elements of a high-performance culture illustrate the inescapable role culture plays in facilitating and sustaining successful change.

Section 2 of the book brings together leadership practices that make a difference in improving adult and student learning, as well as building teams and fostering effective collaborative environments. Leaders and their teams must spend time learning together to build their collective capacity for change. In their meta-analytic study, Marzano, Waters, and McNulty (2005) found that principals need to develop shared or distributed leadership in order to effectively implement improvement practices. The days of the leader as the Lone Ranger are long gone. Leaders must be in place at every level in a school district, and everyone must be empowered to act as a leader based on its vision and mission. Our colleagues at The Leadership and Learning Center have advocated for years that a few best practices, implemented well and monitored well, can result in improved teaching and learning. It is the focus that makes the difference. In Reeves's new book, *Finding Your Leadership Focus*, he argues that even the most committed leaders with the best ideas will fail without the proper focus. He also asserts that when school leaders find their focus, the rewards are rapid and significant (Reeves, 2011).

The chapter authors in Section 2 transition from developing people to implementing leadership practices that facilitate change. Chapter 5 introduces readers to new research on the role of the leader as an evaluator—not just evaluator of staff and student data, but evaluator and decision maker on resource allocation, student course offerings, staff professional development, and the like. The view through this lens magnifies the importance for leaders to consider their role as evaluator much more deeply and thoughtfully to accelerate the change they seek. Also offering a unique perspective on effective leadership practices is the comparison of school leaders to the masters of classical and blues music made in Chapter 6. Using the leadership actions of these accomplished musicians, the author discusses activation of leadership practices that carry into the 21st century. Chapter 7 provides relevant research and action steps for leaders to activate school improvement. The author suggests leadership practices which will facilitate a paradigm shift from compliance to greater levels of staff commitment using the Data Teams process, goals development, and implementation monitoring. In Chapter 8, readers will find a novel approach to using student and teacher perception data, which was employed by the author, resulting in teachers activating a personal impetus for change. The manner in which this data was collected and presented spurred action from staff that otherwise would not have been taken. The chapter also provides insight to leaders on how to lead teachers through drawing inferences and setting priorities when using various data sets. The professional practices advocated in Section 2 will help leaders be thoughtful and strategic about where to direct their attention. In their role as evaluator, school leaders make critical decisions that affect instructional quality in many ways. The actions leaders take to meet the demands of the 21st century and the methods they use to inspire commitment among their people will make the real difference in whether they move forward or lag behind.

The third section of the book weaves in processes that activate collaborative organizations, focused on student and adult learning, through reciprocal accountability and deliberate practice. According to Michael Fullan's (2008) *The Six Secrets of Change*, the key to a successful organization is purposeful peer interaction. Leaders create processes and conditions for effective interaction. This interaction goes far beyond collaboration and serves as the social and intellectual glue of the entire organization. Fullan goes on to suggest that the intent of standardization is not to make work highly repetitive but rather to define best practices for those few elements that are crucial to success. These are tasks that everyone must do well using the best known methods. For these few aspects, which represent less than 20 percent of the daily work of teachers, there is no acceptable deviation from the defined method. In *Change Leadership*, authors Tony Wagner and Robert Kegen (2006, p. 193) suggest that leaders must understand and bring together the challenges of both organizational and individual change to successfully lead improvement processes in schools. They, too, advocate for limiting the number of priorities and staying relentlessly focused on them. They state, "it's true that if we have many improvement priorities, we actually have none" (Wagner & Kegen, 2006, p. 202).

The authors in Section 3 have taken their years of experience in school leadership to develop change processes for school leaders that are practical, focused, and enduring. In Chapter 9, the author outlines a system to connect the work from the superintendent's office to the schools and into the classrooms. Centered around improving teaching practices in all schools, in all classrooms, for all students, teams at all levels are cohesive in their efforts to bring on whole-system reform.

They report and share their work up and down the line in a systematic process of school improvement. Sharing the view of Wagner, Fullan, Reeves, and others, the author illustrates how teams can select and focus on a few high-leverage strategies and how a cohesive system of leadership leverages that work up and down the district line. In Chapter 10, the author shares an effective and practical change readiness process for determining a school's readiness level for change. The Change Readiness Assessment, discussed in this chapter, significantly increases a leader's chances of successfully implementing a change. The process engages leaders in considering context, history, politics, and barriers before getting started. It allows leaders time to pause and predict the future, to a degree, as it relates to the change they hope to initiate. It is a thoughtful, disciplined approach to ensuring successful change and avoiding confusion, miscommunication, and mistrust among stakeholders. The final chapter of the book brings all of the work together using a comprehensive accountability planning process that provides clarity and cohesiveness to the overall mission and vision of the organization. Using real-life scenarios, the author demonstrates how leaders use this assessment to serve as their "North Star" by guiding the work in a deliberate, planned manner.

The bookcases of school leaders are filled with volumes on leadership, change, transformation, and school improvement. The chapters that follow offer an interesting and unique perspective on these subjects by bringing together a cadre of authors who offer a balance of current research, practical applications, and personal experiences designed to help leaders activate skills, practices, and processes to successfully meet the challenges they will soon face. The book is organized to help readers understand and coordinate focus and effort on three critical elements essential for leading change: the development and motivation of people, the implementation of practices that make the biggest difference, and processes and structures for improved results.

References

Alliance for Excellent Education. (2011). [Home page]. Retrieved from www.all4ed.org

Allison, E., & Reeves, D. (2009). *Renewal coaching: Sustainable change for individuals and organizations.* San Francisco, CA: Jossey-Bass.

Drucker, P. (1990). *Managing the nonprofit organization: Principles and practices.* New York: HarperCollins.

Fullan, M. (2008). *The six secrets of change: What the best leaders do to help their organization survive and thrive.* San Francisco, CA: Jossey-Bass.

Marzano, R., Waters, T., & McNulty, B. (2005). *School leadership that works: From research to results.* Alexandria, VA: ASCD.

Pink, D. (2009). *Drive: The surprising truth about what motivates us.* New York, NY: Riverhead Books.

Reeves, D. (2011). *Finding your leadership focus: What matters most for student results.* New York, NY: Teachers College Press.

Wagner, T., & Kegen, R. (2006) . *Change leadership: A practical guide to transforming our schools.* San Francisco, CA: Jossey-Bass.

Wiseman, L. (2011). *Multipliers: How the best leaders make everyone smarter.* New York, NY: HarperCollins.

SECTION 1

LEADERS FOCUSING ON
PEOPLE

CHAPTER ONE

Leading Change:
A Principal's Journey

JAY TRUJILLO

L EADERSHIP IS A FUNNY THING. We work like crazy to arrive. We work like crazy to survive. Some days, maybe even several, we probably wonder, "What in the world was I thinking?" I have found leadership to be lonely, too. Do we ever really share our worries or fears? I think not. We silently shoulder the burden of the position. As I pondered leadership and change content for this chapter, taking into account my experiences as principal and the experiences of other leaders I have known or studied, as well as experts on the subject, I began to formulate a better understanding of why so many leaders fail to enact change. In its primal form, it boils down to fear. It could be fear of the unknown. It may be fear of losing support, losing respect, or losing one's job. It very well may be fear of guaranteed success. It could be fear in any of its manifested forms. Fear of change is powerful and debilitating, taking down competent leaders with ease. My esteemed colleague Doug Reeves (2009, p. 1) goes so far as to say that "fear of pain and death is not, for many people, greater than their unwillingness to change." With fear prominently, or even surreptitiously, present, it is logical that leaders often fail. It is Maslow reincarnate—self-survival.

This battle that rages within, *wanting to do something, but not doing it*, is well documented. Pfeffer and Sutton (2000) identified the "knowing-doing gap," and more recently, Heath and Heath (2010) illustrate it as the internal struggle between our *emotional* and *rational* sides or states of being. To help readers visualize this concept, the authors colorfully name our emotional side the *elephant* and the rational side the *rider.* An example of elephant versus rider Heath and Heath give is the person (let's just say *all* of us) who thoughtfully (this is the rider) sets the morning alarm clock *early* to allow for a stress-free, no-rush morning, only to press the snooze button several times over. The elephant, our always present emotional sidekick, likes the cozy comforts of a warm bed. Heath and Heath further propose that inner battles, especially over the long haul, will likely be won by the very large elephant over the tiny little rider. Size matters.

So there you have it. Leading change is hard, challenging, fearful, perhaps even impossible, unless leaders can solve its mystery. The remainder of this chapter aims to do just that.

Opportunity Knocks

Early in my principal years, I often found myself second guessing my career choice, as well as my ability to lead. After all, I was supposed to be making effective change. I was well read, I was experienced, and, essentially, I knew what to do. "Change was a-coming!" I gave rah-rah speeches. I enlisted suggestions and feedback from trusted advisors. I made what I thought were strategic changes, and I *really* tried hard. I then waited with baited breath for the *real* change to arrive ... and waited ... and waited. It was a yearly cycle of hope and disappoint-ment. Oh, we improved some, but nothing like I had expected. I soon found myself as the recently hired fourth principal in six years in our district's oldest high school. Once again, I/we made a few tweaks here and there and waited. I hated waiting. A voice deep down told me I was waiting for nothing. Had it not been for the dreaded AVIS, which clobbered us head on—no, not the rental car company, but the Accountability Virus Infection Syndrome—I might still be waiting. What I did not know or understand then, I absolutely know and understand now: If I wanted to lead real change, then the person who needed to change the most was me.

Then: 2001—I vividly remember the cool morning when I stumbled upon the morning newspaper: "RUBIDOUX HIGH SCHOOL—SANCTIONED BY THE STATE" was the front-page news. At that moment, I thought this to be the most horrible day of my professional career; this was, after all, my school. I was wrong. The day I had to address my entire staff and essentially tell them we needed to change was worse. We were a school community in mourning for being publicly labeled one of California's worst high schools. Never mind that we felt it was untrue and not representative of our students and community. As far as state officials were concerned, we failed to meet growth targets again, and our overall school ranking validated this status. We ranked in the lowest decile (bottom 10 percent) when compared to high schools across the state, and we ranked equally as low when we were compared to high schools with similar demographic characteristics (e.g., diversity, parent education level, mobility, percentage of students on free and reduced lunch, percentage of English language learners). In my county alone, we ranked number 33 of 36 high schools, as measured by California's Academic Performance Index. My school, then with a population of 2,450 (61 percent Latino, 28 percent white, 8 percent African American, 3 percent other, 19 percent English language learners, 39 percent free lunch recipients), had its charge and challenge—CHANGE NOW.

Five years later: 2006—The journey forward from those seemingly ancient days has been nothing short of sensational. Our immediate response under those dire circumstances was to hire The Leadership and Learning Center, then named the Center for Performance Assessment. Specifically, we contracted professional assistance for the following services: (1) Effective Classroom Assessments, including *Certification Training*; (2) Data Teams and Data-Driven Decision Making, including *Certification Training*; (3) Power Standards; (4) Common Formative Assessments; and (5) on-site coaching or implementation days. We were busy, but the results, in five short years, speak for themselves:

- Rubidoux High School was the most improved comprehensive high school in the entire Southern California Inland Empire (80+ high schools).

- In Riverside County (45 high schools), Rubidoux was the most improved over two, three, and five years (sustained improvement).

- In Riverside County, Rubidoux rose to rank number 19 of 45 high schools, compared to number 33 of 36 schools five years earlier.

- The achievement gap from that of the county's highest scoring school compared to Rubidoux decreased from 215 points to 94 points.

- Postsecondary college enrollment plans increased from 46 percent to 75 percent.

- Students enrolling in Advanced Placement classes increased 300 percent.

- We set three consecutive school records for average daily attendance and recorded four of the top five years of average daily attendance in the school's 47-year history.

- Local educational leaders awarded my school two Model of Excellence Awards in 2007.

- Visitors from across the state and from as far away as Denver and Washington, D.C., have visited our school to see and learn firsthand how we led this remarkable change.

The numbers above do not tell the full story; Rubidoux High School achieved these results despite an ever-changing, diverse student population. Exhibit 1.1 highlights the demographic shifts from 2001 to 2006.

Rubidoux students and staff are the real heroes of this feel-good story. The results shown in the preceding bulleted list are only those most commonly referred to in accountability reports or maintained in data warehouses. The most inspiring accomplishments we achieved were new-found community pride, joy, and vision or hope for a better future.

EXHIBIT 1.1 **Student Population Demographic Comparison, 2001 versus 2006**

	2001	2006
Total Enrollment	2,450	3,140
Latino	61%	67%
White	28%	24%
African American	8%	6%
English Language Learners	19%	24%
Free Lunch Recipients	39%	54%

Leadership and Change Operational Framework

As part of my preparedness training for school leadership, I was fortunate to attend a two-year training program sponsored by the California School Leadership Academy. This experience, coupled with on-the-job training, has provided me with a strong foundation on which to build my leadership actions to tackle change. Exhibit 1.2 represents my operational framework.

As stated earlier, enacting change is a difficult and fear-producing task befalling school leaders today. To surmount this challenge, leaders must be thoroughly grounded in and guided by the three critical interrelated concepts, or big ideas, shown in Exhibit 1.2: vision, data, and relationships. The degree to which leaders can master coordinated and effective implementation of these ideas translates to deeper levels of meaningful and lasting change.

Operational Framework for Leadership Action

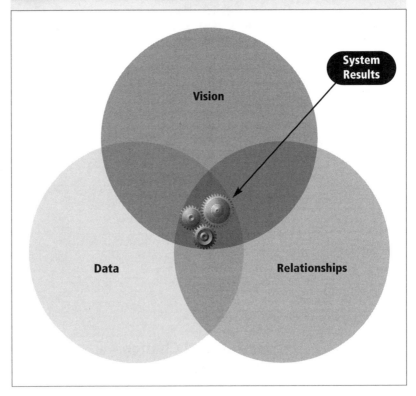

Distinguished change expert Michael Fullan (2008) describes similar ideas in his book *The Six Secrets of Change.* Fullan's Secret #1, love your people, and Secret #2, connect peers with purpose, match perfectly with vision and relationships in the operational framework displayed in Exhibit 1.2. Secret #5, transparency works, which Fullan defines as the importance of measuring what matters, partially embodies my ideas surrounding the use of data. I also contend that Fullan's remaining three secrets (#3—capacity building, #4—learning is the work, and #6—systems learn) fall within the interconnecting area labeled "system results" in the exhibit. Aside from my training, education, and experience, all of which contributed to the creation of this practical framework, it is also personally comforting and helpful to know that others, most notably Michael Fullan, shared complementary viewpoints.

Vision

Vision is nothing new to leaders, schools, or organizations. It is, however, sparingly used as the lightening rod to spark change. On the contrary, No Child Left Behind, test scores, and accountability mandates rule the roost. Certainly, we may see vision statements written on schools' Internet home pages or scrolled across their walls and letterhead, but do staff, students, and the local community really know what the vision is? If asked to tell it, could stakeholders rattle it off? Try it. The answer is a resounding NO, and herein rests a crucial part of our change problem. Unless we know our destination—*really* know—it does not matter where we drive, what we take with us, where we stop, or what type of transportation vessel we mount; the journey is pointless. Vision, like a riverbank, guides us toward a common, meaningful goal. The alternative, a river without banks, is a muddy mess.

Peter Senge (1990), American scientist and director of the Center for Organizational Learning at the MIT Sloan School of Management, reminds us that vision provides focus and energy, compels courage, fosters risk taking, and promotes a "whatever it takes" attitude to attain the change we seek. Surely schools do not exist to meet state accountability targets, federal adequate yearly progress goals, or Common Core State Standards expectations. Yet you do not have to listen very carefully to hear countless cries bemoaning the invasion of test-prep factories into our schools. In truth, schools exist for a far loftier goal: the greater good and the pursuit of happiness for *all* of us, just to name two. John Goodlad (1984, p. 2) wrote in his classic book, *A Place Called School*, "To the extent that the attainment of a democratic society depends on the existence of schools equally accessible to everyone, we are all their clients." As leaders, we are keepers of the vision. We must be steadfast in our constant and effective communication of our school's overall purpose.

A leader's declared vision is foremost for successful change.

Remember, change is hard, but the alternative, the status quo, is unthinkable as long as schools are failing children. Leaders must be the voice for those who cannot speak, do not speak, or will not speak. This is especially critical in lower-socioeconomic-status schools and communities, where vision and hope are like a killer virus—invisible but deadly. Clear and purposeful vision is the antidote.

Acquiring 21st-century workforce skills will require an ability largely absent in many schools and classrooms—critical thinking. Carnevale and Desrochers (2002) found that the percentage of the U.S. workforce with postsecondary education has steadily increased from 28 percent to 59 percent between 1973 and 2000. Similarly, the Partnership for 21st Century Skills (2008) reports that the U.S. Bureau of Labor Statistics has identified more than 250 jobs with high growth potential over the next 10 years. All of these jobs will require a college-educated workforce. Why is clear and purposeful vision for schools a requirement for leaders? Because school change that guarantees *all students* future success is difficult to achieve, and we will need the muscle that vision provides. "Strength comes from a commitment that you are doing the right thing," according to Curwin (1992, p. 96). Leaders must keep the vision up front and personal. Our country and our students are depending on us.

Data

Johnny, please put your toys away.
Johnny, don't make me come over there and . . .
Johnny, one, two . . . thank you.

Countdowns, rankings, and other numbering devices have been around since ancient civilizations first roamed the planet. They are how we launch space shuttles, manage sporting events, celebrate anniversaries, and, yes, measure schools. Data, or simply put, information, is how we keep score. But do we always count the right stuff? Let's look at this another way. The score at the end of a tightly contested basketball game provides a clear indication of the winner and loser, but not much more. Close review of statistics like field goal percentages, assists, rebounds, or turnovers is what gives coaches the information they need to guide their actions—in *practice*, where the majority of coaching occurs. What coaches do in practice ultimately determines wins and losses. Reeves (2006) calls this activity the *antecedents of excellence*. Whereas the educational community is certainly becoming more adept at using student results from either summative or formative assessments to guide our work, by and large we are failing miserably when it comes to collecting, monitoring, and using cause data—adult actions—to guide our decisions.

Given any set of student results—for example, the percentage of students scoring proficient in reading comprehension or solving linear equations—adult actions are attributed as their cause. What we did or did not do, said or did not say day in and day out, as leaders, teachers, or support staff, is largely the reason for student outcomes. Of course, the skills and experiences students bring to the game are relevant. Importantly, however, the specific actions of adults in their "fields of play" are equally significant. Marzano (2007, p. 1) captured this fact when he wrote, "the one factor that surfaced as the single most influential component of an effective school is the individual teachers within that school." What we do in schools matters.

Have you ever walked into a dingy, dirty, or disheveled convenience store or restaurant, one that supposedly caters to customers? You do not have to *watch* the people working there, conducting their daily activities, to derive a thought or two about their vision and corresponding actions. It permeates every nook and cranny of the structure. Margaret Wheatley (1992) describes *vision as a field*. She explains that the people who work in the field are influenced by it, their actions governed by it, whether they are meant to be or not. Stated another way, vision and action go hand in hand. *It's the way we do things around here.* To lead change, I am advocating that leaders must strategically collect data about the relevant adult actions selected in pursuit of the vision.

Going back to the story of my school, the question of which adult actions to monitor was both straightforward and mind-boggling at the outset. Given our welcomed adoption of best practices associated with 90/90/90 schools (Reeves, 2003), there were several adult actions to consider for our data collection and use. Possibilities ranged from the identification and use of priority standards and common assessments to nonfiction writing to collaborative scoring, and more. Once decided, we had to ask ourselves, what, exactly, would be the "data" collected, and how would we collect it? How often would we collect the data? Who would collect it? What would we do with it once collected? What new processes or protocols needed to be established? These were the questions that engulfed our planning sessions. Working through the answers was challenging and invigorating.

We decided to focus a majority of our monitoring efforts and energies on the implementation of the five key steps of our newly created teacher collaboration process—Data Teams.

The five-step Data Teams process involves the following:

1. Charting data

2. Analyzing and prioritizing data

3. Setting SMART (specific, measurable, achievable, relevant, and timely) goals

4. Selecting instructional strategies

5. Determining result indicators

You may be asking, of all the adult behaviors we could have selected to collect and monitor, why did we choose behaviors associated with the implementation of a *process*? The answer takes into account Richard and Rebecca DuFour's and Robert Eaker's (2008, p. 7) belief that teacher isolation is "the single biggest barrier educators must overcome if they are to create PLCs [professional learning communities] in their schools and districts." We wanted to get good at creating or becoming a learning organization. It is a process. We also believed that increased student achievement, the results we were ultimately looking for, would come if we learned, managed, and worked the process. Learning how to learn was our focus.

Initially, we created a generic rubric on "effective collaboration," which specified basic expectations associated with teacher behaviors in the collaborative process. Some of the specific components we targeted were the following:

- Meeting norms
- Agendas and minutes
- Member participation
- Data usage
- Decision making
- Administrative support

Some bulleted points, or behaviors, we expected to influence were as simple as *being on time and prepared for meetings*, while others focused on meeting outcomes such as *agreed-upon teaching strategies* or *expected timelines*. Administrators collected and poured over agendas and minutes, and we visited collaborative meetings throughout the year. Leaders also met regularly with teacher leaders who were charged with facilitating our Data Team meetings. The purpose was to provide feedback and problem solve. All told, an exciting collaborative culture was taking hold throughout the campus. We were pleased with many aspects of our work, but something was missing.

While we saw pockets of excellence in many of the collaborative Data Team *meetings* we observed, there was less evidence of consistent Data Team impact on *instruction* in the classroom. We did see increased focus on teaching Power Standards, teachers monitoring student results, and goal setting, all of which contributed to improvement, but "how" teachers taught was largely the same in many classrooms. Data Teams were saying one thing collectively, but individual teachers were doing something different in the classroom.

After minimally successful attempts to address this harsh reality, including reteaching essential elements of the Data Teams process, engineering and highlighting team/teacher successes, and providing *general* feedback, we started over.

John Hattie (2009, p. 22), author of *Visible Learning: A Synthesis of over 800 Meta-analyses Relating to Achievement*, reminds us of perhaps his work's most important finding: "The biggest effects on student learning occur when teachers become learners of their own teaching and when students become their own teachers." Teachers needed clarity, focus, and *specific* feedback about their actions. We took three critical steps to meet these needs.

1. *Data Team implementation rubric.* We discarded our initial collaboration rubric and borrowed—and significantly expanded upon—the Data Team Implementation Rubric created by The Center. The new rubric outlined specific teacher and Data Team behaviors in each step of the Data Teams process. We wanted to remove any ambiguity about the Data Teams process and its intended purpose: classroom instruction. Our new rubric language was precise, meaningful, and observable—in meetings *and* the classroom.

2. *Self-assessment.* We asked our Data Teams to complete a self-assessment using our new rubric. We asked every teacher to complete the self-assessment individually first, and then come to consensus as a team regarding the level of implementation for each of the five Data Team steps. The idea was to require teaching teams to go deep into their review, discussion, and analysis of each step of the Data Teams process and its implications for classroom instruction. We devised a simple process to obtain a *level of implementation* "score" for each of the five steps as well as an overall implementation composite score. We were committed to become "data driven" in the successful implementation and execution of the Data Teams process.

3. *Action planning.* Once Data Teams completed the self-assessment process, we required them to identify specific areas of need. For example, one team may have identified "setting SMART goals" as its area of focus. Another team may have determined "selecting instructional strategies." With no more than two or three focus areas identified, Data Teams were required to set an implementation improve-

ment goal and to determine specific actions or strategies to reach this goal. Administrators then met regularly with Data Team leaders (DTLs) to review their plans, review progress made reaching their implementation goal(s), and collaboratively plan next steps, as needed.

The essence of this three-tiered process was straightforward: (1) we precisely established which adult actions (i.e., cause data) we wanted to master; (2) we devised a method to help us consistently monitor our progress; and (3) we used progress indicators to adjust our actions. In no uncertain terms, we modeled the data-driven decision-making process. It worked.

Relationships

I recently was in Fort Bend, Texas, assisting a wonderful group of district leaders and principals in their implementation of the Data Teams process. While there, I attended Michael Fullan's keynote address to this room full of leaders. He was unveiling, in part, his findings as an authority on educational reform. He spoke briefly, yet powerfully, on the first of his six secrets of change, "love your employees." The challenge, Fullan (2008) reminds us, is that some of us are unlovable. Though love may not be a necessary element for leading change, trust is. The crux in building relationships with and among staff is building trust.

In his book *On Becoming a Leader*, leadership giant Warren Bennis (1989) identifies qualities possessed by leaders the world over. These include a guiding vision, passion, curiosity and daring, and integrity, which Bennis claims is the foundation of trust. Bennis describes four necessary ingredients to building and sustaining trust (p. 160):

1. *Constancy.* Whatever surprises leaders themselves may face, they don't create any for the group. Leaders are all of a piece; they stay the course.

2. *Congruity.* Leaders walk their talk. In true leaders, there is no gap between theories they espouse and the life they practice.

3. *Reliability.* Leaders are there when it counts; they are ready to support their coworkers in the moments that matter.

4. *Integrity.* Leaders honor their commitments and promises.

Expert opinion on the importance of trust abounds in leadership circles. Reeves (2009, p. 12) profoundly states, "[O]f all the things leaders do in order to create the conditions for change, the most important are their thousands of moments of truth when their actions speak louder than words." In deference to the late W. Edwards Deming, the godfather of total quality management (TQM), my contribution is this: "no TQLS!" No total quality lip service.

At the height of my high school's enrollment, 3,100 students, the number of my staff hovered right around 200 employees. How does one build meaningful relationships with 200+ people? The fact is, you can't. But make no mistake, they see you. Leaders' words and actions are on display daily for the whole world to see. What we do and say matters. Our challenge is to *consistently* do and say the things that support our vision and to collect and use data about high-yield adult actions that help us attain that vision. This was the goal year one, year two, year three, and every year thereafter. We did not deviate. I suppose some staff members may have considered taking medical leave for having grown sick and tired of the *vision-data thing.* Some moved on. Some were moved. But I found that my relationship with staff was becoming stronger every year. Call it the cycle of success. As practitioners, teachers were becoming more savvy on *instruction that works;* as a leader, I was becoming more comfortable with teacher autonomy, authority, and leadership, within, of course, clear parameters. I was, as advocated by the DuFours and Eaker (2008, p. 310), a *leader of leaders* who enthusiastically embraced the idea and practice of "widely shared leadership for both research-based and practical reasons." I could not do it alone.

Despite the small-city atmosphere prevalent in large comprehensive high schools, there existed a critical mass of staff with whom

I worked exceptionally hard to build relationships. This group included my three fellow assistant principals (APs) and 20 DTLs. There was nothing miraculous to my actions. I simply gave them my time and my ear. We met regularly to plan and problem solve, and I did everything possible to support these leaders in their new leadership roles. For example, the APs were now responsible for aiding their newly assigned Data Teams. Assistant principals had to learn the Data Teams process as well as, if not better than, any teacher in the building. They had to devote time and effort to attend Data Team meetings and monitor processes. It was demanding work, for it wasn't like any other duties and responsibilities came off their plates. This effort required continuous communication of expectations, support, and understanding from me, the school principal.

Newly appointed DTLs, too, were charting new territory. This group, I knew, would dictate our Data Team success. "Teachers not only exert significant influence on the performance of students, but they also influence the performance of other teachers and school leaders" (Reeves, 2008, p. 2). Jim Collins (2005, p. 14) describes a parallel idea relative to social-sector organizations, that is, schools: Greatness, he says, "flows first and foremost from having the right people in the key seats." Unlike any teacher leadership position previously known or experienced, DTLs were in the key seats on the bus and charged with challenging the status quo among their peers. Data Team leaders would facilitate the . . . *gulp* . . . sharing of student scores and teaching strategies. They basically would be asking teachers to expose their teaching and learning souls. My teacher leaders, in particular, deserved my unconditional love. They got it.

First and foremost, my DTLs got paid for their new role. I am not talking about controversial "performance pay," but instead "recognition pay." We wanted to elevate the position of DTL to one of significance. Moreover, we were intent on attracting the best possible candidates to serve in this role. We've all heard the refrain, "put your money where your mouth is" or "you get what you pay for" or "success isn't cheap." My administrative team and I were 100 percent in agreement as we created perhaps a crude formula to determine DTL compensation. We felt they needed to be paid the same as, if not more than, athletic coaches. Data Team leaders were going to serve a full year. Their role, arguably, was the most important, next to the principal, in the whole school. They would be collecting data and creating data charts and displays for teacher use. In addition, DTLs would facilitate meetings, twice per month, on top of meeting with the principal or assigned AP. Meeting agendas needed to be made available ahead of time (this was one of our Data Team Implementation Rubric norms), and minutes taken and distributed to stakeholders. In short, DTLs were going to be busy. To support them, it was clear that this principal needed to show the love in order to foster quality working relationships.

I address just one more point as it relates to the compensation of DTLs. Principals, even the great ones, can only push volunteerism so far. The fact that teacher leaders were now to be paid for their new role resulted in two immediate benefits: (1) a higher expectation of quality services for hire and (2) a greater likelihood of the execution of said services.

System Results

"Expectation communication." If I had a dollar for every time I heard this, I'd be a rich man. Come to think of it, I am rich—rich in knowledge and know-how as it relates to expectation theory and application. I largely credit DeWayne Mason, my boss during my formative years as a new principal. DeWayne was a student of Thomas L. Good, who, along with Jere E. Brophy, wrote *Looking in Classrooms* (2000), a respected body of work that provides battle-tested, research-based insight into achieving effective classroom instruction. DeWayne helped me solidify my understanding and use of the notion that what you get is what you expect. This holds true for teachers and principals alike. It is best that we "know a little bit about the Pygmalion effect … understand exactly how to use the Pygmalion effect … as a tool to convey positive expectations and, maybe more importantly, to avoid conveying negative expectations" (Tauber, 1998, p. 1). Leading change is akin to changing culture. Culture begins with deeply held values, beliefs, traditions, and norms—otherwise known as expectations.

The operational framework I have described will only lead to change if leaders are able to consistently communicate an equally high expectation to their staff. "Communicate," by this definition, translates to behavior. In my experience, as both a principal and a consultant, I have found that many leaders know something about the Pygmalion effect, but do we know enough to use its gift as a tool to enact change? Let's see.

Directions: On a piece of paper, please take this four-item Expectation Theory and Application Quiz, one of DeWayne's personal favorites.

1. List three synonyms that define "expectation."
2. List three of the five steps that describe how the expectation theory process works. *(Note the big hint here.)*
3. Identify one leadership behavior you currently consistently practice that communicates a high expectation for your school or staff.
4. Identify one leadership behavior you currently consistently practice that may communicate a low expectation for your school or staff.

Let's check your work.

Question 1. *Answer:* Belief, supposition, hypothesis, theory, assumption, prediction, prophecy. Good and Brophy (2000, p. 74) define expectations as "Inferences teachers [leaders] make about the future behavior or academic achievement of their students, based on what they know about these students now."

Question 2. *Answer:* The five-step expectation process:

1. Leader forms expectation.
2. Leader behaves consistently with this expectation toward teachers, students, etc. This "treatment" communicates to

others, explicitly or implicitly, how they are expected to behave or perform (recipient's perception is key).

3. Consistent treatment (without mediation) affects teachers, students, others.

4. Effects reinforce leader expectations (sustains expectation held).

5. Ultimately, sustained expectations, congruent treatment, and recipient conformity lead to major outcome effects (self-fulfilling prophecy in progress).

Question 3. *Answer:* High expectation behavior responses can vary. It may be as simple as providing feedback to the teacher who consistently arrives late to work. If his behavior does not improve, then the leader with high expectations displays increased attention and follow-up action.

Question 4. *Answer:* Low expectation behavior responses can vary. A common low expectation leadership behavior is visiting a classroom and noticing several students off-task for the majority of the period, and *not* doing anything about it in response—either immediately during the leader's visit or later, perhaps during an impromptu or scheduled meeting with the teacher.

The critical point is this: What leaders say and, more importantly, what we do speaks volumes about our expectations and beliefs. If the vision for your school is to be data driven, what leadership behaviors will follow? If your vision is to ensure that all students learn, what leadership behaviors will ensure the creation of safety nets for struggling students?

Understanding expectation theory and application processes can help leaders successfully respond to low or incongruent expectations held by others. It may be natural for a teacher to question, or perhaps even argue, a point of contention relative to a leader's request (e.g., bell-to-bell instruction). This teacher may not possess the same level of knowledge, know-how, or sense of efficacy, or the teacher simply may not agree to its importance. It does not mean this individual is a "bad teacher." The artful yet clear expectation delivered by the leader, one aligned to his or her own belief system, will ultimately determine this teacher's final behaviors. Concerning matters of critical importance, such as ensuring equitable learning opportunity for all students, supporting equal treatment and fairness for staff, and making sure others' behaviors represent institutional values, leaders must clearly reveal their expectations. Whether you realize it or not, they will be on display.

Conclusion

I began this chapter by highlighting impediments to change. I suggested that fear is largely at the root of change resistance. Closely related to fear is the issue of "buy-in." I wonder if the two are not interchangeable, or go hand in hand, though I have never heard a leader espouse fear as the reason for inaction. Buy-in, on the other hand, is a totally different story.

How can leaders overcome the buy-in dilemma? We don't. Here is what we can do. First, develop and communicate a clear vision. Second, develop meaningful relationships with staff. Third, use data, both cause and effect data, to drive leadership actions. I have tried to present a strong case and authentic examples for this operational framework for leading change. Not one to be too naive—I am a high school principal, after all—I am fairly certain this buy-in fixation will creep into the change picture and deter otherwise competent leaders. Here is a dose of change reality: Behavior precedes belief. The research on this topic has been consistently reported. In the *New York Times* best seller *Influencer: The Power to Change Anything*, authors Patterson, Grenny, Maxfield, McMillan, and Switzler (2008, p. 51) remind us that verbal persuasion is the most common yet unsuccessful tool used to help change behaviors; instead, "The great persuader is personal experience." In a simplified tribute to Pythagoras, I like to put it this way: A + B = C. Actions + Benefits = Change. Don't be duped by buy-in.

I consider myself simple in most respects and my abilities not too far ahead. There is not much more to my personal story or journey to leading change. I made neither earth-shattering discoveries nor rip-roaring changes. My transformation and that of my school were taken one step at a time. We focused on deep implementation of a few key big ideas. *Good to Great* author Collins (2001, p. 91) describes a comparable idea: the hedgehog approach. "It doesn't matter how complex the world, a hedgehog reduces all challenges and dilemmas to simple—indeed almost simplistic—hedgehog ideas."

Similarly, McKenna and Maister (2002, p. xxviii) describe "victory change" this way: "success in helping your group succeed is mostly about *you*. Not them." I agree. Change, and the change you seek shall come.

References

Bennis, W. (1989). *On becoming a leader.* Reading, MA: Addison-Wesley.

Carnevale, A., & Desrochers, D. (2002). *The political economy of labor market mediation in the United States.* Princeton, NJ: Educational Testing Service.

Collins, J. C. (2001). *Good to great: Why some companies make the leap . . . and others don't.* New York, NY: Harper Business.

Collins, J. C. (2005). *Good to great and the social sectors: A monograph to accompany good to great.* New York, NY: HarperCollins.

Curwin, R. L. (1992). *Rediscovering hope: Our greatest teaching strategy.* Bloomington, IN: National Education Service.

DuFour, R., DuFour, R., & Eaker, R. (2008). *Revisiting professional learning communities at work: New insights from improving schools.* Bloomington, IN: Solution Tree.

Fullan, M. (2008). *The six secrets of change: What the best leaders do to help their organizations survive and thrive.* San Francisco, CA: Jossey-Bass.

Good, T. L., & Brophy, J. E. (2000). *Looking in classrooms* (8th ed.). New York, NY: Longman.

Goodlad, J. I. (1984). *A place called school: Prospects for the future.* New York, NY: McGraw-Hill.

Hattie, J. (2003). *Visible learning: A synthesis of over 800 meta-analyses relating to achievement.* New York, NY: Routledge.

Heath, C., & Heath, D. (2010). *Switch: How to change things when change is hard.* New York, NY: Broadway Books.

Marzano, R. J. (2007). *The art and science of teaching.* Alexandria, VA: ASCD.

McKenna, P. J., & Maister, D.H. (2002). *First among equals.* New York, NY: Free Press.

Partnership for 21st Century Skills. (2008). *21st century skills, education & competitiveness: A resource and policy guide.* Retrieved from http://www.21stcenturyskills.org/documents/21st_century_skills_education_and_competitiveness_guide.pdf

Patterson, K., Grenny, J., Maxfield, D., McMillan, R., & Switzler, A. (2008). *Influencer: The power to change anything.* New York, NY: McGraw-Hill.

Pfeffer, J., & Sutton, R. I. (2000). *The knowing-doing gap: How smart companies turn knowledge into action.* Boston, MA: Harvard Business School Press.

Reeves, D. B. (2003). *High performance in high poverty schools: 90/90/90 and beyond.* Englewood, CO: Leadership and Learning Center.

Reeves, D. B. (2006). *The learning leader: How to focus school improvement for better results.* Alexandria, VA: ASCD.

Reeves. D. B. (2008). *Reframing teacher leadership to improve your school.* Alexandria, VA: ASCD.

Reeves, D. B. (2009). *Leading change in your school: How to conquer myths, build commitment, and get results.* Alexandria, VA: ASCD.

Senge, P. M. (1990). *The fifth discipline: The art and practice of the learning organization.* New York, NY: Doubleday Currency.

Tauber, R. (1998). *Good or bad, what teachers expect from students they generally get!* ERIC Digest (Number ED426985). Washington, DC: ERIC Clearinghouse on Teaching and Teacher Education.

Wheatley, M. J. (1992). *Leadership and the new science: Learning about organization from the orderly universe.* San Francisco, CA: Berrett-Koehler.

CHAPTER TWO

Leadership Through Coaching and 100-Day Projects

ELLE ALLISON

M Y FAVORITE QUESTION to ask leaders and decision makers is this: What could happen if more individuals supported others in accomplishing the most important goals of the organization? In educational organizations, answers paint a promising picture and include the following outcomes:

- "We would retain our best principals."
- "Teacher effectiveness would increase."
- "We would develop better leaders from within our teacher ranks."
- "Student achievement would improve."

More research is needed about the impact of coaching on these key indicators in education. In an exit survey of educational leaders who worked with coaches from The Leadership and Learning Center, many said they completed the project they asked to be coached on sooner than they would have without a coach, and they felt more confidence in their ability to do their work. They also said they believed their organization benefited directly from the projects they were coached on (Allison, 2009).

Coaching is a particularly effective approach for developing leaders. Leaders who coach more, lead more (Allison, 2010), and leaders in education have ample opportunities to coach peers, colleagues, and the people they supervise. In their excellent book, *Execution: The Dis-*

cipline of Getting Things Done, Bossidy and Charan (2002, p. 74) say, "Good leaders regard every encounter as an opportunity to coach."

Opportunities to Coach

Educational enterprises abound with opportunities to coach, every day. In educational systems where coaching is a widely accepted practice, individuals in all roles can coach the people they work with. Certainly, new leaders benefit from opportunities to reflect and make decisions, in the company of a leader who is devoted to helping them think, not provide them with answers that shortchange the potential in the moment for growth. In organizations where coaching is a cultural norm, we see professionals in different roles coaching each other that go way beyond coaching new leaders who wish to move from the classroom to an administrative position. Relationships where coaching is possible in the educational setting include but are not limited to the following:

- Principals coaching teachers as they solve challenges of student learning in the classroom
- Principals and other administrators coaching colleagues who seek them out for professional discourse and problem solving
- Teacher leaders coaching team members; specialists coaching principals and teachers alike
- Colleagues coaching each other on curriculum projects
- Cabinet members coaching each other to make great decisions about policies and procedures

Leaders already wear many hats; they carry out the work of their positions through many roles. Leaders in educational systems must fluidly move between roles of mentor, supervisor, teacher, collaborator, and consultant. When coaching is the most effective way to support others, the outcomes are extremely positive for the coachee and for the organization. Leaders who embrace coaching as a way of supporting others notice opportunities to coach during the workday and choose to do so as often as possible.

When to Coach

Even though coaching might initially take more time to conduct than, say, just giving an opinion would take, leaders who coach recognize that coaching may in fact be the best job-embedded professional development approach available, especially after teachers have learned new ideas and now want to apply them in their work and practice. In their now famous 1995 study about the impact of coaching on teachers implementing new skills to create change in teaching and learning, Bruce Joyce and Beverley Showers have shown that without coaching, only 5 to 15 percent of what teachers learn in other models of professional development (presentation, modeling, practice, and low-risk feedback in a workshop) make it to the classroom.

As great as coaching is, it is not a panacea. It cannot possibly replace other forms of supporting people, such as mentoring, teaching, collaborating, or supervising, when they are undeniably more appropriate to the coachee and to the situation. Leaders who coach develop a knack for recognizing when coaching is the best leadership approach to offer.

Here are some conditions that make coaching a powerful way to influence others (Allison, 2010):

1. **When coachees have projects in mind and feel excited about seeing them implemented.** Coachees who express passion for carrying out a project under their responsibility are rewarding to coach. Coachees who invite leaders to coach them are more likely to participate fully in each coaching conversation and take action to create change after each conversation. Leaders who coach might also seek out and offer coaching to those who have a passionate project but may not know that they can ask for coaching.

2. **When coachees come to the leader with a specific situation or dilemma and they also have ideas for proactively**

addressing it. Sometimes on-the-job coaching is more situational than project based. Even so, to qualify as coaching, it must lead to action taken by coachees. In school systems, leaders at all levels run into situations that are barriers to them as they work with others and carry out their responsibilities. Some barriers are limited resources, changing personnel, revised roles, and schedule and time changes. Individuals who desire to remove these barriers but who also want to learn from the experience will welcome coaching.

3. **When development of coachees is just as important as, or more important than, completing the projects or tasks.** Leaders know that one of their primary responsibilities is to develop other leaders. Moreover, they seek ways to provide leadership development opportunities on the job where the context provides "real time" situations that demand attention, decisions, and action. What could be more perfect than to have the opportunity to coach someone who is knee deep in the work of the district? Yet, task completion is usually time bound, and the coaching process takes more time than it takes to simply tell someone what they should do. Leaders who coach more often choose to take more time and allow a task to be completed a day late rather than compromise a perfect opportunity to facilitate meaningful on-the-job development with a person who shows great promise as a leader. Sure, coaching might take longer and important tasks might be delayed a day or two, but the gains that come from coaching bring compounded returns. Not only are tasks accomplished but they are often accomplished better than they would have been without coaching, *and* the coachee's capacity for accomplishing this task and similar tasks in the future increases.

4. **When coachees are dependent on answers and advice from others and lack confidence in their ability to know what to do and how to take action.** Some adults become so afraid of making a mistake that they will not make a move

unless they consult the person they see as being in charge or the person who will criticize them, or worse, if they fail (Mezirow, 2000). Leaders who coach seek to elevate the capabilities of those around them by empowering them with pathways to discover their own answers to the dilemmas they face. As with most outcomes of coaching, both parties—leaders who coach and their coachees—enjoy reciprocal benefits (Reeves & Allison, 2009). Leaders who coach the people around them, especially those who can become more independent, eventually gain more time and energy to lead, and their coachees gain more ownership and accountability for their actions.

5. **When coachees ultimately need to take responsibility for how their projects turn out or how situations are addressed and resolved.** Leaders who coach and who become known for coaching within their organization are sought after by peers and colleagues who need to accomplish projects that could make or break a career, a program, or even the mission of the school and district. Although leaders rarely carry out high-stakes projects alone, they are often at the helm of highly visible projects in the district or organization and they will receive both the accolades for things that go right and the criticism for things that go wrong, with the latter making for more interesting news fodder than the former. Coaching does not guarantee that high-stakes projects will run perfectly or turn out exactly as visualized. But coaching does build in important time for reflection that most leaders rarely have as they make crucial decisions, work with others, and carry out important work. At the very least, leaders who have a coach to consult as they implement high-stakes projects have a deeper understanding of the reasoning and data behind each of their decisions. This gives coachees greater confidence as they convey information to others or are asked to justify the decisions made.

Coaching is about developing other people; it is not the process of dispensing advice and making recommendations. Of course, there are times when coaching simply is not the best method for supporting individuals in the organization. Leaders who coach must develop a level of discernment that guides them to know when coaching is not the best model for supporting a colleague or someone they supervise.

When Not to Coach

Certain situations to which coaching is not the appropriate response are obvious. These include emergencies, when policies and procedures dictate what needs to be done, or when an immediate answer is required and time is of the essence. Other situations to which coaching may not be the right response are more nuanced and require a contextual decision. Here are some of the conditions in which educational leaders often choose not to coach:

1. When the leader has strong opinions about the coachee's project or plan and what should be done, or he feels there is only one "right" answer

2. When a personality conflict exists between the two parties

3. When potential coachees have performance problems and need direction and supervision

4. When potential coachees are new to the requirements of a project and they do not have transferable skills

5. When potential coachees refuse to be coached

When coaching is the appropriate method of support, leaders who coach within the educational system where they work provide their colleagues and direct reports with one of the best job-embedded professional development models known.

Foundational Coaching Skills

Coaching provides a performance edge to those who want to go beyond the limits of their own mind. It is a strategy for accomplishing remarkable outcomes. To coach is to partner in thought with individuals who want to accomplish important outcomes in their work.

Leaders who coach learn to use coaching skills they can employ within their daily work. These skills include:

- *Listening.* Leaders who coach listen more often and for longer time periods. When leaders listen, colleagues often arrive at important insights and begin to solve their dilemmas.

- *Deepening understanding.* Leaders who coach are skilled at asking questions that clarify information and provide details. Often, a single clarifying question such as, "You mentioned that students are not using the strategy as you expected. Can you give me an example from the class you are most concerned about?" reveals where leverage for changing a troubling situation exits.

- *Asking open-ended questions:* Open-ended questions are not meant to be answered as much as they are to be explored. Leaders who coach are skilled at asking these types of questions in place of giving advice. Open-ended coaching questions are highly contextual. Coaches must ask them in the moment to match the specific situation of the person they are coaching. Some examples of open-ended questions are "How will you know when the strategies are working?" "What will these strategies make possible for this group of students?"

- *Asking for action.* Leaders who coach end most coaching conversations with the question: "What will you do?" This final question reveals the heart of coaching, which is to support individuals in accomplishing what they feel is important, not what the leader deems important.

Trust

Leaders who coach within the organization where they work must take extra care to create conditions of safety and trust whereby coachees feel they can, within the confines of coaching, say whatever needs to be said. This level of trust demands that leaders who coach do not judge or criticize coachees or the ideas of their coachees. In addition, coaching leaders must keep their opinions and war stories to themselves.

It should go without saying that leaders who coach must have a reputation for being confidential and trustworthy, not just when they are in coaching mode but in all aspects of their leadership work. Leaders who coach cannot expect to be utilized as coaches if they demonstrate untrustworthiness when they are not wearing the coaching hat. Most people will not and should not give a second chance to a coach who cannot keep confidences.

Action

According to the 2008 International Coach Federation's Global Coaching Client Study, people are motivated to seek coaching over other forms of support when they want to accomplish important projects and goals. The report says, "A key differentiator for the industry is that coaching is seen as an 'action plan' rather than an exploratory process."

Leaders have many options by which to approach coaching the people they work with. On a daily basis, leaders can use single coaching skills (listening, asking questions) when interacting with others. They can also make themselves available for single coaching conversations whereby colleagues and direct reports can stop in for a 20-minute coaching session as they process a dilemma. Leaders who coach might also have the opportunity to coach a colleague or direct report through a long-term coaching project.

Long-term project coaching takes place within a series of conversations, all focused on the important matters that come up as the coachee works on a specific project. An important tool used in this type of coaching is the 100-day project framework (Reeves and Allison, 2009, 2010). The 100-day project requires individuals to premeditate high-impact actions to move their project forward and reflect on the consequences of those actions. Coaching conversations focus on how the project is going and on identifying the actions that will keep it moving in an effective direction.

100-Day Projects

The 100-day project is a plan that declares high-impact actions to launch a leadership project and create early wins within 100 days (Reeves and Allison, 2009, 2010). The 100-day project provides a system for educational leaders to think in advance about the actions they need to take to get their project under way. When the 100-day project is combined with coaching, leaders have an extra advantage: They have a coach who will skillfully create conversations for the leader to think through each action and reflect on its impact. Through these coaching conversations, leaders have time and energy to understand their plans, develop effective and innovative ideas, consider ways to enhance their success, and reflect on and learn from whatever happens.

What the 100-Day Project Is and Is Not

The 100-day project focuses the coaching conversations between leaders and their coaches on high-impact actions. It is a simple project management system that reveals what leaders intend to do in the first 100 days of beginning new projects or revitalizing existing projects. Educational leaders are often surprised to know that certain actions taken in the first 100 days of launching initiatives can create success for the project during the implementation phase as well (Watkins, 2003).

As can be seen in Exhibit 2.1, the 100-day project is an adaptive project management tool that provides leaders and their coaches with a single location for planning actions and reflecting on the impact of those actions. To be of value, the 100-day project must align with the mission and goals of the organization. Furthermore, to be valuable to the leader, it must be practical, personal, and mutable in order to reflect the changing needs of the organization as the project unfolds (Allison, 2010).

EXHIBIT 2.1 **Characteristics of the 100-Day Project**

The 100-day project is...	The 100-day project is not...
A call for action over inaction to produce early results that suggest how to revise and respond.	A useless exercise in writing yet another plan that has little impact on the real work of leaders.
A "living" project management tool. The 100-day plan is not written in stone. In fact, coachees will revise it as needed at the end of coaching sessions.	Put in a file after it is written or tossed into a trash can once the project is executed.
Action that clearly aligns with the mission of the organization.	Based on goals and strategies different from the coachee's organization. Leaders already have many important projects on their plates that they need to start or revitalize. Pick one you feel passionate about.
A single place where leaders personally record and track the actions they plan to take to move their project forward.	An accountability document written to comply with mandates.
A starting point for every coaching conversation.	A plan submitted to the coach, never to be consulted and revised.
A learning journal that captures and holds historical information about what it took to implement the project.	An exercise that reduces time available for learning and reflection.

Exhibit 2.2 depicts a sample 100-day project for a high school principal who wants to build teacher leadership through action research about school-wide practices to positively impact student learning in language arts and math classes. His project involves find-

Sample 100-Day Project

Project Title: Teacher Leadership Through Action Research	
Date	**Action**
6/27/09	Share my vision of how action research develops teacher leaders. Obtain feedback via a survey done in the staff meeting.
6/27/09	Start of 100-day leadership plan.
6/30/09	Look at student achievement data and establish baseline scores.
7/3/09	Invite volunteer teachers to team up as the first to do action research on one of three strategies: grading, teacher assignment, and common formative assessment.
7/7/09	Provide professional development on how to conduct action research.
7/14/09	Teams calendar the events of their project.
7/14/09	Teams develop their agreements and protocols for their project.
7/17/09	Teams prepare project progress presentation for stakeholders.
7/22/09	Analyze policies and procedures that affect all three areas.
7/28/09	Distribute findings and refer again to the vision that paints a picture of hope.
8/4/09	Teams begin the action research project. Identify research questions and methods.
8/7/09	Support and feedback meeting for teams.
8/13/09	Identify milestones for tracking small wins.
9/1/09	Visit classrooms as projects begin. Start to collect impact stories as students respond.
9/4/09	Strategy team check-in and midcourse corrections.
9/7/09	Update superintendent and senior leadership team.
9/11/09	Second presentation from action research teams, focused on evidence of student learning, engagement, and faculty morale.
9/15/09	Teams meet to refine procedures and protocols.
9/18/09	Second assessment of student learning in targeted areas.
9/22/09	Analysis of data with a focus on evidence of student learning, engagement, and faculty morale.
9/27/09	Technology support person conducts a comparative analysis looking at student achievement, engagement, and morale in the classes that did not use the strategies.
10/1/09	Action research teams meet to analyze and interpret the data.
10/3/09	Announce with complete transparency what worked, what failed. What did we learn? How will next semester be different? What can we apply now on a school-wide or system-wide basis?
10/6/09	Debrief of lessons learned with the core action research teams, including feedback on the impact and the process.

ing teacher leaders who would like to learn and use the process of action research in order to make recommendations about how to improve teacher assignment, grading, and common formative assessment. In addition, this principal identified two areas where he wanted to improve as a leader: sharing the vision and following up on details.

Notice that this plan contains just 24 high-impact actions, all of them written at a macro level of detail. Clearly, the 100-day project is not a tome. Nor is it a tedious task analysis of each and every step that this principal will need to do during the course of his project. What the 100-day project does accomplish is to develop a description that creates a flow of movement toward getting this project out of the mind of the leader and into the physical world where action can occur. In addition, someone coaching this principal can read his 100-day project and begin to understand what he wants to accomplish, and what he thinks is the best way forward.

100-Day Project Strategies

No two 100-day projects are alike. Because every educational system has different cultures and contexts, even if two leaders undertake a 100-day project with the same title and to accomplish the same outcomes, their strategies or approaches for getting the project off the ground are likely to differ. Strategies are the main approaches leaders use to focus the actions they intend to take to implement their project and meet milestones and deadlines (Allison, 2010; Reeves and Allison, 2010, 2009). For example, Exhibit 2.3 compares the strategies selected by two different elementary school principals, both with the same project of to "build teacher networks that use data to improve student achievement."

By looking at the project strategies employed by the two principals in Exhibit 2.3, we can make a few inferences about the context surrounding each leader. In the case of Principal A, we get the notion that this elementary school requires initial professional development in the work of Data Teams and structures for leading Data Team meetings and sharing findings. In the case of Principal B, we glean the idea

Comparison of Strategies for Two 100-Day Projects with the Same Aim

School Principal A: "Build teacher networks that use data to improve student achievement."	School Principal B: "Build teacher networks that use data to improve student achievement."
Strategy 1: Provide professional development about school-based Data Teams and the five-step process to all teachers.	**Strategy 1:** Revise the schedule to ensure three hours of common planning time for teachers of the same courses to meet together.
Strategy 2: Identify grade-level Data Team leaders and provide them with specialized training for efficiently running Data Team meetings.	**Strategy 2:** Select four courses in math and language arts in which teachers will develop and give common assessments on the Power Standards.
Strategy 3: Hold an "in house" data fair at the end of the first quarter so teams can share their strategies and results so far.	**Strategy 3:** Share the results of this work through multiple public methods, for example, prominently displayed Data Wall, presentation to school board, write-up in parent newsletter, presentations by the teachers at faculty development meetings.

that this school context requires schedule refinements so that teachers have time to meet together to develop common formative assessments and share the results after students take them in select classes of math and language arts.

Principals are responsible for implementing projects with awareness of and concern for the context of the organizational system surrounding them. To not be aware of where projects can begin within the system is to set the project up for failure. Coaches can help individuals set up their projects with effective opening strategies by asking some of the following questions:

- Where do you see an invitation within the system for this project to start?

- What seems the natural place for the people in your system to become involved in this project?
- What currently exists in the system to support this project?
- Where can this project begin to take hold?
- Who wants to take part in this project? What do they bring to the table?
- Where are the greatest learning needs related to this project?
- What would get this project off the ground?
- Where are people in the system ready to begin in this project?

Project strategies are the opening approaches leaders find to get their project moving. As projects progress, the approaches leaders use to keep them moving will change. Leaders should start with just three opening strategies that match the context and climate of the system they work within. Once the opening strategies are identified, leaders identify high-impact actions to get the strategies working.

High-Impact Actions

The actions written into the sample plan depicted in Exhibit 2.2 can be sorted into four broad categories: *learning, evidence, attitudes,* and *decisions*—otherwise known as L.E.A.D. (Allison, 2010; Reeves & Allison, 2009):

Learning: Leaders of successful projects ensure that they and others build their knowledge and expertise. This category serves as a reminder that the best leaders engage in learning in order to make wise decisions that lead to excellence. Populate your 100-day project with actions that require yourself and others to learn. Here are some examples of learning actions:

- Plan and implement professional development experiences geared to the roles and needs of each stakeholder group.
- Engage in book and article studies.
- Hold focus groups and conversations about the ideas in the project.

- Conduct action research projects.
- Explore Web sites and visit other exemplary programs.
- Be mentored by someone who is an expert in the topics of the project.

Evidence: The evidence category reminds leaders to consider relevant information from multiple points of view in order to fully illuminate the issue. Leaders who take time to analyze and discuss relevant evidence create more accurate and complete pictures for themselves and others to see. Populate your 100-day project with actions that require yourself and others to collect, analyze, report, and post data (quantitative and qualitative). What evidence do you have to inform your decisions (data, examples, facts from different points of view)? Here are some examples of evidence actions:

- Determine what student achievement and adult action data to analyze.
- Convene focus groups about the topics in the project, and analyze the transcripts for trends and themes.
- Create mini–case studies.
- Display data.
- Maintain logs of strategies and their impact.
- Identify the key indicators to identify and monitor.
- Celebrate early wins.

Attitude: The attitude category reminds leaders that human beings respond emotionally to projects and the changes they bring. During any change process, emotions play a role. Sometimes individuals and teams are eager to improve but are afraid of how their roles will change. Leaders must remember to look at how their attitudes impact their projects as well. Populate your 100-day project with actions that take into account the emotional side of motivating people to change. Here are some examples of attitude actions:

- Communicate the vision early and often. Be sure to describe how the new initiative benefits all stakeholders.

- Involve individuals and teams in designing their roles and responsibilities in the new reality.
- Keep a journal of the implementation process, noting how you feel about events.
- Set personal learning goals and ask others to do the same.
- Identify the potential challenges and brainstorm ways to mitigate them.
- Establish supportive relationships and networks.

Decision: Projects require action. Ultimately, decisions reveal exactly what has changed. Once the learning, evidence, and emotions have been considered, decisions show that the project is moving forward. Populate your 100-day project with actions that create a new result or represent a choice. Examples of decision actions include:

- Roles and responsibilities
- Policies, guidelines, and practices
- Resources
- Teams
- Schedules
- Deadlines
- Data to monitor
- Information to share and receive
- Program structures

Leaders who premeditate actions that are known to move projects forward and reflect on them through coaching conversations put themselves ahead of the curve.

L.E.A.D. as a Parallel Process during the Coaching Conversation

Coaches can also use L.E.A.D. during the coaching conversation in order to guide them as they develop strong mediating questions to engage their coachees. Questions about learning, evidence, affect, and decisions cause coachees to *think about* learning, evidence, affect, and decisions. For example, coaches could say:

1. "Tell me more about what you see as the greatest learning needs of each stakeholder group." (Example of a "learning" question)
2. "How do you envision using the data to guide and reflect on this project?" (Example of an "evidence" question)
3. "Who else in the school cares deeply about making this project a success?" (Example of an "affect" question)
4. "How could these decisions leverage resources and systems for future projects?" (Example of a "decisions" question)

Similarly, the L.E.A.D. framework guides coachees to think deeply about how to make focused headway in their project. Coaches who use the L.E.A.D. framework in their coaching practice feel confident that the questions they ask coachees to encourage reflection will truly be in service to the coachees.

One hundred–day projects are personal working plans for leading projects that align with the mission of the organization. They should never be an exercise in compliance. If leaders develop 100-day projects simply to satisfy a requirement for someone else, the plan becomes impractical and ineffective. Ideally, leaders who work with a coach use their 100-day project to focus the coaching conversations. One hundred–day projects combined with coaching provide the opportunity for deep reflection about learning as a leader.

A Call to Coaching

If coaching is a development model for supporting good leaders in doing more of and better at the best work aligned with the mission of the organization, then imagine *your* educational organization filled with leaders who seek coaching and who provide coaching for their peers, their colleagues, and the people they supervise. Imagine the outcomes coaching will produce for these leaders, their teams, staff members, and students.

Every time a leader chooses to coach instead of give advice or give the "right" answer, they open a window and invite fresh thoughts into the room. Coaching is like taking a deep breath. In an era of "busyness," where many people feel overwhelmed and overworked, coaching provides time and space for renewal.

References

Allison, E. (2009). Introduction to coaching. *The Reeves report.* Retrieved from http://www.leadandlearn.com

Allison, E. (2010). *The foundations of great coaching for sustainable change and a greater good.* Salem, MA: Orange Dog Press.

Bossidy, L., and Charan, R. (2002). *Execution: The discipline of getting things done.* New York: Crown Business.

International Coach Federation. (2008). ICF professional coaching core competencies. Retrieved from www.coachfederation.org/includes/media/docs/CoreCompEnglish.pdf

Joyce, B., & Showers, B. (1995). *Student achievement through staff development.* White Plains, NY: Longman.

Mezirow, J. (2000). Learning to think as an adult: Core concepts of transformation theory. In J. Mezirow & Associates (Eds.), *Learning as transformation* (pp. 3–34). San Francisco, CA: Jossey-Bass.

Reeves, D. B., & Allison, E. (2009). *Renewal coaching: Sustainable change for individuals and organizations.* San Francisco, CA: Jossey-Bass.

Reeves, D. B., & Allison, E. (2010). *Renewal coaching workbook.* San Francisco, CA: Jossey-Bass.

Watkins, M. D. (2003). *The first 90 days: Critical success strategies for new leaders at all levels.* Boston, MA: Harvard Business School Publishing.

CHAPTER THREE

Leadership Mindset

AINSLEY ROSE

I ADMIT TO A WEAKNESS for big-box shopping centers, particularly those that house a Home Depot, Barnes & Noble, or Chapters Indigo, if in Canada. If you are like me, you have a hard time passing by without glancing at the latest in business books or browsing the litany of magazines or shelves replete with books on leadership—not unlike Home Depot with 15 different models of hammer drills. I have come to realize that the business section beckons each time, and I take the bait. I must say, though, little has changed from the last time I stopped by to browse—I rarely buy, being an educator; I have come to value the community library. Leadership books abound, whether in the library or at the bookstore, but seldom do I see any titles that are vastly different from the last time I dropped by, save that most of the best sellers now appear to be one-word titles: *Switch, Drive, Outliers,* and so on.

That said, here I am trying to engage you by offering you a chapter in this leadership book that I hope will display fresh thinking more than that which is available in your favorite big bookstore. In all my reading about leadership, I have come to realize that most leadership books are written for the business world. Then, we in education try to fit those theories into our work in schools and classrooms. By now, some, like me, have tired of the notion that business clairvoyance should drive our beliefs and values about best practice in education. After all, we have the world of business to thank for strategic planning, zero-based budgeting, total quality management, site-based management, among other innovations that have long since been outsourced or passed on to the innovation graveyard. That is not to say, as educators, we have not benefited from some of the business world's innovations. Jim Collins (2001) is still cited extensively, and I for one continue to examine and laud strategies using the concepts I gained from his valuable contribution in *Good to Great*. Other beneficial contributions garnered from the world of business writing have led education to adopt SMART (specific, measurable, achievable, relevant, and timely) goals and mission and vision statements that have proved useful over time.

At the risk of offending our business colleagues any further, then, I move on to establish the premise upon which this chapter is based. As with my learned peers, some of whom have authored other chapters in this volume on leadership, it has become more clear to me that leadership is much like a chameleon and takes the shape and colors of its surroundings. As Deutschman (2007, p. 163) says, "After all a company is no more than a bunch of people united by common practices, beliefs, and 'frames.'"

The words "leadership" and "change" have become synonymous to some degree. If you are a leader, you must be either initiating, leading, or resisting some form of change and, for the most part, struggling all the while doing so in the midst of making that change. So, too, might you be trying to get others to make the changes that you so desperately need or feel are necessary to fulfill a mandate that you may have inherited and for which you are being held accountable. Your ability to make those changes might stem from your innate ability, your apparent charisma, or your passion to make a difference (Chase, 2010). Whatever the impetus, the common factor is one's ability to move an organization that is replete with individuals, all of whom possess a variety of opinions, beliefs, and values, many of which may not concur with those of the leader.

What, then, compels us to do this work, let alone be successful at it, and to whom can we turn as models of our efforts? Reeves (2009, p. 54) offers one response: "Although we can certainly learn from the lives of Harriet Tubman and George Washington, Martin Luther King Jr. and Simón Bolívar, Abraham Lincoln and Susan B. Anthony, we are poorly advised to compare our leadership efforts to these historical ideals." Kotter (2005, p. 132) suggests there are two aspects that determine our success or lack thereof. He says that first, thinking differently can change behavior and lead to better results, and second, feeling differently can change behavior more and therefore lead to better results.

In most instances you may have the competency to pull off the change effort, or at the very least the character to do so. Character and competence, then, are your only choices, or so it seems. Reeves (2009, p. 54) makes the point more clear: "The complexities of change leadership require not the perfect composite of every trait, but rather a team that exhibits leadership traits and exercises leadership responsibilities in a way that no individual leader, past or present, possibly could."

This notion might help to explain why some leaders are so effective while others struggle, or why some leaders are successful while others with the same conditions—dare I say a similar staff—are unable to make the necessary changes required in a school bereft of student and adult success. Whitaker (2003, p. 13) asks similar questions: "What really makes the difference between two schools? What matters most in the classroom? Effective principals understand the answer to these questions; indeed, they know that the real issue is not *what* is the variable, but *who*." Could it be that too many of our school leaders are more concerned with trying to change those around them than looking inward at themselves? I have come to believe that who you are shapes your thinking about things, people, and situations around you. Covey (1989, p. 24) first drew my attention to the possibility when he wrote, "Each of us has many maps in our head, which can be divided into two main categories: maps of the way things are, or realities, and maps of the way things should be, or values. We interpret everything we experience through these mental maps. . . . We simply assume that the way we see things is the way they really are or the way they should be. And our attitudes and behaviors grow out of those assumptions. The way we see things is the source of the way we think and the way we act." Ralph Waldo Emerson is said to have declared, "Who you are speaks so loudly I can't hear what you are saying." This suggests to me that we need to pay far more attention to the beliefs and values of leaders than we do presently. When a leader is hired, often too much of the emphasis is on competence rather than character. What "mental maps" do leaders hold dear, and how do those maps drive their work and their interactions with the staff of a school or the workers in their business—both places where their focus should be? The notion of mental maps leads me to Covey's circular model, which is best illustrated by the terms "see-do-get." In other words, how you see the world determines what you do and the results you get from what you do.

I share an example to illustrate this important principle. As a former elementary and secondary school principal, I was expected to resolve a long-standing tension between the extracurricular arts and physical education activities (sports teams practicing or playing during class instructional time) and the instruction of academic classes. As a former physical education teacher, I knew the benefits of participation in extracurricular activities, but all the academic teachers held a different belief, a belief about the value of students participating in class instruction, particularly when they were failing a given course or subject. How I saw student participation in extracurricular activities led me to generate policies that continued to permit students to participate on an athletic team despite a failing grade in one course. As a result, what I *got* was widespread, continuous, and at times vitriolic pressure to discontinue my approach.

I came to realize that the academic teachers and the extracurricular teachers had different "*sees*," which led them to *do* and *act* differently, getting results that in some cases put students in a tenuous position when they had to choose either to play the sport and risk failing or drop the sport to save the grade, making matters worse. My task, I now understood, was to create a new "*see*," which both groups could share, leading them to *do* things differently in order to *get* different results that would not put students, or their coaches, in a compromising situation. Over time we reframed our thinking about the purpose and value of student participation in extracurricular activities and the need to balance that with the need for students to meet their academic obligations. This led us to create a policy that blended the value of student participation with the commitment to maintain passing grades in all their courses. In other words, as a school, we changed our *see* that led us to *do* something different and as a result *got* a different outcome that benefited all groups.

I also held a belief that, as a principal, I was to try to change some of my teachers who, I believed, exhibited a "negative attitude." For years I thought, if only I could change the teacher's attitude, all would be perfect in the school. Needless to say it took some time, years in fact, to come to the conclusion that my attempt to change attitudes was a losing cause. With experience, and a lot of reading and studying, I came to understand that my attempts to change attitude would never achieve the desired results for those teachers who I felt required an attitude adjustment. A change in attitude follows, rather than precedes, a change in behavior. Reeve's (2009, p. 10) supports my contention when he says, "Change leaders know that they do not change organizations without changing individual behaviour, and they will not change individual behaviour without affirming the people behind the behaviour."

Deutschman (2007, p. 201) takes the point further. He says, "While the medical model assumes that people are sick or disabled and need to be cured, the three keys to change assume that people are well or capable but need to learn habits, skills, and mindsets they don't have yet."

My notions of what really drives leadership ability and the impact or effect on a school or a business have been shaped and consolidated by Carole Dweck's work. Dweck (2006) says, "For twenty years, my research has shown that *the view you adopt for yourself* profoundly affects the way you lead your life." I suggest that when she refers to life, she means all aspects—both personal and, for the purpose of this chapter, professional. Her abiding passion to understand how people cope with failure drove her to conduct the research that led to the theory of mindset. The notion is that we all have a predisposition to either one of two mindsets—a fixed mindset or a growth mindset—

each with a set of predispositions that determine how we respond when faced with a challenge or problem. As leaders' lives are filled with challenges hourly, daily, monthly, and beyond it behooves us to consider the impact of a leader's response and the effects of those decisions and how they might be different.

Earlier in this chapter I posed questions about why some leaders are effective while others struggle. Others have asked the timeless question, are leaders born or made? Similarly, the work on mindset began with questions about why some students thrive on challenges while others who are just as intelligent appear to give up, withdraw, or resist even trying under similar circumstances. The answer to the latter question appears to lie in our understanding about the characteristics of mindsets as either fixed or growth. For example, a leader with a growth mindset believes that leadership abilities can be learned through experience, effort, and hard work in time, even though the individual may not have those abilities. In other words, good leaders are made. Fixed mindset leaders view leadership as an innate attribute, believing that leaders are born, not made.

Consider for a moment how this framework would play out for those respective leaders in their companies or schools. What might be the impact of policies and procedures in those schools where the leaders happen to be of a fixed mindset and the school was underachieving or stagnant in terms of student achievement? What of the fixed mindset principal in the high-achieving school whose student achievement scores began to regress? Can we anticipate how a principal with a growth mindset might shape the school with a high rate of free and reduced lunch and a high English language learner population? We could imagine many different permutations and combinations of schools and mindsets of leaders that would dictate the outcomes of the actions of each. Indeed, that type of imagining is precisely what we should do. I suggest that the mindset of the leader is a critical component in deciding and even predicting the success, lack of success, or eventual success of that school.

More important, we need to train and develop our educational leaders to be much more attentive to their own characteristics in order to help them change their outlook and perspective, given the impact their outlook has on the choices they might make and on their ability to lead. In support of my assertion Deutschman (2007, p. 199) says, "When you're locked into the mindset that helped you succeed, then it's difficult even to think about the profound changes you'll have to respond to. But if you practice change, if you keep up your ability to change, if you use it rather than lose it, then you'll be ready to change whenever you have to." Whitaker (2003, p. 19) places similar emphasis on the need to be more introspective when he writes, "Success in any profession starts with a focus on self. After all, we are the one variable that we can most easily and most productively influence." Our ability to look inward becomes primordial in growing not only our competence but also our character, as both are essential to the function of leadership. Simply, there are two kinds of leaders: those who want to get things done and others who don't want to make mistakes (Maxwell, 2007).

One of the prime functions of a leader is the role that he has in shaping the vision, mission, values, and goals of the organization. Furthermore, in order to bring the individuals of the organization to share that vision, mission, values, and goals the leader needs to be able to influence those for whom he has responsibility in the organization. Doing so requires that the leader be clear about his beliefs and values in order to demonstrate them to his colleagues by acting accordingly. We have all heard the now-famous phrase, you need to walk the talk. To do so necessitates a clear understanding of one's own principles and values. Kouzes and Posner (2007, p. 50), prolific and well-respected authors on the subject of leadership for several decades, say, "To act with integrity, you must first know who you are. You must know what you stand for, what you believe in, and what you care most about. Clarity of values will give you confidence to make the tough decisions, to act with determination, and to take charge of your life." Does it make a difference, then, whether the principal is characterized as having either a fixed or a growth mindset if she is unable to articulate her beliefs? Or is it more likely that the growth mindset principal would be able to do so whereas the fixed mindset principal, by her very nature, would not be able to do so? These are intriguing and important questions that I rarely hear being asked. I expect that part of the answer stems from what Kouzes and Posner (2007, p. 344) say in their popular treatise on leadership: "The instrument of leadership is the self, and mastery of the art of leadership comes from mastery of the self."

Similarly, Collins (2001, p. 13), in his work, in which he identified what good companies and businesses did to make themselves great, was somewhat surprised to find that a different type of leadership was required to turn a good company into a great one. Conventional wisdom has always held that charismatic leaders made the best leaders, when in fact what Collins found was that the good-to-great leaders were "self-effacing, reserved, even shy—these leaders are a paradoxical blend of personal humility and professional will. They are more like Lincoln and Socrates than Patton or Caesar." Collins's research led him to formulate the notion of a Level 5 leader as a person who blends extreme personal humility with intense professional will (p. 21). This is hardly a description of a fixed mindset person, but there is nothing to say that a growth mindset person necessarily possesses these attributes, either. What I would say, however, is that it is more likely that a growth mindset person would be more sensitive to whether or not he has these attributes and what he would do to acquire them if he found himself lacking them. Even Collins postulates that there are two categories of people: those who are not Level 5 leaders, nor do they have the potential to be so, and those who have the potential to be Level 5 leaders, which sounds very much like the growth and fixed mindset principle Dweck outlines. Collins writes, "The first category consists of people who could never in a million years bring themselves to subjugate their egoist needs to the greater ambition of building something larger and more lasting than themselves" (p. 36). Those in the second category of people have the potential to become Level 5 leaders. Collins says, "under the right circumstances—self-reflection, conscious personal development, a mentor, a great teacher, loving parents, a significant life experience, a Level 5 boss, or any number of other factors—they begin to develop" (p. 37).

My experience after almost 39 years in education, most of which were spent in some leadership capacity, supports Dweck's statement, quoted above, that "the view you adopt for yourself profoundly affects the way you lead your life." My own mentor, a friend, former educator, and former area superintendent in his 80th year, is just one example of what Dweck would call a growth mindset person and to which Collins would attribute the Level 5 leader characteristics. I first met him as a result of a series of interviews with associates of his, principals, all of whom named him as the person who had the greatest influence on their lives and careers. He was, and is to this day, a self-effacing, humble individual, devoted to his faith, family, and friends, as he was as a teacher, principal, and area superintendent. I can also point to my predecessor, the principal of the high school to which I was finally assigned, as he was a person of high moral character, an effective administrator with a remarkable sense of humour, and highly principled. Both these individuals were instrumental in my own success. One is still alive and continues to shape my thinking and beliefs about education and leadership, which to some extent prompted me to write this chapter.

What they have led me to understand is that there is another aspect of a leadership mindset that bears examination—the degree to which influence shapes a leader's ability to cause other people to want to do what otherwise they might not. I have often joked with principals for whom I was responsible that you are only a leader if someone is following.

Influence

So what causes people to want to follow someone? Cialdini (1984, p. xi) wrote, "Just what are the factors that cause one person to say yes to another person? And which techniques most effectively use these factors to bring about such compliance?" While I do not care for the word "compliance," there is a certain mystery in this notion of influence. To help us understand how influence can change people's behavior, I refer you to the fascinating work of Patterson, Grenny, Maxfield,

McMillan, and Switzler (2008), who have written extensively on this subject. In order to truly understand the magnitude of influence and the impact for leadership behavior, I encourage you to read their work. They have documented intriguing accounts and examples of change efforts around the world, all of which they attribute to one's ability to influence behavior using various strategies, which they claim we too can learn. Deutschman (2007, p. 151) makes a similar claim when he writes, "Change is a paradoxical process, and trying to change your own life means opening up to new ideas and practices that may seem illogical or even insane to you, at least until you have experienced them long enough to develop a new understanding."

My thought is that to change someone or something requires an ability to influence the person to act in a new way. Patterson et al. (2008, p. 26) say that influence geniuses focus on behavior. They recount the intriguing case of Dr. Mimi Silbert, the director of the Delancey Street Foundation in San Francisco, who works extensively to rehabilitate psychotic criminals, most of whom have reoffended. Silbert says, "The hardest thing we do here is to try to get rid of the code of the street. It says, 'care only about yourself, and don't rat on anyone.'" However, "If you reverse those two behaviors you can change everything else" (p. 29). Another case they cite involves the story of Dr. Ethna Reid from Salt Lake City, who as part of her doctoral studies examined strategies to improve students' poor reading habits. What she discovered in her research was what Patterson and colleagues refer to as vital behaviors, in this instance, the use of praise versus punishment. The best reading teachers, probably having a growth mindset, rewarded positive performance more frequently than did other teachers.

The Heath brothers say that to change someone's behavior one needs to get her to act in a new way or, more specifically, to change her situation (Heath & Heath, 2010). The brain is of two minds, as it were: one is the rational side, and the other is the emotional half. It may be a stretch to suggest that both of Dweck's mindsets, fixed and growth, may be ascribed to either the emotional brain or the rational brain, but it is an intriguing thought nonetheless. Would a fixed mindset leader have the capacity to influence another when he himself sees no reason to try? Does the growth mindset leader always find it easier to influence behavior in those individuals with a need to change certain patterns or habits? It seems that, as Deutschman points out (above), one has to be able to change one's own life before one has any hope of changing (influencing) others' lives. Heath and Heath (2010) refer to this as self-supervision. Once again introspection is shown to be the hallmark of effective leaders. Now you might say this is not new or startling evidence, but I say why, if we know this, do we still encounter leaders who do not apply these approaches? Kotter (2008, p. ix), in his book *A Sense of Urgency*, suggests that if the sense of urgency is not high enough and complacency is not low enough, everything becomes more difficult to change. Change will not occur unless people see the need to change.

Concluding Thoughts

So what might these concepts look like from a practical standpoint? First, a leader needs to have a clear sense of who she is, what she believes, and where she wants to go. To achieve this clarity, leaders need to ask themselves the following questions:

1. What's sacred around here?

2. What could be changed?

3. What am I prepared to do to help bring this change about?

Dweck (2006, pp. 6–7) puts it this way: "We need leaders to create transformed schools using a new growth mindset: The passion for stretching yourself and sticking to it, even (or especially) when it's not going well, is the hallmark of the growth mindset. This is the mindset that allows people to thrive during some of the most challenging times in their lives. This *growth mindset* is based on the belief that your basic qualities are things you can cultivate through your efforts. Although people may differ in every which way—in their initial talents and aptitudes, interests, or temperaments—everyone can change and grow through application and experience."

Second, we turn once again to Kouzes and Posner (2007, p. 14), who write extensively about leadership traits. They identify five practices that good leadership is built upon, which are consistent with many of the notions outlined above:

1. Model the way.
2. Inspire a shared vision.
3. Challenge the process.
4. Enable others to act.
5. Encourage the heart.

Finally, the words of my friend, colleague, and mentor Gordon Elhard ring loudly as I conclude with some principles of leadership that he has coined and shared generously with me, which have created a mindset for my work over the years. He says:

1. People are more important than things.
2. The individual is more important than the group.
3. Relationships are more important than skills.
4. Values are more important than knowledge.
5. Feelings are more important than facts.
6. Giving is more important than receiving.
7. Listening is more important than talking.
8. Developing people's strengths is more important than correcting their weaknesses.
9. Purpose is more important than position.
10. The walk is more important than the talk.

References

Chase, M. (2010). Should coaches believe in innate ability? The importance of leadership mindset. *Quest, 62,* 296–307.

Cialdini, R. B. (1984). *Influence: The psychology of persuasion* (rev. ed.). New York, NY: HarperCollins.

Collins, J. (2001). *Good to great: Why some companies make the leap . . . and others don't.* New York, NY: HarperCollins.

Covey, S. R. (1989). *The 7 habits of highly effective people: Powerful lessons in personal change.* New York, NY: Simon & Schuster.

Deutschman, A. (2007). *Change or die: Could you change when change matters most?* New York, NY: HarperCollins.

Dweck, C. S. (2006). *Mindset: The new psychology of success.* New York, NY: Random House.

Heath, C., & Heath, D. (2010). *Switch: How to change when change is hard.* New York, NY: Broadway Books.

Kotter, J. (2005). *Our iceberg is melting: Changing and succeeding under any conditions.* New York, NY: St. Martin's Press.

Kotter, J. (2008). *A sense of urgency.* Boston, MA: Harvard Business School Press.

Kouzes, J. M., & Posner, B. Z. (2007). *The leadership challenge* (4th ed.). San Francisco, CA: Jossey-Bass.

Maxwell, J. C. (2007). *Talent is never enough: Discover the choices that will take you beyond your talent.* Nashville, TN: Thomas Nelson.

Patterson. K., Grenny, J., Maxfield, D., McMillan, R., & Switzler, A. (2008). *Influencer: The power to change anything.* New York, NY: McGraw-Hill.

Reeves, D. B. (2009). *Leading change in your school: How to conquer myths, build commitment, and get results.* Alexandria, VA: ASCD.

Whitaker, T. (2003). *What great principals do differently: Fifteen things that matter most.* New York, NY: Eye on Education.

CHAPTER FOUR

Leadership for a High-Performance Culture

CATHY J. LASSITER

I F YOU HAVE SERVED IN PUBLIC EDUCATION for any number of years, chances are you have been involved in an initiative that never fully materialized. The district's top leadership staged an exciting kick-off, followed by everyone going to training and gung-ho support being offered by the building's leaders. But soon after, inevitably, teachers lose touch with the training, and although they try to implement what they have learned, they do not receive quality feedback for improvement. Leaders, often fuzzy themselves on what is expected, focus on the initiative less and less, and before long the new program fades away. Why does it happen? Why does it keep happening? How can it be stopped?

The answer is simple, but the work is complex. The new programs failed because the culture of the organization could not support them. The leaders did not take into consideration the current culture, that is, "the way we do business around here." According to Reid and Hubbell (2005), "Culture is the learned assumptions on which people base their daily behavior. Culture drives the organization, its actions and results." The authors note that hospitals, financial institutions, government, and many types of organizations are increasingly paying attention to the effectiveness of their performance management, which includes creating a culture of high performance. However, many leaders, whether they are in business, nonprofit organizations, medicine, or education, demonstrate over and over that they would rather do anything than address culture as a core strategy for success. They consider culture a "soft" indicator, one that will come along once their strategies are in place and working well. Nothing could be further from the truth.

The literature in business and education, as well as analyses of published studies on motivation, human behavior, and leadership, is clear: High-performing organizations go the extra mile to create cultures where people are prepared for and expect change. The culture supports risk taking, expects mistakes during the learning phase, and supports individual growth and development. Peter Drucker, the organizational and performance management guru, is credited with saying "Culture eats strategy for breakfast." In this chapter we examine culture as a core strategy for schools and classrooms and apply five core elements of creating a high-performing culture to meet the wave of demands coming in the next decade for schools across the nation.

Culture Change

Much has changed in public education since 2000. Public schools have become much better at collecting and charting data, and they have disaggregated their data to highlight student achievement in various sub-group categories. Districts and schools have developed standards-based curricula aligned to their state's standards. Many schools and districts have developed or purchased formative assessments, aligned to their district and state standards, to regularly monitor student achievement. Teachers and administrators have begun to shed their isolationist ways and routinely work in teams to solve their student achievement challenges. Principals and teachers are increasingly placing the responsibility of student learning on themselves as opposed to the students, their families, their socioeconomic condition, or their home language. These changes represent significant progress in just 10 years.

Heifetz and Linsky (2002) categorize these changes into two types: adaptive and technical. Most of the change seen across schools over the past decade can be considered technical. Block scheduling, com-

mon planning, double dosing in reading or math, new reading programs, new evaluation systems, school improvement planning, and
data analysis are all technical changes. They require a change in the
way educators *do* their job. On the contrary, adaptive changes require
a fundamental shift in the way educators *think and feel* about their
work. Adaptive change includes what teachers believe is possible and
how they view students who struggle, what limitations they place on
themselves and the children, and their belief in their own ability to
make a difference. In short, adaptive changes involve changing the
culture (Heifetz & Linsky, 2002). Adaptive changes have occurred less
frequently than the technical changes over the past decade. In the
coming decade, most districts will have to climb higher and stretch
harder to achieve the adaptive changes needed to create a high-
performance culture capable of meeting new challenges.

New Demands

The demands of the next 10 years will require deeper, sustainable
change, not surface change. At the time of this writing 41 states and
the District of Columbia have adopted the nation's Common Core
State Standards (CCSS). These standards were developed by educators from states around the country with support from the Council of
Chief State School Officers and the National Governor's Association
(2010). Having a set of national standards does not, on the surface,
present a new challenge to the current and future adopters. However,
the challenge will become clear once states and districts begin to
"unwrap" the standards to determine the level of rigor and skill
required to teach and learn them. The Thomas B. Fordham Institute,
an organization that has been studying state standards since 1997,
released a new study of the state standards and the CCSS in July 2010.
It found that the CCSS in English language arts are clearly superior to
existing standards in 37 states and too close to call in 11 other states.
It further determined that only California, Indiana, and Washington,
D.C., had existing standards that were clearly superior to the CCSS. In
mathematics, it found the CCSS to be clearly superior to 39 state stan-

dards and too close to call in 11 states (Carmichael, Martino, Porter-Magee, & Wilson, 2010). As states begin to unveil their plans to implement the CCSS, districts and schools will endeavor to rise to new expectations. By 2014 national assessments will measure school, district, and state effectiveness in teaching the standards to all students. Of course, the media, both local and national, will provide comparisons from state to state, district to district, and school to school. They will entice readers with headlines proclaiming states as best in the nation and worst in the nation. They will undoubtedly make the same pronouncements with districts and individual schools. In this environment, performing at high levels will be of paramount importance to governors, senators, state superintendents, local superintendents, and mayors, resulting in intense pressure on school leaders and teachers to produce results.

Additional pressure is brewing courtesy of the Race to the Top competitive grants being offered by the federal government. The Race to the Top program, launched by the U.S. Department of Education in November 2009 through the American Recovery and Reinvestment Act of 2009, provides $4.35 billion for the Race to the Top Fund, a competitive grant program designed to encourage and reward states that are creating the conditions for education innovation and reform; achieving significant improvement in student outcomes, including making substantial gains in student achievement, closing achievement gaps, improving high school graduation rates, and ensuring student preparation for success in college and careers; and implementing ambitious plans in four core education reform areas (U.S. Department of Education, 2009). The application criteria for states to receive a Race to the Top grant are the following:

- Adopting standards and assessments that prepare students to succeed in college and the workplace and to compete in the global economy;

- Building data systems that measure student growth and success, and inform teachers and principals about how they can improve instruction;

- Recruiting, developing, rewarding, and retaining effective teachers and principals, especially where they are needed most; and

- Turning around our lowest-achieving schools.

To date, two rounds of funding have been completed, with one round to go. Thirty-five states and the District of Columbia originally submitted applications for the funds, 19 finalists made the first cut, and 11 winners were awarded money (UPI, July 27, 2010). In the first round, Tennessee was awarded $500 million and Delaware was awarded $100 million. In round two, ten additional winners were announced with all of the fanfare of a Powerball Lottery event; they included New York and Florida ($700 million each); Georgia, Ohio, and North Carolina ($400 million each); Massachusetts and Maryland ($250 million each); and Hawaii, Rhode Island, and Washington, D.C. ($75 million each) (UPI, August 24, 2010). The losing states put forth great effort to compete for the funds, but they walked away with nothing. For example, the state of New Jersey submitted a 1,000-page application; Governor Chris Christy grabbed headlines for his comments about New Jersey losing in the competition. Indeed, the stakes are high.

This level of government spending during the nation's economic crisis has become a political powder keg. Every day citizens are unemployed at rates not seen since the Great Depression, and record-breaking rates of home foreclosures continue to challenge the fragile U.S. economy. Fueled by the media, which have their own survival at stake, communities and parents are demanding more for their investment. A term not often heard in education before, ROI, or return on investment, is at the forefront of discussions on education both nationally and locally. Large urban divisions, where spending is high and results are low, are the focus of much of the attention. This point of view was poignantly illustrated in the film *Waiting for Superman*, in which few schools were shown to have cultures of high performance or excellence; in fact, most, according to the film, do not (Weber, 2010). The movie offers viewers heartbreaking scenes of students trying to get into high-performing schools, only to be disappointed when not selected in the various lottery processes. The movie provides graphs and visuals that show a decline in America's ability to compete globally, and pushes a reform agenda. The film also takes direct aim at the two teacher unions and the teacher tenure system, as well as how teachers are evaluated for effectiveness. Following are the alarming statistics highlighted in the film (Weber, 2010):

- Eight years since the passage of the No Child Left Behind Act, and with four years left to reach the 100 percent proficiency goal, most states hover around 20 to 30 percent proficiency in math and reading.

- Among 30 developed countries, the United States is ranked 25th in math and 21st in science. When the comparison is restricted to the top 5 percent, the United States ranks last.

- Barely half of African American and Latino students graduate from high school.

- Most middle-class American high schools still track their students based on the old economy, but by 2020, 123 million American jobs will be in high-skill, high-pay occupations, from computer programming to bioengineering, but only 50 million Americans will be qualified to fill them.

- In 1970, the United States produced 30 percent of the world's college graduates. Today it produces only 15 percent.

- Since 1971, education spending has more than doubled from $4,300 per student to more than $9,000 per student. Yet, in the same period, reading and math scores have remained flat and they have risen in every other developed country.

Despite the film's message, there are many outstanding schools in the United States, and many are nested in low-performing districts. There are many wonderful, effective teachers who happen to work in low-performing schools. How does a school principal isolate her team from the ineffective policies of a low-performing district and create a school where all students receive a world-class education? How does a principal in a high-performance district create a sense of urgency to improve? Researchers like Karin Chenoweth with the Education Trust have chronicled these schools in numerous reports and books, showing that schools are breaking the mold in the most unlikely places. The research being conducted at Mid-continent Research for Education and Learning (McREL), Harvard University, Public Agenda, The Leadership and Learning Center, and various projects sponsored by the Wallace Foundation support the notion that high-performing schools exist in very challenging neighborhoods. What makes these schools high performers? How do they create and sustain a high-performance culture in the face of many challenges? There are indeed common characteristics or elements of these high-performance cultures that enable their teachers and leaders to work together, sustain commitment and engagement, prepare them for new demands, and propel them to higher performance, no matter what challenge they encounter. The core, common elements of these high-performance cultures can best be detailed under five main headings:

1. Communicating a clear, purpose-driven vision and mission

2. Growing and refining teaching talent

3. Developing *before* distributing leadership

4. Analyzing progress data for adults and students

5. Creating an internal accountability system

Core Element 1:
Purpose-Driven Vision and Mission

Nonprofit institutions exist for the sake of their mission. They exist to make a difference in society and in the life of the individual. The first task of the leader of such an organization is to make sure that everybody sees the mission, hears it, and lives it (Drucker, 1990). But the reality today is that leaders develop and distribute a mission statement and *assume* they will go forth and make it happen. The daily work of all staff is not explicitly linked to the mission, people do not know their individual roles in achieving the mission, and they see no real connection in their work to a higher purpose or greater good. This is a huge missed opportunity for leaders, especially school leaders. Drucker argues that the mission has to be clear and simple. It has to be bigger than any one person's capacity. It has to lift up people's vision. It has to make each person feel that he or she can make a difference—that each one can say, I have not lived in vain (Drucker, 1990). Researchers in education make similar arguments about the impact of creating a clear, shared vision and mission in a school setting.

In 2001 McREL conducted a four-year study to determine how high-poverty, high-performing schools beat the odds. The study's findings support the importance of vision to school improvement efforts. It identified 739 high-performing schools and 738 low-performing schools, all of which had 50 percent or more of their students on free or reduced-price lunch. The beat-the-odds schools developed, with input from teachers, a vision of success and a clear focus for their improvement efforts (Goodwin, 2010). The study found that both the high- and low-performing schools focused on many of the same strategies for improvement, such as assessment, monitoring, collaboration, and professional development. But it was the culture in which this work takes place that separated the high- from the low-performing schools. The high performers' vision and mission enabled them to assemble a package of reform strategies that helped establish a purpose motive. It provided a clear answer to why we do the work we do and set a clear goal and destination, as opposed to an isolated set of actions for teacher compliance. An organization's vision and mission should compel employee commitment and engagement. Engaged employees want their organization to succeed because they feel connected emotionally and socially to the mission, vision, and purpose.

Research is also emerging that shows all professionals, but especially teachers, want a sense of purpose and challenge in a job. Education is already infused with an important moral and policy purpose, but it is critical that explicit links be made between the daily work of teachers, the purpose of the school, and greater good to the community (Curtis & Wurtzel, 2010). This greater-good theory was tested in two separate studies conducted 25 years apart in the United Kingdom and Sweden by separate researchers involving blood donation. The conclusions, as described in *Drive*, by Dan Pink, are that people are more strongly motivated to donate blood if they feel as though it is for the good of the citizenry. It is their contribution to something bigger than themselves, something for the greater good that serves as a strong motivational force. Donating blood voluntarily provides donors with what the American Red Cross describes as a feeling money cannot buy (Pink, 2010). School leaders are in a prime position to provide this feeling that money cannot buy for their faculties by keeping the purpose and mission alive in their actions; recognizing team members for work aligned with the mission, including examples of "good work" in all communications; and making all decisions through the lens of the purpose or mission. Doing good work feels good. As long as the job provides clear goals, immediate feedback, and a level of challenge matching our skills, we have a chance to experience work as "good" (Gardner, Csikszentmihalyi, & Damon, 2001). Failure to make this connection will lead to the continued exodus of veteran and new teachers for jobs that provide a stronger sense of purpose, challenge, and recognition of good work (Curtis & Wurtzel, 2010).

About a year ago, the Coca-Cola Company created its long-term vision project entitled 2020 Vision. The resulting work provides an interesting example of how a highly profitable, global brand has capitalized on the research on what motivates human beings to engage in good work with a clear purpose motive. The company's Web site includes this statement about its mission: "Our roadmap starts with our mission, which is enduring. It declares our purpose as a company and serves as the standard against which we weigh our actions and decisions." It goes on to describe the three components of the Coca-Cola mission, which contains three clear, powerful statements that are purpose driven: (1) Refresh the world, (2) inspire moments of optimism and happiness, and (3) create value and make a difference. These statements have little to do with beverage distribution, but they provide a challenge and purpose to Coke workers world-wide that engages them in working toward the greater good (Coca-Cola Company, 2010). Remember, this is a soft drink company, not a nonprofit community service organization. Clearly, company leaders are leveraging the human desire for good work and yearning for purpose and challenge on their jobs. Schools, by nature of the work, have a more direct connection to the greater good and therefore should be able to match or exceed the mission and vision of a soft drink company.

Sandra Thorstenson, superintendent of Whittier Union High School District (WUHSD, 2010) in California, meets the mission criteria provided by Drucker for her school district. The mission for this high-performing district is to "achieve & maintain excellence in providing a comprehensive education for all students." In short, this district strives to provide an excellent education for each student it serves. In addition to the mission, the district has a set of belief statements that describe how its mindset about the teachers and leaders, their colleagues, the students, and their parents will impact their achievement of the mission. The district believes every student can learn, every student has worth and dignity, and every student must be prepared to meet the challenges and changing needs of society (WUHSD, 2010). In her letter to the community to kick off the new school year, Superintendent Thorstenson writes, "I want you to know that all of us at Whittier Union remain steadfastly dedicated to doing everything we can to ensure our students' well being and academic achievement and that they not only attain, but also surpass our expectations of what they can achieve" (WUHSD, 2010). Through these beliefs and this mindset, along with the district's purpose-based mission, it has established a strong foundation for a high-performance culture. And its results speak loudly to this fact. Whittier Union's five comprehensive high schools were ranked among the top third of all of California's schools with similar demographics. Additionally, three of the district's high schools made *Newsweek*'s America's Best High Schools List; less than 6 percent of the nation's high schools made the list. The superintendent was quoted as saying, "We will continue to set the bar high for all of our students and do 'Whatever It Takes' to help them reach those goals so that they may leave us well prepared for the challenges of college and beyond" (WUHSD, 2010).

Vickie Fleming, former superintendent of Redmond School District, Oregon, also understands mission and vision as the guiding force behind the work of a successful school district. She engineered a district mission and vision project known as the Redmond Educational Vision (REV): A Blueprint for Action. The development of this comprehensive vision project involved all stakeholders in imagining the future for students in Redmond and answering the question, Why do we exist? The Redmond vision is "Leading for Success in the 21st Century," and the mission is "Ensure a rigorous and relevant education that develops productive citizens for a local and global economy" (Redmond School District, 2007). Like Whittier Union and the Coca-Cola Company, REV explicitly details the shared beliefs, values, and commitments it expects from its people. An entire blueprint for action was developed around this work, which includes clear and urgent themes, student knowledge and skills, instructional core, programmatic focus, and stakeholder connections. A five-year strategic plan covering years 2007–2012 was also developed, with the mission serving as the guiding light. The results in Redmond are impressive. The district was recognized by the state of Oregon for "closing the achievement gap" in elementary schools (Redmond School District, 2009).

How can school principals establish a clear, purpose-based mission and vision for their schools, and what benefits will they reap? The good news is that people coming into education do so to make a difference in the lives of children. However, in order to create a culture centered around a purpose-driven mission, the principal must articulate it, celebrate it, and constantly communicate it to everyone touched by the school. Principals should engage their staffs in regular conversations about the mission of the school. They should constantly ask, Why do we exist? School leaders must listen to the thoughts, dreams, and vision of the people who work with them and demonstrate how they are all connected. A great exercise for any school faculty is to reflect on why they became teachers. Teachers will respond that they wanted to make difference, they wanted to pay back, they want to improve their community, and so on. The responses will not differ among grade levels, content, or geographic location. It is the responsibility of the principal to take these responses, marry them with his own, and craft a mission and vision that answer the question, Why do we exist?

But the work cannot stop here. As Drucker (1990) argues, the first task of the leader in a nonprofit organization is to ensure that everybody sees the mission, hears it, and lives it. The leader must use the mission as the filter for all decisions, all expenditures, and all communications. A well-articulated, purpose-driven mission will keep the team focused on the right work. It will enable them to see the big picture. It will provide them a "North Star." It will satisfy their desire for a challenge and their need to contribute to the greater good. And it will serve as the vehicle for struggling schools to become high performing and propel high performers to greater levels of success. Leaders who invest the time to do this work well will have engaged teams that are prepared and eager to tackle the ever-increasing demands of educating America's children.

Core Element 2:
Developed and Refined Teaching Talent

Vision alone does not make a culture high performing. In a school it is essential that every classroom is occupied by skilled and promising teachers. Good teachers seek work in high-performance cultures, where all students are expected to achieve at high levels and where all teachers and administrators focus on effective teaching as the core function of the school. Unfortunately, far too few teachers find work in such environments, which contributes to the loss of millions of teachers to retirement and new teacher attrition at the entry level. In fact, we are at a critical juncture with the teaching force in this country. We currently have 1.8 million baby boomers in the classroom. We are expected to lose 1.5 million of them in the next eight years. Added to this exodus is the annual loss of 2.5 million teachers of all ages due to job dissatisfaction (National Commission on Teaching and America's Future, 2010). Sadly, American schools are increasingly without great teaching talent at a time when it is needed more than ever. The statistics show that young teachers are 184 percent more likely to leave the profession than are middle-aged teachers, and the attrition rate for teachers with one to three years experience has risen to 40 percent. The annual cost of this constant teacher churn exceeds $7 billion and has no end in sight (National Commission on Teaching and America's Future, 2010) Ultimately, every district in the nation will be affected by the shrinking pool of qualified teachers, and the competition for good teachers is in full swing. Principals and central offices must act now to ensure their students will be taught by high-quality teachers. Contrary to the past practice of just recruiting new people to replace the old, they must concentrate their efforts on developing teaching talent in the staff they have and on retaining those teachers who show promise. High-performing schools have been doing this for years, and forward-thinking principals are well positioned to meet the new expectations of the 21st century. The rest will need to catch up quickly in order to have any hope of meeting the new demands and realizing success toward their mission.

Human capital management is not a required course in any graduate program that prepares school principals. Therefore, we must look to the private sector for strategies and structures to manage human capital to meet goals and realize the mission. Many successful companies use the "workforce of one" philosophy for developing talent. They consider each new and current employee on an individual basis, determining their strengths, setting goals for improvement, determining career interests, and sharing career paths that match those interests. They provide professional development targeted to specific skills, and they provide regular feedback for growth. Schools have not traditionally developed people in this manner. In fact, traditionally schools have followed the sink-or-swim mentality, and have lost many promising teachers in the process. Times have changed, and we cannot afford to lose any teacher with promise. The research today is clear: The quality and competence of the teacher makes the biggest difference in student achievement. However, we do not invest enough time, effort, and energy into developing talent in each teacher we hire.

What actions can a principal take to develop and retain teaching talent? First, a decision that it is worth the effort is necessary. Then a shift in the way professional development is delivered is essential. School leaders should forget the sink-or-swim approach they were trained with and adopt the "platinum rule" for teacher talent development: Do better for others than we would expect them to do for us (Allison & Reeves, 2009). According to Doug Reeves, author of more than 20 books on education, including *Transforming Professional Development into Student Results*, effective teaching comes from practice, in the classroom, with quality feedback for improvement. Developing talent in our teaching force is not about all-inclusive checklists that administrators use for compliance. Rather, teachers develop skill by focusing on a few strategies that they practice again and again with feedback on their progress from instructional masters. Reeves (2010, p. 66) states that the components of deliberate practice include performance that is focused on a particular element of the task, expert coaching, feedback, careful and accurate self-assessment, and the opportunity to apply feedback immediately for improved performance. Marzano (2010) is also a proponent of deliberate practice. He argues that teachers and principals in a school need a common language by which to discuss and describe instruction in their school. It is this common language that allows a staff to clearly know what good teaching looks like and to establish learning goals for themselves in becoming effective teachers. Marzano states, "Expertise does not happen by chance. It requires deliberate practice" (p. 82).

Clearly, principals cannot provide this type of support alone. But they can create structures and schedules that allow the most effective teachers and administrators to work with a small number of teachers in a community of learning around effective teaching practices. The principal should participate in these communities and develop one of her own whenever possible. The inclusion of this work in the school improvement plan, accountability plan, or strategic plan is recommended. Indicators of success should be created and tracked on a regular basis. For example, metrics could be collected on the number of mentoring hours performed, number of peer observations and support sessions provided to teachers, scores on climate surveys, proficiency levels of teachers as they work to master a few new skills, and the quality of feedback provided for improvement. When the quality and competence of the teachers improves, so does the student achievement. Investing in the development of teacher talent will also increase retention and attract promising teachers to the school. Finally, school leaders must realize that teaching talent is walking out the door en masse. Potential talent is not staying long enough to mature, and veteran talent is retiring. We must develop, nurture, and refine teaching talent if we are to provide a great teacher for every child in the United States (Curtis & Wurtzel, 2010).

Core Element 3:
Leadership That Is Developed
Before It Is Distributed

Good leaders make everyone around them smarter. They are what Liz Wiseman (2010) calls "multipliers." After a two-year study of more than 150 leaders, Wiseman concludes that leaders with a multiplier mindset have significantly better results because they get twice as much from their people. These leaders have a rich view of the intelligence of the people around them, and they know how to revitalize the intelligence of those in their organization. Wiseman found that employees who identified their leader as a multiplier gave 120 percent to their jobs every day.

How did the multipliers build this kind of culture? Wiseman identifies four practices of the multiplier that have great relevance to building a high-performance culture in a school. Leaders who are multipliers (1) look for talent everywhere—they watch and identify the native genius that people bring to the job; (2) they label that genius and talk with the individual about it; (3) they find a way to maximize the genius to the organization's benefit, connecting people with opportunities and shining a spotlight on their work; and (4) they remove barriers and let the people do their work. Multipliers' efforts to amplify their teams' intelligence and capacity motivate staff to work harder, seek challenges, and freely give their best. "It isn't how intelligent your team members are; it is how much of that intelligence you can draw out and put to use" (Wiseman, 2010, p. 10).

Multipliers are leaders who constantly seek to develop other leaders. In schools, this involves not only the identification and promotion of aspiring administrators but, more importantly, the development of teacher leadership (Reeves, 2010). School leaders today have recognized the importance of distributing leadership among staff members, as they have realized there is too much work to do for one person to do it all. However, the problem has been that leadership is distributed *before* it is developed in the people who show potential and/or interest in new challenges. The results of this "tag, you're it" method of distributing leadership are frustration, self-doubt, and feelings of inadequacy among the very people we wish to support and keep in our schools. Richard Elmore warns against this haphazard method of distributive leadership. In *Building a New Structure for School Leadership*, Elmore (2000) contends that in distributed leadership we want to avoid asking people to perform tasks they do not know how to do or have had no occasion to learn in the course of their careers.

Beyond the aspiring administrators in a school, which staff members should be considered for new challenges? Isn't teaching a tough enough job without adding more responsibilities to overburdened teachers? Harvard researcher Susan Moore Johnson argues in favor of additional responsibilities for second-stage teachers, those who are in their fourth to tenth year of teaching (Curtis & Wurtzel, 2010). Second-stage teachers have mastered the tough job of teaching, and they are best positioned to assist other teachers in the classroom by mentoring, modeling, and supporting newer and struggling teachers. They love teaching but are looking for new challenges. They want to make a greater contribution to the school and their communities. They *need* a change to stay engaged in the work. Johnson contends that second-stage teachers are motivated by two drivers: improvement and advancement. At the second stage they are coming into their own, and they want leadership responsibility to improve instructional practice (Curtis & Wurtzel, 2010). They are the grease in the machine of the high-performance culture.

Reeves (2010) agrees, and argues that sustained capacity building for high-impact learning depends upon the development of teacher leadership. Specifically, successful teaching focus, including deliberate practice, videotaping, and incremental improvement in the art and science of teaching, depends upon teacher leaders who provide feedback to help their colleagues and who receive feedback on the impact of their coaching (p. 71). Given the current climate in education today, second-stage teachers will prove to be worth their weight in gold to their principals and must be supported and developed based on their strengths and individual goals, as well as the goals of the school.

The power of being a multiplier and believer in leadership development can be seen through the work of Terri Tomlinson, principal of George Hall Elementary School in Mobile, Alabama. She credits the school's remarkable success to the many layers of leaders in her school. She spends much of her time developing leadership among her team and feels confident that the high-quality work and dedication continues on a daily basis whether she is in the school or out at a meeting (Education Trust, 2010). George Hall was recently awarded the national Blue Ribbon Award, and Secretary of Education Arne Duncan visited the school and declared it a national turnaround school (Phillips, 2010). The turnaround at this school is commendable and worth noting, from one of the lowest-performing schools in the state to one of the highest-performing, due to smart leadership focused on developing talent and distributing leadership. This principal, and many like her, have learned important leadership lessons along the way. Leadership in high-performance cultures does not reside only at the top of the organization. It must emerge from, and cascade down to, those closest to the student, and it is incumbent upon leaders to build support structures and scaffold tasks for staff to develop, and then distribute, leadership at all levels of the organization. People who learn and grow together can conquer challenges that seem impossible.

All school leaders would do well to develop leaders among them, starting with the second-stage teachers in their school, recognizing that each teacher has different interests, strengths, and career aspirations. Applying the "workforce of one" concept to these valuable staff members will benefit the school immeasurably, if done right. That means knowing each person and matching the person to the appropriate task to develop leadership skill. Dan Pink, author of *Drive* and *A Whole New Mind*, calls it the Goldilocks approach. He states that we frequently have a mismatch between what people *must* do and what people *can* do (Pink, 2010). In developing leadership in schools we must match the strengths and aspirations of each teacher to the task that will stretch her, but not overwhelm and frustrate her. This can be accomplished through deliberate practice on sharply defined elements of performance but within the current job. Furthermore, leadership development should be part of an organization's culture (Colvin, 2008). If school leaders do not implement a plan for leadership development, teachers' collective talent will be squandered and the best teachers will leave to find positions in which feedback for improvement is provided and opportunities for advancement are available.

Exhibit 4.1 shows a sample leadership development organizer to help school leaders get started with this effort. The time devoted to the front end of this endeavor will pay great benefits in the long term, as more and more staff members are able to step into leadership positions, perform them well, and contribute to the high-performance culture in a school. The organizer is not intended to be all inclusive, but rather a way to organize the work and initial thinking. It can and should be modified to meet the unique needs of schools and districts. To get started, list all second-stage teachers, veteran staff, and new teachers with high potential down the left-hand side of the chart. Complete the chart by filling in years of experience, strengths, career interests, current leadership duties, development stretch task, support person to guide them through the task, review dates, and progress results for each teacher. This requires the principal and/or school leaders to look at each teacher as an individual and match him to the appropriate tasks. It also requires principals to talk with teachers to share the plan and learn more about where they want to start, a conversation that is centered on improvement and advancement.

In addition to the organizer, a sample assignment menu (Exhibit 4.2) is provided to assist in selecting tasks that can be delegated, with support, under three major headings: instructional, operational, and organizational. It is important for school leaders to compile such a menu to keep track of what tasks are being considered and to whom the task is best suited. Principals should create their own menu based on what makes sense for their schools.

Organizing and planning for the development of leaders within a school serves numerous purposes. First, it supports the development

 EXHIBIT 4.1   Sample Leadership Development Organizer

Teacher	Years Experi-ence	Strengths	Career Interests	Current Leader-ship Duties	Stretch Task or Duty	Support Person	Review Dates	Results
Jones	5	Excellent teacher Great rapport Strong classroom routines High expecta-tion for self and students	Assistant prinicpal	New teacher mentor Data Team leader	Lead develop-ment of school discipline plan	AP	Sept. 30	

EXHIBIT 4.2   Sample Assignment Menu

Instructional	Operational	Organizational
Grade-level chair	Cafeteria operations	School calendar—sports, clubs, holidays
Department head	Buses AM and PM	Master schedule
Data Team leader	Fire drills	Class coverage schedule
New teacher mentor	Inclement-weather plan	Professional development logistics
University cooperating teacher	School safety plan	After-school tutoring coordinator
Curriculum development	Morning routines	Testing coordinator
Demonstration lessons	School discipline plan	Coordination of daily substitutes
Content coach—reading, math, etc.	School climate coordinator	Parent & community programs
Teacher support group leader	Student incentive programs	Data manager

of a strong cadre of committed teachers who contribute to the school's vision through teaching and leading. This development process satisfies the teachers' need for a sense of challenge in a job and accomplishment of developing new skills. The staff will come to believe that they are seen as individuals and that their work is being recognized as value added to the school. Using the leadership development process assists hard-to-staff schools by keeping good teachers and developing them to their full potential. The process also attracts promising new teachers as the word gets out that the school invests in the development of its teachers and supports them with their career interests and aspirations. Principals who invest in creating a reliable and consistent pipeline of good teachers and leaders are well positioned to meet new challenges and create a high-performance culture in their schools.

Core Element 4:
Progress Data for Adults and Students
That Are Analyzed and Acted On

As far back as 1995, Darling-Hammond and McLaughlin argued that habits and cultures inside of schools must foster critical inquiry into teaching practices and student outcomes. The school culture must be conducive to the formation of communities of practice that enable teachers to meet together to solve problems, consider new ideas, and evaluate alternatives (Darling-Hammond & McLaughlin, 1995). Since that time districts collect more data than ever thought possible, and, in fact, many suffer from data overload. What distinguishes high-performing schools from low-performing schools is the manner in which they organize, analyze, and act upon their data. High-performing schools have Data Teams and/or professional learning communities that follow a consistent cycle of inquiry into how students are progressing on learning goals and how staff are progressing with their teaching techniques. Conversely, in low-performing schools, teams of teachers and administrators meet to make sense of the data, but without a set process or cycle of inquiry and with little to no direction or training on how to proceed. After several frustrating meetings, with no clear plan of action for improvement, teachers see data analysis as a waste of their valuable time and slip back to going it alone in the classroom.

Several factors separate the high- from the low-performing teams. Schools with effective Data Teams engage in the regular practice of teamwork and collaboration, and they regularly track student and adult performance indicators to drive their work. The Data Teams process enables teachers to work together and learn from one another. The very structure of the Data Team facilitates the development of teaching talent while providing opportunities for distributive leadership. The communities of practice discussed by Darling-Hammond and McLaughlin (1995) are present in Data Teams and maximize the knowledge and skill of a collective faculty for improved student learning and achievement. This invigorating process empowers teachers to act in the best interest of all of their students. Without the Data Teams process, teachers drown in their data and gain no benefit from the experience. They are not learning or improving their teaching, and their students do not benefit from the collective knowledge of their teachers, thus their progress is in jeopardy.

The primary purpose of the Data Team is to improve student learning (Allison et al., 2010, p. 3). This is accomplished by improving the quality of teaching and leveraging leadership to facilitate learning for staff and students. The structure of Data Teams allows for acceleration and intervention in a systematic manner, and the process makes learning visible (Allison et al., 2010, p. 4). The Data Teams process involves a six-step cycle, which is followed consistently by the team at each meeting (Exhibit 4.3). The first step is to chart and display data from formative assessments to illustrate achievement of individual students on specific skills or standards. The next step in the cycle is to analyze and prioritize the needs. Teams look concurrently at student strengths and weaknesses and draw inferences from both, then they use the student strengths to build a bridge to address the weak areas. In step three, the teachers determine short-term SMART (specific, measurable, achievable, relevant, and timely) goals by which to measure the success of their intervention strategies. These goals detail current student proficiency rates, desired proficiency over the short term, measurement tools, and intended assessment dates. The fourth step is the team's selection of instructional strategies that each member of the team agrees to use in his instruction, including how often the team members will use the strategy and the duration, based on the SMART goal. In step five, the team determines its results indicators, which provide its members a vehicle by which to monitor the use of the strategies and determine the impact of the team's work on student achievement. Finally, teams monitor and evaluate results and determine if their goals were met. They start the process anew each time they have new data. Effective use of the Data Teams process can be the great equalizer for students, as it exposes the learning needs of each student and compels consistent, strategic action on the part of their teachers and principals.

Principals must be mindful, however, that just putting people together does not make them a team. All teams go through various stages of development, which school leaders must anticipate in order to have well-functioning teams. The most well-known model of team development is the one offered by Bruce Tuckman (1965). In Tuckman's model, teams go through four stages of development, including forming, storming, norming, and performing. It is important for the

EXHIBIT 4.3   The Data Teams Process

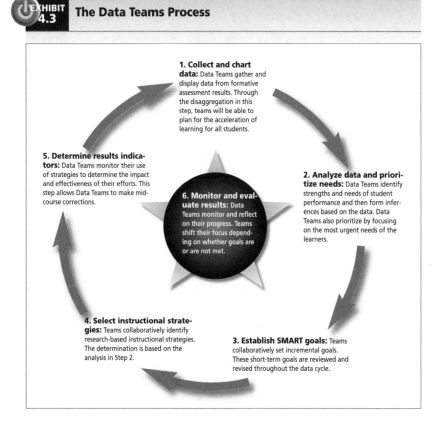

1. **Collect and chart data:** Data Teams gather and display data from formative assessment results. Through the disaggregation in this step, teams will be able to plan for the acceleration of learning for all students.

5. **Determine results indicators:** Data Teams monitor their use of strategies to determine the impact and effectiveness of their efforts. This step allows Data Teams to make mid-course corrections.

6. **Monitor and evaluate results:** Data Teams monitor and reflect on their progress. Teams shift their focus depending on whether goals are or are not met.

2. **Analyze data and prioritize needs:** Data Teams identify strengths and needs of student performance and then form inferences based on the data. Data Teams also prioritize by focusing on the most urgent needs of the learners.

4. **Select instructional strategies:** Teams collaboratively identify research-based instructional strategies. The determination is based on the analysis in Step 2.

3. **Establish SMART goals:** Teams collaboratively set incremental goals. These short-term goals are reviewed and revised throughout the data cycle.

team members to be aware of the stages they will experience so that when times get rough, they understand that it is simply part of the process all teams go through when first working together. In the forming stage, team members are generally polite, as they gain an understanding of the work the team is expected to do and where they fit in. At this stage, it is important for the principal or school leaders to provide clear instructions, provide structures such as a meeting calendar, and discuss the team's goals and objectives. Next, the team will experience the storming phase. In this phase, members confront their confusion about how to proceed, they question their leaders as to the purpose of the work, they experience the uncomfortable feeling of not knowing the process well, and they fear being exposed for not being competent. The leader of the Data Team must be able to persist through the storming phase of the work and reassure all members that they are learning something new and it will take time to become proficient. Making mistakes is expected, and learning as they go forth is the only way to become an efficient Data Team. As members become more comfortable with the process and learn from their mistakes, they begin to experience a flow or rhythm to their work, known as norming. They have a process. They follow the process. Their roles are known, and meaningful work is taking place. Finally, as all members gain their confidence and the work pace picks up, the team is in the performing stage. It fully understands the process, its data is driving the work, its members trust one another to come prepared and follow through, and team members feel energized by working together. A team cannot get to this performing stage, however, without the pain of experiencing the previous stages to get it there. If one member of the team is replaced by someone else, the team goes back to the forming stage and starts the process over again.

Alfie Kohn (1999) also argues that simply putting people in groups does not ensure cooperation and that considerable effort and organizational commitment are required to turn a group into a team. The benefits to collaboration and teamwork are such that the opportunity to collaborate should be the default condition in classrooms and schools, Kohn contends. People are able to do a better job in well-functioning groups than they can on their own. They are also more excited about their work. Both effects are due to the exchange of talent and resources that occurs as a result of cooperation. This argument is supported by the research of Curtis and Wurtzel (2010), authors of *Teaching Talent*, who argue that principals are managers of human capital and leaders of learning. As such, they must establish conditions for a community of adults to continually build the knowledge and skills that most effectively generate student learning. Building structures for teachers to collaborate, to improve practice, and to create a culture of continuous learning and improvement is critical to their success (p. 91).

Lauren Campsen, principal of the national Blue Ribbon school Ocean View Elementary, in Norfolk, Virginia, understands the power of teacher collaboration and process-based inquiry around data. She suggests that the principal is the key to success. She states that a principal must know what challenges are occurring, who needs more support, what additional resources are needed and how the current ones are being allocated, and when to be ready to intervene before any potential roadblock becomes an obstacle to implementation (Allison et al., 2010, p. 124). Campsen credits Ocean View's success—a school with 64 percent of its students on free lunch, a high minority population, a high English language learner rate, and high mobility due to the large surrounding military population—to the consistent and proficient use of the Data Teams process at all grade levels. She shares that the initial implementation came as a mandate from her, but over time the process has become part of the culture and identity of the school. Every teacher in the school serves on a Data Team, which include horizontal grade-level teams and vertical content teams. Ocean View's high-performance culture was built from these teams over time. They have learned that the data is trying to tell them something about what they are doing, and if they listen to it, reflect on it, and give it voice, it will help them understand what to do next. The Data Teams process has built a collective efficacy at the school, and each teacher knows her work makes a difference in the performance of all students.

Core Element 5:
Internal System of Shared Accountability

"One essential lesson of the research ... is that schools with strong internal accountability—a high level of agreement among members of the organization on the norms, values, and expectations that shape their work—function more effectively under external accountability pressure" (Elmore, 2004, p. 134). Contrary to the popular view held today, teachers and administrators do not resist being held accountable for their work. But, as Elmore and his colleagues found in their studies, when external accountability measures are applied to schools, often teachers and leaders do not understand the full scope of what they are being held accountable for and to whom they are accountable (Elmore, 2004). The isolation of classrooms and schools from state and federal education policymaking, and the manner in which governments communicate with districts and schools, usually means that very little changes at the classroom level when external accountability policies are adopted. In many schools, accountability is determined by the individual teacher's sense of responsibility to the students and the community. Accountability is not collective or shared. But, in schools that respond well to external accountability, strong internal accountability systems are in place. These internal systems define the schools' vision, mission, and shared beliefs. They link a few, but powerful, specific teaching and leadership actions to the vision, and they clearly articulate the accountability metrics, timelines, and responsibilities. The plan provides the staff clarity on the purpose of the work, what they are held accountable for, and to whom they are accountable.

Doug Reeves and colleagues at The Leadership and Learning Center have been assisting districts for years in developing internal systems of accountability, with great results. In his book *Accountability in Action* a framework for accountability planning is provided (Reeves, 2005). The framework engages an entire team at the district or school level in the development of a few, very specific strategies that are targeted and tailored to the organization's needs. Similarly, Reeves argues that accountability *for* learning is much more effective than systems designed to punish and humiliate. He contends that accountability for learning equips teachers and leaders to transform educational accountability policies from destructive and demoralizing accounting drills into meaningful and constructive decision making in the classroom, school, and district (Reeves, 2004, p. 1).

A school-based accountability plan acts like a school charter that establishes the purpose and vision, the customs and culture, and the functions and roles of each member of the team. The accountability plan establishes the culture of the school and determines "how we do business around here." Not only will a few but powerful strategies guide the actions of adults, the plan is constructed to build reciprocity of accountability. According to Elmore (2004), everyone is accountable to someone for the work, and each person holding others accountable has an equal and reciprocal obligation to provide support, resources, and guidance to assist those doing the work. Elmore suggests, "For each unit of performance I demand from you, I have an equal and reciprocal responsibility to provide you with a unit of capacity to produce that performance" (pp. 244–245). The actions of adults are targeted toward improving student learning, and data is collected and analyzed on these actions to ensure a cycle of continuous improvement. In high-performance cultures everyone knows the vision, he understand his role in achieving the vision, and he continuously builds his capacity to perform tasks in line with the vision.

The most common mistake, and one made by most low-performing districts and schools, is including far too many strategies, goals, and initiatives in their annual plans. Many of these plans are hundreds of pages long, and they are so inclusive that it is impossible for any staff member to focus on a few things and do them well. The sheer number of goals, strategies, and initiatives proposed in most strategic plans detracts from the ability to focus, and it is often unclear how implementation will lead to improved outcomes for students (Chauncey, 2010). According to Elmore (2004), low-performing schools do not know what to do to turn around their schools. If they did, they would be doing it. Thus, the hundred-page plans including every educational approach known is offered in order to give the appearance that these schools do know what to do and they are working hard at doing it.

The truth is the opposite: A few strategies, implemented well and monitored well, can go a long way in turning around an underperforming school. It goes back to the deliberate practice, suggested by Reeves, Colvin, and Marzano, to improving the quality teaching, thus improving student learning. Harvard Business School's Stacey Childress, quoted by Curtis and City in *Strategic Priorities for School Improvement*, edited by Caroline Chauncey (2010, p. 170), states, "Deliberate actions are puzzle pieces that fit together to create a clear picture of how the people, activities, and resources of an organization can work effectively to accomplish a collective purpose." Curtis and City also argue that, "Without systems in place for discussing implementation, learning from it, and refining the strategy accordingly, the effects of the work are diminished and the plan becomes irrelevant" (p. 172). And Brent Stephans, quoted in the same volume, agrees stating, "The manner in which a school describes the source of its poor performance is a telling indicator of its location on the trajectory towards internal accountability" (p. 149).

An effective accountability plan enables a school leader to pull together all of the five elements of a high-performance culture in a way that makes sense to everyone in the school. Internal accountability plans establish the purpose-driven vision and mission, include efforts to develop talent in all teachers, describe how leadership is developed and distributed to individuals who are ready for a new challenge, and provide a structure for organizing and analyzing progress data for staff and students in teams where professional learning is of paramount importance. An accountability plan improves student achievement by improving teaching and leadership practices. The accountability plan creates the structures for a dynamic learning organization that continually assesses its own effectiveness in concrete and measurable ways. This is emerging as the core of local, state, and national accountability efforts (Curtis & Wurtzel, 2010).

Conclusion

Demands of greater accountability for student results and global competitiveness require that districts and schools address culture as a core strategy for accelerating and sustaining improvement. School and district leaders who continue to focus on the "low hanging fruit" or technical changes will soon find themselves left behind and outperformed by colleagues who made the shift to culture as their core strategy to take them to higher levels of student achievement. The five core elements discussed here can be found in high-performance schools across the country. School leaders, both central office and school based, must recognize that a school's culture is what enables it to respond quickly and flexibly to challenges. It sets the tone, determines the work pattern, and dictates the level of effort individuals put forth in their work. The school's culture touches on the emotional longing in human beings to be part of something bigger than themselves, and it enables them to perform work for the greater good.

But having a sense of purpose and engagement in a meaningful challenge by itself does not make a school high performing. Time, energy, focus, and effort must be dedicated to developing the instructional skills and talents of the staff. Teachers are leaving the profession in droves. We cannot close our teaching gap by simply recruiting more new teachers. We must develop talent in the teachers we have now and make career development programs part of the culture. This will serve as a magnet to attract more teachers with promise and result in greater capacity to teach and lead. Progress in these areas, along with the progress of students in their learning, must be measured, analyzed, and acted upon by teams of educators. School-wide and grade-level Data Teams follow the same cycle of inquiry detailed in this chapter. They use evidence to draw conclusions about strengths and areas for growth and follow through with intervention strategies designed to improve performance. Internal accountability plans provide the big picture, and they demonstrate how all the pieces of the work fit together to move the school to greater levels of achievement. This understanding and collective efficacy is an adaptive change of great significance. It requires careful attention and persistence.

Without the five core elements of a high-performance culture, new strategies have little chance of making a difference in the quality of our schools.

Complete the questionnaire below to determine the status of your school in becoming a high-performance culture. Based on the five core elements, your score will help you determine where to begin.

Creating a High-Performance Culture

The idea that a single teacher, working on her own, can do everything to meet the diverse needs of many learners is an idea whose time has passed. Our teachers and youth deserve an opportunity to draw on the collaborative power of teamwork that has become the key to success in every high performing organization in our economy. (National Commission on Teaching and America's Future, 2010)

Leading learning ... means creating the conditions for a community of adults to continually build the knowledge and skills that most effectively generate student learning. It is an ongoing process of building structures and opportunities for teachers to collaborate, to improve practice, and to create a culture of continuous learning and improvement. The goal is not just to ensure that all individual teachers in the school are effective; it is to create a school environment where learning—for children and adults—is fostered, developed and celebrated. (Curtis & Wurtzel, 2010)

Your Performance Culture Index

Statements for Reflection	Agree	Disagree
My classroom/school has a clear purpose and vision focused on all students learning at high levels.		
All work by adults and students is aligned with achieving the vision and purpose.		
My school/district has high expectations for staff and provides structures that foster team learning and collaboration aimed at improving instructional practice.		
My school/district values my work and provides learning opportunities aimed at my personal development in the profession.		
Teachers at my school/district have a sense of empowerment, teamwork, and community. They embrace new challenges with a can-do attitude.		
Teams at my school/district routinely examine student data, determine trends and patterns, and make agreements to implement instructional practices matched to the needs of the students.		
Teams in my school/district reflect on the impact of these practices by using frequent formative assessments to determine student learning progress and use the results to make adjustments in teaching practice.		
My school/district routinely collects and shares data on adult practices to ensure deep implementation of specific strategies and to support all adults toward improving student learning.		
The school improvement plan at my school is a working document used by all staff to monitor the effectiveness of adult actions on student learning.		
The leadership in my school/district sets challenging goals and provides an equal level of support and feedback to assist teams in meeting the challenges.		
Totals		

References

Allison, E., & Reeves, D. (2009). *Renewal Coaching.* San Francisco, CA: Jossey-Bass.

Allison, E., Besser, L., Campsen, L., Cordova, J., Doubek, B., Gregg, L., ... White, M. L. (2010). *Data Teams: The big picture.* Englewood, CO: The Leadership and Learning Center.

Carmichael, S., Martino, G., Porter-Magee, K., & Wilson, W. (2010). *The state of the state standards—and the Common Core in 2010.* Washington, DC: Thomas B. Fordham Institute.

Chauncey, C. T. (Ed.). (2010). *Strategic priorities for school improvement.* Cambridge, MA: Harvard Education Press.

Coca-Cola Company. (2010). Mission, vision & values. Retrieved from www.thecoca-colacompany.com

Colvin, G. (2008). *Talent is overrated: What really separates world-class performers from everybody else.* New York, NY: Penguin.

Council of Chief State School Officers & National Governors Association Center for Best Practices. (2010). *Common Core State Standards initiative.* Retrieved from www.corestandards.org

Curtis, R., & Wurtzel, J. (Eds.). (2010). *Teaching talent: A visionary framework for human capital in education.* Cambridge, MA: Harvard Education Press.

Darling-Hammond, L., & McLaughlin, M. W. (1995). Policies to support professional development in an era of reform. *Phi Delta Kappan, 76*(8), 597–604.

Drucker, P. (1990). *Managing the nonprofit organization: Principles and practices.* New York, NY: HarperCollins.

Education Trust. (2010). [Webinar]. Washington, DC: Author.

Elmore, R. (2000). *Building a new structure for school leadership.* Washington, DC: Albert Shanker Institute.

Elmore, R. (2002). *Bridging the gap between standards and achievement: The imperative for professional development in education.* Washington, DC: Albert Shanker Institute.

Elmore, R. (2004). *School reform from the inside out: Policy, practice and performance.* Cambridge, MA: Harvard Education Press.

Gardner, H., Csikszentmihalyi, M., & Damon, W. (2001). *Good work: When excellence and ethics meet.* New York, NY: Basic Books.

Goodwin, B. (2010). *Changing the odds for student success: What matters most.* Denver, CO: Mid-continent Research for Education and Learning.

Heifetz, R., & Linsky, M. (2002). *Leadership on the line.* Boston, MA: Harvard Business School Press.

Kohn, A. (1999). *Punished by rewards.* Boston, MA: Houghton-Mifflin.

Marzano, R. (2010). What teachers gain from deliberate practice. *Educational Leadership, 66*(4), 82–84.

National Commission on Teaching and America's Future. (2010). *Who will teach? Experience matters.* Washington, DC: Author.

Phillips, R. (2010, August 28). Education secretary visits George Hall Elementary, says Mobile school is model of improvement. *Press Register,* p. 1.

Pink, D. (2010). *Drive: The surprising truth about what motivates us.* New York, NY: Riverhead Books.

Redmond School District. (2007). Welcome to the Redmond Educational Vision Report! Retrieved from http://www.redmond.k12.or.us/14541013164911523/site/default.asp?1454Nav=|&NodeID=242

Redmond School District. (2009). Redmond schools shine at central Oregon Scholastic Art Awards. Retrieved from www.redmond.k12.or.us/rsd/cwp/view.asp?A=3&Q=322598&C=53713

Reeves, D. (2004). *Accountability for learning: How teachers and school leaders can take charge.* Alexandria, VA: ASCD.

Reeves, D. (2005). *Accountability in action.* Englewood, CO: Advanced Learning Press.

Reeves, D. (2010). *Transforming professional development into student results.* Alexandria, VA: ASCD.

Reid, J., & Hubbell, V. (2005). Creating a performance culture. (Ivey Management Services Reprint No. 9B05TB10). Retrieved from www.iveybusinessjournal.com

Tuckman, B. W. (1965). Developmental Sequence in Small Groups. *Psychological Bulletin,* no. 63, 384–399.

United Press International (UPI). (2010, July 27). 18 states, D.C., Race to the Top finalists. Washington, DC: Author.

United Press International (UPI). (2010, August 24). States win grants for education reform. Washington, DC: Author.

U.S. Department of Education. (2009). Race to the Top program executive summary. Washington, DC: Author.

Weber, K. (Ed.). (2010). *Waiting for Superman: How we can save America's failing schools.* New York, NY: Perseus.

Whittier Union High School District (WUHSD). (2010). [Home page.] Retrieved from www.wuhsd.org

Wiseman, L. (2010). *Multipliers: How the best leaders make everyone smarter.* New York: HarperCollins.

LEADERS FOCUSING ON

PRACTICES

CHAPTER FIVE

School Leaders as Evaluators

JOHN HATTIE and JANET CLINTON

I N THEIR SEMINAL REVIEW OF EVIDENCE about how school leadership affects student outcomes, Robinson, Hohepa, and Lloyd (2009) commenced by noting that the more recent reviews of the literature lead to disparate conclusions (see also Robinson, Lloyd, & Rowe, 2008). For example, Witziers, Bosker, and Krüger (2003) conclude that the impact is minimal; Hallinger and Heck (1998) and Leithwood, Seashore, Anderson, and Wahlstrom (2004) conclude that it is modest but important; and Marzano, Waters, and McNulty (2005) conclude that it is substantial. A major problem with such reviews, claim Robinson et al. (2009), is that the studies do not distinguish between two major forms of leadership: transformational and instructional.

Transformational leaders aim to inspire their people with a vision that energizes and encourages others to work collaboratively toward a common good. The leader specifies what is expected and provides consequences for meeting or not meeting those expectations. Transformational leadership involves setting direction (vision, expectations), helping people (intellectual stimulation), redesigning the organization (building collaborative cultures), carrying out transactional and managerial duties (contingent rewards), monitoring school activity, and buffering staff from external demands (Leithwood, Tomlinson, & Genge, 1996). *Instructional,* or pedagogical, leaders establish learning environments with minimal disruption, set up systems of clear teaching objectives, and promote high teacher expectations of students. These attributes relate to principals being involved in classroom observations, reviewing and interpreting test information with staff, having a clear mission about learning gains and high expectations about achievement, and attending to the opportunity to learn. Instructional leaders are more directly involved in learning, whereas transformational leaders are more indirect in their involvement toward enhanced learning outcomes. From their meta-analysis of 12 studies (188 effects), Robinson et al. calculated an overall effect size from transformational leadership of 0.11 and from instructional leadership of 0.42 (Exhibit 5.1; see also Elmore, 2004; Marks & Printy, 2003).

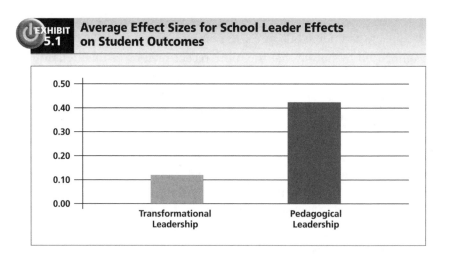

EXHIBIT 5.1   **Average Effect Sizes for School Leader Effects on Student Outcomes**

Specifically, they report substantial effect sizes ($d = 0.84$) for promoting and participating in teacher learning and development; 0.42 for establishing goals and expectations; 0.31 for strategic resourcing (e.g., aligning resource selection to priority teaching goals); 0.42 for planning, coordinating, and evaluating teaching and the curriculum; and 0.27 for ensuring an orderly and supportive environment. Their conclusion was that instructional leaders give greater emphasis to setting, communicating, monitoring, and reporting school goals, especially those that are related to student achievement. They work more often with teachers or departmental heads to plan, coordinate, and evaluate teachers and teaching; ensure that student progress is monitored and the results are used to improve teaching; and are actively involved with teachers in professional learning.

Leaders as Activators: Leaders as Evaluators

The argument presented in this chapter is that a more effective metaphor than "instructional leaders" for explaining the effectiveness of school leaders is "leaders as evaluators." The attributes and their effect sizes, mentioned above, that most directly lead to enhancing student outcomes include the thinking and skills involved in *evaluating*—the processes, programs, people, and products (in this case student achievement and learning). They involve the underlying competencies of evaluation and highlight the two key attributes of evaluation: determining and making a judgment about the merit and worth of the effects of their leadership. Furthermore, by assuming this "persona," school leaders can be active in ensuring, with the highest possible probability, that the students in their school are maximizing their achievement, learning, and progress. This notion of leaders as *activators* implies deliberate change, directing of learning, and visibly making a difference to the experiences and outcomes for the students (and for the teachers)—and the key mechanism for this activation is a mind frame that embraces the role of evaluation.

We cannot underestimate the importance of school leaders to lead discussions and make decisions about what topics and programs have the most merit in a school; what leaders are seen to value is critical to the success of the school, provided this valuing significantly relates to the learning of students. The manner in which effective leaders conduct their evaluation talk is via establishing goals and expectations, making decisions (most often between competing demands to strategically provide resources), evaluating teaching and the curriculum, promoting and participating in providing evaluative evidence relating to teacher learning and development, creating educationally powerful connections, ensuring that all in the school are engaged in constructive problem talk, and using evaluative evidence (e.g., from test scores, student work) as the underpinning of this talk. Such talk begs the question as to which outcomes, and these decisions and engaging in debates about worthwhile outcomes play a key role of the evaluating leader. The notion of leader as evaluator, then, is primarily about the leader setting up a learning organization that embeds the ideas of evaluation so that change can occur to maximize the positive impact on all in the school. As Senge (1990) demonstrated, this notion requires school leaders who are sincerely interested in the world of practice, who are highly respectful of that world, and who are sincerely interested in using evaluative methods to make that world better for all—and in the case of schools particularly, for the success of the students but not excluding the teachers as learners as well. Leaders as evaluators require engagement of all in the school to learn, to review and revise, and to become evaluators of themselves and their impacts on students. "It is no longer sufficient to have one person learning for the organization, a Ford or a Sloan or a Watson. It's just not possible any longer to 'figure it out' from the top, and have everyone else following the orders of the 'grand strategist.' The organizations that will truly excel in the future will be the organizations that will truly tap people's commitment and capacity to learn at all levels in an organization" (Senge, 1990, p. 4).

School leaders are evaluators of themselves, as well as of their teachers' (and other school personnel) impact on their students, and they are involved in sharing, valuing, and acting on these evaluations. The key questions for the school leader include, How do I know this is working? How can I compare "this" with "that"? What is the merit and worth of this influence on learning? What is the magnitude of the effect? What evidence would convince me that I am wrong? Where is the evidence that shows "this" is superior to other programs? Where have I seen this practice installed so that it produces effective results? Do I share a common conception of progress?

The Role of School Leader as Evaluator

There are many models of evaluation, and while this notion does not lead to endorsement of any particular model, a major implication of this argument for leaders as evaluators is that principals could profitably learn much from the models and methods of evaluation and could be most effective if they adopt one of the more successful models most suited to their context. The claim is about school leaders understanding and embracing the roles of evaluators. There are many possible roles for the leader as evaluator:

1. **Sense making**. The evaluator can be critical in making sense not only of his own theories of action but also those of others. Along with helping others, making their program logic transparent can often be a first and critical step in understanding how a school's staff see "what is" and "what could/should be." As teachers have very strong (although not always explicit) theories of their actions, it is often necessary to start by understanding this situation if change is to have any chance of success.

2. **Priorities**. A key role for the school leader is ascertaining the key issues in often contested territory. Leaders have many pressures and pulls on their time and expertise; hence, a major role is determining the problems and pressures that are best worth investing time and effort into. Schools are full of contests, pluralistic values, power differences, vulnerabilities, and real-life implications for resource allocations. The usual claim that all these factors need time and resources to accommodate often ignores the reality that all school leaders have similar amounts of these—it is more about how the time and resources are needed, hence determining priorities to be subject to evaluation is an important role of the effective school leader.

3. **Equity**. School leaders can rarely afford to "lose" players in schools (teachers, parents, students), and often schools, and the culture in which the school lives, have established critical equity goals. Hence, ensuring multiple views are considered, and privileged cultural norms are recognized, can lead the school leader to more effectively implement and inter-

pret the best processes, people, and impacts on all students and participants in a school. House and Howe (1999), for example, have detailed evaluation principles based on "democratic deliberative evaluation" to ensure that all views are included in the debates and decisions as to the positive impacts on student learning.

4. **Coaching**. Fetterman (2001, p. 123) considers the norm in his model of evaluation as "an immersed coach or facilitator," but the coach role may also include giving advice, offering recommendations, and seeing change through to successful completion. Reeves (2008) has elaborated on this coach role extensively and documented the success of leaders taking it on in their leadership of schools.

5. **Critical social scientist**. Segerholm (2002) has argued how essential it is for evaluators to see their role as critical social scientist with the skills of asking and framing questions; seeking evidence; and, most important, interpreting this evidence to have the greatest impact on students.

6. **Reflexivity**. The evaluator always needs to consider the impact of herself on the context, her influence on the participants, and the impacts on the students. There is no one evaluation role that the school leader can adopt; being aware of her influence in different circumstances, in different parts of the transformation process, and on the impact on the players (teachers, cleaners, and students) is important.

Other roles that the school leader as evaluator can take on (depending on situation and context) include advocacy, technical assistance, strategic planning, consulting, serving as program advisor or evaluation advisor, collaborating, developing partnerships, networking, peer reviewing, validating models, providing evaluator credibility, engaging in the community, facilitating, developing workforce capacity, determining priorities for acquiring and distributing resources, serving as knowledge broker, and forward thinking. The foregoing is a formidable list, indeed, but in part or together, the purpose of all of these roles is to create a learning environment in which multiple individuals and organizations can learn from each other, and from successes and challenges, to continuously improve quality (see Clinton, Appleton, Cairns, & Broadbent, 2009). These roles should highlight that it requires more than one person to enact them, it requires sharing of these roles, and it requires a learning environment in which evidence from evaluations is interpreted to improve the system rather than being a source of tension.

The imperative, then, is to facilitate the emergence of school leaders as knowledge managers (capturing, organizing, and storing knowledge and experiences of people within an organization and making this information available to others in the organization), knowledge brokers (bringing people together to help them build relationships, uncover needs, and share ideas and evidence that will increase the chances of having a positive impact on student learning), and engaging in knowledge transfer (transferring good ideas and evidence about the impact on the various people in the school that can then lead to impacts on students). By including these roles the school leader can create a learning environment. The center of the model (see Exhibit 5.2) includes the four major evaluation standards: propriety (is the evaluation conducted legally, ethically, and with due regard for the welfare of those involved in the evaluation, as well as those affected by its results?), accuracy (does the evaluation reveal and convey technically adequate information about the features that determine worth or merit of that being evaluated?), utility (does the evaluation decision serve the information needs of intended users?), and feasibility (will the evaluation be realistic, prudent, diplomatic, and frugal?).

School leaders as evaluators not only must adopt certain roles but they also need to have interpretative evaluation skills and methods to help ascertain the impacts on the learning and achievement of the students in the school. Many schools are awash with data and become data graveyards; the effective leader is concerned with interpreting the data and ensuring defensible consequences and actions (Hattie, 2003; Reeves, 2004). As Schwandt (2002) argued, the role of the evaluator is one of "performing evaluation." In these days, where "performance,"

EXHIBIT 5.2 **A Model of Evaluation That School Leaders Can Use to Develop a Learning Organization**

"data," "evidence," and "test scores" are the norm, the role is not merely collecting performance evidence but questioning the values and criticalness of what is to be performed. It is critical to see achievement as more than test scores; to help students develop and use effective learning strategies; to foster high retention rates in school; to promote student commitment to reinvesting in their practice of learning; and to include outcomes such as respect of others, managing self, and developing critical evaluation skills. These outcomes lead to students having challenging minds and dispositions to become active, competent, thoughtfully critical in our complex world, and imaginative when thinking about what is "good" for self and others (see Nussbaum, 2010). This requires school leaders to develop students' capacity to see the world from the viewpoint of others, understand human weaknesses and injustices, and work toward developing cooperation and reciprocity; develop genuine concern for self and others; teach evidence to counter stereotypes and closed thinking; promote account-ability of the person as a responsible agent; and vigorously promote critical thinking and the importance of dissenting voices.

The evaluator role is more than one of using the skills and tools developed within evaluation or social science; in fact, it is primarily about deciding which are the critical analyses to be pursued and ensuring they are indeed pursued in the context of the impact of school personnel, programs, and processes on students' learning and achievement. The evaluator is engaged in making reasoned moral choices within the context and history of a school. Schools are in a constant state of flux, and much change is demanded and inflicted upon schools. Thus, the leader as evaluator needs to be as concerned with change processes and effects of change as with having skills to decide on which changes have the optimal probability of positively enhancing these many outcomes.

Note, the argument is *not* that there is a particular method of eval-uation that the school leader needs to adopt. The model and methods of evaluation are hotly debated, and the invitation is not to advocate a particular method(s). Instead, the claim is that leaders as evaluators need to consider the "goodness of fit" notions of asking and deciding the best methods that led to judgments of merit, worth such that there is sufficient and appropriate rigor to defend the evaluative claims. Thus, given any request for evaluation of any product, personnel, pol-icy, or people, the question is about how adequate and effective are the chosen evaluation methods in leading to the quality and suffi-ciency of the evaluation questions and conclusions. In this way method does not become dominant (as it often becomes), but the choice of method is justified to the degree there is optimal goodness of fit between this choice and the evaluation needs.

The next sections of this chapter illustrate some of the more important notions of the school leader as evaluator. The evaluator is keenly interested in evaluating success, developing some fundamen-tal evaluation tools, and evaluating the major components of schools that aim to enhance the impact of the various parts of the school on the learning and achievement of the students.

Evaluating Success

What Does Success Look Like?

In any evaluation a key question relates to the outcomes, and in schools there are often many—getting the buses running on time, ensuring the food is healthy for lunch, having sufficient teachers for classes, and so on. Notwithstanding that these kinds of outcomes must be attended to, the key role for a school leader is communicating clearly that the learning and achievement outcomes of students are a priority in any list of outcomes. This begs the question, how would you determine the nature of the outcomes? The suggestion here is that these outcomes can be expressed in test scores, but this application is far from sufficient. One of the key outcomes should be retention, as one of the most successful predictors of health, wealth, and happiness in adult life is not achievement at school but the number of years of schooling (Levin, 2008). Many students begin to make decisions about staying in this task of school learning between the ages of 10 and 14, so considerations about retention are key in both elementary and high school learning.

There are other critical outcomes, such as respect for others, managing self, perseverance, efficacy, and so on. These outcomes are related to students, although there can be many other outcomes that are more teacher related. In consideration of these, teachers' working conditions are important, but they are not to be confused with student outcomes; at best they can be correlates of student outcomes. For example, creating homogenous rather than heterogeneous groups (as per streaming or tracking) may be conducive to teachers' working conditions, but there is little evidence that this makes a difference to student outcomes. The mistake is in believing that streaming is a decision about enhancing student outcomes rather than related to teachers' beliefs about their ability to achieve efficiency (see Hattie, 2002).

Who Is in Charge of Success?

Many schools determine priorities, develop vision plans, ascertain what success looks like, and then nothing much happens in action.

An important question for any school is, "Who is in charge of success in this school?" Everyone, of course, but this is not what actually happens. Many schools have deans or year coordinators who often are more responsible for "failure" than for success. They deal with problem students, absenteeism, bullying, and so on. As well as attending to these roles, a person or group needs to be in charge of success, as this drives the evaluative mission of ensuring that success is dependably monitored and esteemed. This "student success" person or group needs to monitor and provide information to all about who is on and who is off track to success (e.g., completing appropriate number of credits, grade point average, retention), who needs credit recovery or rescue, and so on. One test of ensuring success is to ask each student "Who knows in this school how you are doing?" and "Who cares how you are achieving?" As Reeves (2008) has noted, searching for success is a treasure hunt, not a witch hunt; rather than leading to embarrassment and humiliation, collaborative teams that are invested in developing data interpretation competencies can lead to high levels of encouragement, reinforcement, and innovation.

What Is Your Dashboard of Success?

Does the school have a set of criteria for establishing success, which is then appropriately evaluated? We have spent much time determining how to make this dashboard (Hattie, Brown, & Keegan, 2005) and providing it to schools. For example, the school achievement profile (from asTTle; Hattie, Brown, & Keegan, 2005) in Exhibit 5.3 shows the average performance of a school (years 4–8) as indicated by the arrow, relative to the norms for the country (in shaded background) for various dimensions of mathematics and attitude toward mathematics. The box and whiskers show the average performance (and spread) of each class (bold in front) relative to the national norms (shaded in background). In this school, while there is an increase between years 4 and 5, there is no change in the average performance in years 4 to 8. It is clear that there is a problem—no change for four years—and inviting debate about this lack of change. Of course the dashboard begs, but does not

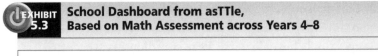

EXHIBIT 5.3

School Dashboard from asTTle, Based on Math Assessment across Years 4–8

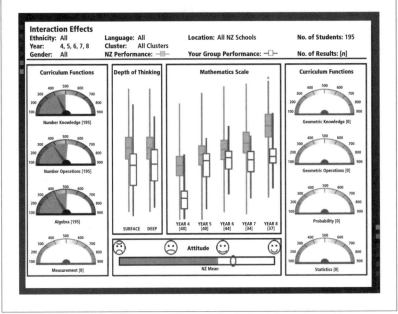

answer, the question. A major function of data to the leader as evaluator is to help determine the right questions.

Another example is the dashboard of comparisons of student outcomes across teachers. A large (3,000+ student) high school has created a dashboard for regularly asking questions about the impact of teachers on students. The 15+ teachers of the subject in any year level meet and decide on appropriate assessments for the work over a two-month period, which are then administered to all students, and repeated two months later. The effect sizes for each teacher are calculated, displayed (via box and whiskers format), and used to ask questions as to what worked, with whom, and what to do next. In our work in many schools we also calculate effect sizes at the individual level (by using the group standard deviation as a proxy for the standard deviation of each student). While this is far from a robust method, it can serve as a prompt for dialogue about whether the teaching impacted some students and not others, which leads to debates about why some are more impacted than others. From the synthesis of meta-analyses presented in *Visible Learning* (Hattie, 2009), an effect size of at least 0.40 is desired. If the effects are >0.40, then the debate is to understand the success indicators and process; if they are <0.40, then changes are the issue. Such dashboards merely create the questions and are examples of evidence into action. An important implication is that such methods place more emphasis on school leaders to use test scores for creating questions and debates about the impact of teaching than using test scores merely to make statements about students.

The Power of Adaptation

Fuchs and Fuchs (1986) completed a meta-analysis of 21 studies that focused on ongoing formative evaluation and modification of proposed programs. Integrating formative evaluation into instructional programs led to a $d=0.70$ increase in student achievement. Programs that depended more on evidence (0.91) were more powerful than those that depended on teacher judgments (0.42) and those that were graphed (0.70); hence, aiming to influence interpretation was more effective than those programs that just recorded (0.26), highlighting that the interpretation is much more important than the gathering of evaluative evidence. The effects were similar across grades (K–3 = 0.50, grades 4–6 = 0.68, grades 7–12 = 0.87), across measurement frequency (twice per week = 0.85, three times per week = 0.41, daily = 0.69), and across treatment duration (<3 weeks = 0.50, 3–10 weeks = 0.50, >10 weeks = 0.70). The art for school leaders is to use such evaluation for their own and teacher formative assessments and not merely summative purposes. Often any whiff of accountability can close formative debates about the impact of teaching on student outcomes. The leader as evaluator is key in ensuring appropriate adaptation to the programs and methods used in a school and is the "keeper" of program fidelity.

The Power of Feedback

Feedback about the impact of schools on students is powerful (Hattie & Timperley, 2007). School leaders can invoke many forms of feedback to create the right debates within schools about how to enhance student outcomes. One of the dilemmas in using feedback is that while it is among the most powerful influences on student learning, it is also one of the most variable. To resolve this dilemma we have devised a four-level model of feedback crossed with three key feedback questions. Feedback can work at the task (e.g., content), process (e.g., strategy), regulation (e.g., self-monitoring), and self (e.g., praise) levels, and the three questions are, Where am I going? How am I going? and Where to next? (Hattie, 2011; Hattie & Gan, 2010). This model of feedback can be used at the school level to determine the effects on task, process, regulation, and self and relating to the three questions. A major role of the evaluating leader, therefore, is to seek, provide, and use feedback at the right level(s) addressing the three questions in a constructive manner to enhance the outcomes and impacts on students.

Evaluating the Major Curriculum Decisions

Curriculum is a major issue for schools. While many jurisdictions determine core standards, standardized tests, and so forth, there are still critical decisions to be made about curriculum. In the StarPath project (www.education.auckland.ac.nz/uoa/home/about/research/ starpath-home/), for example, the effects of curriculum choices was shown to be a major barrier for many minority students having opportunities to graduate and move beyond to tertiary studies. The StarPath team tracked students across many schools as to their achievement levels and the effects that choosing differing subject options had on their achievement and then opportunities to choose more challenging courses. The conclusion was that schools often provide (limited) choices to these students that aim more to "meet their current needs" than challenge them toward courses that lead to tertiary studies. For example, Madjar, McKinley, Jensen, and van der Merwe (2009) found that most subject choice was not necessarily student driven. Schools play a strong mediating role, determining which subjects are available and how they are timetabled, which standards within individual subjects are selected, which prerequisites have to be met for progression to more advanced study, and how students are selected for different versions of the core subjects. They report that students who lacked informed adult support were more likely to make nonstrategic choices early in their school career and were at particular risk of failing to achieve their academic potential or of failing to gain entry to those qualifications that lead to their preferred careers. Schools often seek to maximize students' immediate success but are not always aware of the longer-term significance of their choices— particularly the impact of choosing courses that can block options to more challenging subjects later. School leaders who evaluate the impact of curriculum options, pathways, and levels of difficulty can make more informed decisions to optimize the pathways of all students, but especially students who may be less informed of longer-term implications or who may lack informed adult intervention to optimize future options. The message is that school leaders need to evaluate the choices of curriculum and the impact that these choices have not only on immediate student impact but on the students' future options for learning.

Evaluating the Expectations

School leaders, just as teachers, parents, and students, have expectations about what they can accomplish. These expectations can influence what we teach, how we teach, and many other critical decisions that affect students. Variations in expectations can lead to variations in what is taught, which ultimately will lead to variations in what is learned (Brophy, 1982). Rubie-Davies (2009) and Rubie-Davies, Hattie, and Hamilton (2006) have demonstrated that when teachers have high expectations they typically have them for all their students, and similarly those who have low expectations have them for all their students. High-expectation teachers expect improvement; see the errors of their teaching; and seek evidence about what did not work, for whom, and about what. They see all students as capable of learning and improving and their role as active change agents; they have less differentiation in the kinds of activities that students of differing abilities complete in a class; they see confidence, motivation, persistence, and attitude toward work as keys to engagement in learning; and they have effect size for achievement outcomes in the 0.50–1.50 range. Low-expectation teachers, contrarily, expect low performance and see such low performance as evidence to reinforce their views about student success; they see their role as facilitators and socializers; they see and allow for much differentiation between students in class and believe learning styles cause these differences; they do not see all students as able to improve; and they see lack of ability, low effort, poor class behavior, and difficult parental/social forces as explanations for the lower achievement. These teachers have effect size for achievement outcomes in the 0.00–0.20 range. A key role of school leaders is to evaluate the expectations of all in the school and then use this information to make key decisions to set appropriately challenging goals for all in the school.

Some Basic Evaluation Tools

This is not a chapter about evaluation methods, but three are mentioned to illustrate the kinds of tools that we have used in supporting the leader as evaluator: program logic, which can be used to address "Where am I going?"; the cross-walk, which can be used to address "How am I going?"; and the effect sizes, which can be used to address "Where to next?"

Where Am I Going? Program Logic

One of the difficulties in determining the maximum impact of teaching on students is that there are many possible causes and influences. As President John Kennedy noted, success has a thousand fathers and failure is motherless. One way to determine impact on students is for "evaluator leaders" to develop a program theory to understand success, which not only helps participants articulate and hypothesize the factors and directions of causal change but also allows the development of a causal model that can be used to determine the nature of the evaluation and outcomes. A logic model is a theory of action (Chen, 2005) that can assist those in schools to identify the mechanisms of change (from inputs, processes, and strategies to outcomes) and thus ultimately evaluate and improve a program or project. Evaluation can be conceived as a goodness-of-fit equation—Interventions + Dosage × Processes of implementation + Evaluation influence—that can then lead to a program effect or outcome. The issue that program logic addresses is the nature of each part and the nature of the links between the parts. The discussion and work in devising a program logic are exciting, involve much transparency in individual claims about factors and directions of change, and help clarify the intent of any intervention. The process also helps avoid the "Christmas tree" model of school improvement—when increasing numbers of interventions are put into a school like another bauble on a Christmas tree, often with no anticipated causal effect or with no detailed monitoring of the expected effects (Sebring & Bryk, 2000). For example, in one of our evaluations, the final model (which went through regular reviews and changes) is presented in Exhibit 5.4. This model was modified on many occasions during the five years of the project, which involved introducing many initiatives into five low-socioeconomic schools. As is normal, all initiatives were seen as essential to add into the schools, and there were many numerous claimed outcomes. The development of the model assisted in placing priorities on implementation and resources, on developing the evaluation tools and reports, and on ensuring attention was paid to the mechanisms of change from the antecedents and inputs through to the short- and long-term outcomes.

The Cross-Walk

The evaluation cross-walk is a technique for demonstrating to all involved how evaluation questions are linked to data collection strategies (O'Sullivan, 2004). Across the top of the matrix are the various

A Program Logic Relating Many Interventions into Five Schools to Short- and Long-Term Outcomes

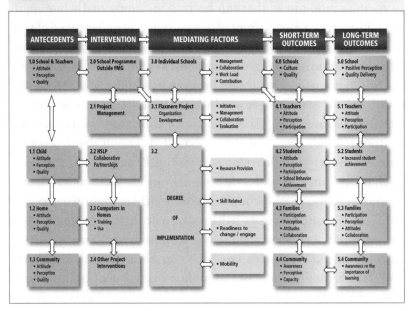

methods such as test scores, student perceptions of learning, observation methods, teacher overall judgments, and student artifacts from lessons. Down the side are the components of the evaluation questions, and these can be subdivided as the participants designing the cross-walk and involved in the interpretations of the evaluation desire. The completion ensures appropriate and sufficient evidence from a variety of sources for each evaluation question. Exhibit 5.5 is part of a cross-walk we developed for innovations in five schools; it shows the nature of the evaluation questions and the types of evidence we then collected. It is organized using Stufflebeam's (2003) CIPP (Context, Inputs, Processes, Product) model, which separates the evaluation questions into four parts: the context, the inputs, the processes, and the product. Each cell includes a tick; a comment; or, in an Internet version, a link to the details of the method of evidence evaluation. By school leaders devising a cross-walk with key participants and

EXHIBIT 5.5 — Example of (Part of) a Cross-Walk That Evaluates a Number of Initiatives Introduced across Five Local Schools

Specific Evaluation Questions for Local Schools	Focus Groups	Databases	Interviews	Standardized Testing	Existing Documentation	Survey
Context						
What are the program goals?					✔	✔
What are the target population and sample characteristics?		✔	✔			
What are the existing initiatives available in schools?					✔	
Describe current achievement levels of students.		✔				
Describe current attitudes to learning.		✔	✔			
Describe current access to information technology in school.					✔	
Input						
What specific activities are to take place?	✔				✔	
What is the degree of implementation?	✔			✔		
Which staff are involved?					✔	✔
Which students are involved?				✔		✔
Process						
Describe the degree of collaboration.	✔		✔			
Describe the degree of organizational development.	✔				✔	
What are the barriers to implementation of the project?	✔		✔			
What are the barriers to the evaluation?	✔		✔			
Monitor the feedback loop.	✔					✔
Product						
What changes in student achievement are evident?		✔		✔		✔
Describe any changes in student behavior.				✔		✔
Describe any changes in student attitudes.				✔		✔
Describe specific contribution for Maori.		✔		✔		

those who are to interpret the evidence, it can lead to more defensible decisions and more decisions that enjoy consensus as to evaluation and methods of analysis, plus allow for costs and reasonableness to be controlled.

The Use of Effect Sizes

A major advantage of using effect sizes is that they are scale free—they do not depend on the scale of any test and can be compared across subjects, teachers, and schools. Just as important, the effect sizes can be compared to the various influences in *Visible Learning*, which details more than 50,000 effect sizes relating to 138 major influences on student achievement. School leaders can calculate effect sizes across teachers, programs, and years and use this information to devise questions about and possible explanations for the impact on student learning. If the effects are >0.40, this probably suggests that the program or other activity is having the desired effect—the impact is at least greater than the average effect of 138 influences on achievement (based on about 240m students, as outlined in *Visible Learning*). Further, by using the pooled standard deviation for the class(es) as a proxy for the standard deviation for each student, it is possible to see effects of teaching on each student.

Take, for example, a class of students who have been administered the Australian National Assessment Program—Language and Numeracy assessments (www.naplan.edu.au) over a two-year period. The class average is 364 (sd = 78) in 2008 and 420 (sd = 51) in 2010. The effect size is 0.87, which is close to expected (2 years × 0.40 for each year = 0.80). If student A scores 345 in 2008 and 385 in 2010, this leads to an individual estimate of ES of 0.54 (385 − 345 = 40/average of 78 and 51, which results in 40/64.5 = 0.62). This is both below the mean for this class and, as critical, below the desired 0.80 over two years. This outcome begs the question, why did the teacher and the program have greater-than-expected effects on some students (those $d > 0.80$) and not on others (those $d < 0.40$)? It is not always as simple as ability or effort, and if students who are not making appropriate progress are detected early enough, alternative programs can be directed to these students—but it is the right question. The major initiatives under the Data Teams approach are key for taking such data and helping teachers and school leaders make the most defensible interpretations that then lead to actions and decisions (see Chapter 8 in this book).

Conclusions

The argument presented in this chapter is that, to be effective in terms of positively impacting student learning and achievement, school leaders need to conceive their role as evaluators. It is important to appreciate that school leaders include more than principals; they may be any driver or champion who performs a leadership role in a school. There is much to be learned from not only the roles and outcomes of evaluations but also the methods and techniques developed in evaluation that can help school leaders perform this role most effectively. Developing shared understandings, based on evidence, of the impact on student outcomes is the key role, but attention is also given to sustainability of the evaluation focus, questions asked, and methods used throughout the school leading to the school becoming a learning organization. The learning comes from the focus on evaluation of the impact that all have on the learning and achievement of the students, while not forgetting the impact on their parents and community as well as on the learning of the systems at the district or state level.

Further, these claims can apply to students. We can teach students to evaluate their own performance, to establish mastery goals about their learning, to set goals that are challenging yet achievable; they need to know someone will support them in their pursuit of success, they need to know what it looks like when they are successful, and they need to have information along the way to recognize progress. This is the essence of self-regulation, students as assessment capable, and lifelong learning (Absolum, Flockton, Hattie, Hipkins, & Reid, 2009).

Most critical is that the two core notions of evaluation, judging merit and worth, highlight the importance of articulating what is valued in a school that is subjected to evaluation. As well, one of the major issues in any evaluation study is how to *relate* the inputs, processes, and outcomes. The message in this chapter is that this involves school leaders being more transparent about how they, and their colleagues in the school, see these components and the relationship between them. Often these are the hidden part of learning in a school; as a result, learning is often attributed to the factors schools have least control over (e.g., student ability, effort, home factors). Articulating the process (e.g., via a program logic), agreeing on targets (for potential, progress, and performance), and interrogating the meaning of the effect sizes can be critical to evaluating success. These are the important issues.

In the book *Visible Learning* (Hattie, 2009), the aim was not to devise a league table and then for the influences at the top of the table to be "ticked off." Instead the aim was to craft a story about the practice of teaching. An important part of this story is about the mind frames of school leaders and teachers, as such attitudes and expectations are among the most powerful. It is not primarily the presence or absence of particular programs or curricula, but it is the mind frame that the school leaders and teachers have when implementing these programs. These include the mind frame that my role is to be an evaluator, particularly of my impact on student learning and achievement. More than evaluation is involved in effective teaching, as, unlike the evaluator, the school leader cannot walk away saying I did my best in seeking and interpreting the evidence but nothing changed for the better. There are other mind frames such as "my role is as a change agent"; determining appropriate challenge and not allowing "do my best"; seeing assessment as feedback to the teacher; and creating class environments that not only tolerate but welcome errors, which are the essence of learning.

Rather than assuming the role of leader as evaluator, it is so much easier to be the leader as visionary leader. Yes, the effects on students from these transformational leaders is positive ($d > 0.0$) but well below the average effects of all other influences ($d = 0.40$). To be an evaluation leader will lead to change, lead to questioning teachers about their teaching and influence, lead to identifying cohorts and individual students where different rather than more is needed, bring into question the curriculum offerings, and ask as to whether teachers have common conceptions of progress. These are challenging efforts that require high levels of trust, involve making a school "evaluation ready," and need gentle pressure relentlessly applied.

Note

Thanks to Andy Cawthera for comments on this chapter. Thanks to Debra Masters and Julie Schumacher, the core members of the Visible Learning Lab, for their improvements to this chapter after having listened to the "standard talk" so many times.

References

Absolum, M., Flockton, L., Hattie, J. A. C., Hipkins, R., & Reid, I. (2009). *Directions for assessment in New Zealand: Developing students' assessment capabilities.* Retrieved from http://assessment.tki.org.nz/Assessment-in -the-classroom/Directions-for-assessment-in-New-Zealand-DANZ -report

Brophy, J. E. (1982). How teachers influence what is taught and learned in classrooms. *The Elementary School Journal, 83*(1), 1–13.

Chen, H. T. (2005). *Practical program evaluation: Assessing and improving planning, implementation, and effectiveness.* Thousand Oaks, CA: Sage.

Clinton, J. M., Appleton, S., Cairns, K., & Broadbent, R. (2009, September). *How does stakeholder engagement in program evaluation really work?* Paper presented at the Australasian Evaluation Society Conference, Canberra, Australia.

Elmore, R. F. (2004). *School reform from the inside out: Policy, practice, and performance.* Cambridge, MA: Harvard Education Press.

Fetterman, D. M. (2001). *Foundations of empowerment evaluation.* Thousand Oaks, CA: Sage.

Fuchs, L. S., & Fuchs, D. (1986). Effects of systematic formative evaluation: A meta-analysis. *Exceptional Children, 53*(3), 199–208.

Hallinger, P., & Heck, R. H. (1998). Exploring the principal's contribution to school effectiveness: 1980–1995. *School Effectiveness and School Improvement, 9*(2), 157–191.

Hattie, J. A. C. (2002). Class composition and peer effects. *International Journal of Educational Research, 37*(5), 449–481.

Hattie, J. A. C. (2003, October). *Teachers make a difference: What is the research evidence?* Keynote presentation at the Building Teacher Quality: The ACER Annual Conference, Melbourne, Australia.

Hattie, J. A. C. (2009). *Visible learning: A synthesis of 800+ meta-analyses on achievement.* Oxford, UK: Routledge.

Hattie, J. A. C. (2011). The power of feedback in school settings. In R. Sutton, M. Douglas, & M. Hornsey (Eds.), *Feedback: The handbook of criticism, praise, and advice.* London: Peter Lang.

Hattie, J. A. C., Brown, G. T., & Keegan, P. (2005). A national teacher-managed, curriculum-based assessment system: Assessment Tools for Teaching & Learning (asTTle). *International Journal of Learning, 10,* 770–778.

Hattie, J. A. C., & Gan, M. (2010). The use of feedback to make learning visible to the teacher and learner. In R. Mayer & P. Alexander (Eds.), *Handbook of research on learning and instruction* (pp. 249–271). New York, NY: Routledge.

Hattie, J. A. C., & Timperley, H. (2007). The power of feedback. *Review of Educational Research, 77*(1), 81–112.

House, E. R., & Howe, K. R. (1999). *Values in evaluation and social research.* Thousand Oaks, CA: Sage.

Leithwood, K., Seashore L. K., Anderson, S., & Wahlstrom, K. (2004, September). *How leadership influences student learning.* Retrieved from http://www.wallacefoundation.org/NR/rdonlyres/E3BCCFA5-A88B-45D3-8E27-B973732283C9/0/ReviewofResearchLearningFrom Leadership.pdf

Leithwood, K., Tomlinson, D., & Genge, M. (1996). Transformational school leadership. In K. Leithwood, J. Chapman, D. Corson, P. Hallinger, & A. Hart (Eds.), *International handbook of educational leadership and administration* (pp. 785–840). Dordrecht, the Netherlands: Kluwer Academic.

Levin, B. (2008). *How to change 5000 schools: A practical and positive approach for leading change at every level.* Cambridge, MA: Harvard Education Press.

Madjar, I., McKinley, E., Jensen, S., & Van der Merwe, A. (2009). *Towards university: Navigating NCEA course choices in low-mid decile schools.* Retrieved from www.education.auckland.ac.nz/uoa/home/about/research/starpath-home/starpath-research/towards-university

Marks, H. M., & Printy, S. M. (2003). Principal leadership and school performance: An integration of transformational and instructional leadership. *Educational Administration Quarterly, 39*(3), 370–397.

Marzano, R. J., Waters, T., & McNulty, B. (2005). *School leadership that works: From research to results.* Aurora, CO: ASCD and Mid-continent Research for Education and Learning.

Nussbaum, M. C. (2010). *Not for profit: Why democracy needs the humanities.* Princeton, NJ: Princeton University Press.

O'Sullivan, R. G. (2004). *Practicing evaluation: A collaborative approach.* Thousand Oaks, CA: Sage.

Reeves, D. B. (2004). *Accountability for learning: How teachers and school leaders can take charge.* Alexandria, VA: ASCD.

Reeves, D. B. (2008). *Reframing teacher leadership to improve your school.* Alexandria, VA: ASCD.

Robinson, V. M. J., Hohepa, M., & Lloyd, C. (2009). *School leadership and student outcomes: Identifying what works and why best evidence synthesis iteration.* Retrieved from www.educationcounts.govt.nz/publications/series/2515

Robinson, V. M. J., Lloyd, C. A., & Rowe, K. (2008). The impact of leadership on student outcomes: An analysis of the differential effects of leadership types. *Educational Administration Quarterly, 44*(5), 635–674.

Rubie-Davies, C. (2009). Teacher expectations and labelling. *International Handbook of Research on Teachers and Teaching, 21*(8), 695–707.

Rubie-Davies, C., Hattie, J. A. C., & Hamilton, R. J. (2006). Expecting the best for students: Teacher expectations and academic outcomes. *British Journal of Educational Psychology, 76,* 429–444.

Schwandt, T. A. (2002). Traversing the terrain of role, identity and self. In K. E. Ryan & T. A. Schwandt (Eds.), *Exploring evaluator role and identity* (pp. 193–207). Greenwich, CT: Information Age.

Sebring, P. B., & Bryk, A. S. (2000). School leadership and the bottom line in Chicago. *Phi Delta Kappan, 81*(6), 440–443.

Segerholm, C. (2002). Evaluation as responsibility, conscience, and conviction. In K. E. Ryan & T. A. Schwandt (Eds.), *Exploring evaluator role and identity* (pp. 87–102). Greenwich, CT: Information Age.

Senge, P. M. (1990). *The Fifth Discipline.* New York, NY: Doubleday/Currency.

Stufflebeam, D. L. (2003). The CIPP model for evaluation. In T. Kellaghan & D. L. Stufflebeam (Eds.), *International Handbook of Educational Evaluation* (pp. 31–62). Dordrecht, the Netherlands: Kluwer Academic.

Witziers, B., Bosker, R. J., & Krüger, M. L. (2003). Educational leadership and student achievement: The elusive search for an association. *Educational Administration Quarterly, 39*(3), 398–425.

CHAPTER SIX

Bach, Beethoven, and the Blues: B³ Leaders for the 21st Century

DOUGLAS B. REEVES

LEADERS CANNOT ENGAGE IN ACTIVATION, the theme of this book, if they are paralyzed by fear and plagued by impossible demands. They cannot inspire and engage others if they are emotionally withered and physically exhausted. That is particularly true in the second decade of the 21st century, with financial crises looming, political demands increasing, and job security a long-forgotten pipedream for educators, administrators, and employees throughout the ranks of state and local governments. In challenging times, popular leadership literature can drift into the absurd, seeking lessons from such thoughtful and nuanced characters as Attila the Hun and Alexander the Great, both of whom devoted their lives to proving the maxim of Thomas Hobbes (1651) that life is "nasty, brutish, and short." This chapter offers an alternative to the cynicism and despair that can so easily triumph in challenging times. The lessons from the great masters of music, including Bach, Beethoven, and a host of contemporary blues artists, provide not only solace for the weary leader but a guide for transforming ideas into action even in the midst of the greatest challenges. These women and men, Europeans and African Americans, not only give us tunes and lyrics that resonate across the ages but also help us understand how leaders can better cope with new challenges.

B³ Leaders, the term I apply to leaders who effectively apply these lessons, are needed by every educational institution. These lessons do not depend upon a technical knowledge of music, the ability to play an instrument, or even an appreciation for Bach, Beethoven, or the blues, although I hope that the following pages might inspire readers to listen to all three. Rather, B³ Leaders apply and communicate essential lessons about risk and value in a powerful and effective manner.

William Congreve (1697) observed that "music has charms to soothe a savage beast, to soften rocks, or bend a knotted oak" and, we could add, to settle the jangled nerves of a leader beset by staff anxiety, parent discontent, and student unrest. Neurologist and author Oliver Sacks (2007) confirmed the observation, noting that music reaches the human mind in a manner unlike any other stimuli. But music can do far more for educational leaders than serve as an audible substitute for Prozac. This chapter suggests that the musical masters, from the Baroque era to contemporary jazz, from Johann Sebastian Bach to Wynton Marsalis, can provide a blueprint for the challenges of 21st-century leadership. The goal of great music is not harmony but meaning. We can train a pigeon to play a chord on the piano, but animals, including the vast majority of *Homo sapiens*, lead only with brute force. Threats, force, and the granting or withholding of vital resources are the stock-in-trade not only of alpha-male gorillas but also of politicians who, defying all evidence to the contrary, seek to motivate through fear and intimidation. Bullies succeed, at least in the short term, because they can count on other people to submit to their demands. However, great musicians and great leaders take risks, challenge tyrants, suffer the disapproval of both the powerful and the crowds, and endure endless pronouncements of their doom and irrelevance. Because these negative forces are so powerful, most musicians and leaders succumb to the pressure and are soon forgotten. But the reason we still listen to Bach 500 years after he composed and the reason the blues will be sung 500 years from now is that great musicians do not entertain their audiences but challenge them. Great musicians and leaders do not seek to satisfy their contemporaries but give them meaning, insight, and inspiration.

This chapter advances four arguments. First, B³ Leaders embrace appropriate and essential risks. Although they are not reckless, these leaders push the boundaries of prevailing prejudices and elevate the impact of their work over their personal popularity. Second, B³ Leaders make connections. Rather than managing discrete tasks and projects, they place every action in the context of a broader whole. Every piece of music Bach wrote, including those without words, was attached to meaning in a theological, political, educational, or social context. The blues repertoire includes not only lamentations about relationships gone wrong but the wailing sounds unreachable with words, recalling the bitterness of oppression. While most people can recall the thundering chorus of Beethoven's Ninth Symphony, *"Alle menschen werden brudern"*—all mankind will be brothers—we seldom recall the historical context in which this was not a noble nostrum but was, to the European hierarchy of the day, a threatening and dangerous notion (Sachs, 2010). Third, B³ Leaders communicate purpose and meaning in a variety of obvious and subtle ways. Sometimes Bach shouts his message, with the chorus singing a message in unison, every voice articulating the same message at the same time. At other times, however, the messages are subtle and complex. It is the same message, but the hands and feet of the organist, the bows of the string, and the breaths of the woodwinds are expressing that message in different forms. Similarly, B³ Leaders understand that communication of purpose and meaning is always important, but effective communication requires engagement of the listener, not mindless repetition by the orator. Fourth, B³ Leaders add value. Just as a concerto is more than the sum of the 88 keys on a piano, leaders challenge the "zero-sum" hypothesis in which the gain of one is equal to the loss of another. The chapter closes with some thoughts regarding the next generation of leaders and the essential influence of music on them.

Appropriate Risks

It is not difficult to imagine the following conversation. The chairman of the board announces, "We really need some radical change in this institution. Our weekly meetings are boring, and we've spent decades employing the same old teaching strategies and getting the same old results. But this new fellow, Mr. Bach, appears to have some innovative ideas, so let's bring him in as our new leader." Taking the directives of his superiors seriously, Herr Bach does precisely as he was told, and presents a bold new idea to the community. He calls it "*Wachet Auf*"—"Sleepers Awake"—a work designed to start the official new year of his institution, the emerging Lutheran church, for the first Sunday of Advent. The cantata, scored for chorus, soloists, organ, and orchestra, is based on a simple, well-known melody composed decades before Bach put pen to paper. Unlike the original familiar hymn, the new cantata is replete with the innovations that Bach's employers had sought. In addition to religious themes, his work includes secular, educational, and philosophical implications (Greenberg, 1995, 1998). After Bach's presentation of his innovative work, some people are amazed; others are a bit overwhelmed; and others not only boo and hiss but they throw their shoes, shout in anger, and beat their fists into the wind. One of 11 board members offers meekly, "He was only doing what we hired him to do." Bach's employment, like that of many leaders who engage in bold and innovative change, is terminated. Half a millennium later musical groups, from high school choirs to professional choruses, regularly perform the work in both religious and secular settings.

Wynton Marsalis, director of Jazz at Lincoln Center and one of the leading musicians of the 21st century, is not only heir to an extraordinary musical heritage rooted deeply in American and, in particular, African American music, but he is also a multicultural innovator who, within minutes, moves from the classic and familiar strains of blues and jazz standards to the most original and challenging improvisations. Maria Schneider leads an eponymous orchestra that includes songs based on bird calls from the Brazilian rainforest, fusing the music of mechanical instruments with the music of nature. What do Bach, Marsalis, and Schneider have in common? None conducts from a podium; each leads from the sidelines—Marsalis plays 4th trumpet in his band; Bach played in churches where the organist was, by design, invisible to the congregation; Schneider starts her musicians with a beat, and then withdraws to the sidelines to play, observe, and affirm. When things go right, they share the credit. When things go wrong, they take the heat.

What can educational leaders learn about risk from these examples? First, innovation and change are never risk-free endeavors. Even when boards, employers, bosses, and political leaders promise change and offer preliminary support to change agents, what they really mean is, "We'll support you until the tide of public opinion turns, and then you're on your own." B³ Leaders accept that risk, knowing that if they enjoy universal popularity, they have probably compromised their commitment to change. Two leaders I have known for more than 20 years, one a school superintendent and one an orchestra conductor, asked the same question: "Will I always have to move every five to seven years? Will I never be able to simply stay and enjoy the changes that I have created?" The orchestra conductor built his audience fivefold and transformed a dying community orchestra into a regional symphony. The superintendent improved student achievement, strategy, and operational effectiveness in four consecutive school systems. By any measure, they were successful, but in both cases, the complaints about their changes diminished their popularity with their boards. These leaders could certainly have chosen stability over change, but I knew them well enough to know that such a choice would have made them miserable. More importantly, the profound and important changes that benefited the communities they served would have been lost had they heeded the siren song of popularity.

Note well that B³ Leaders are neither reckless nor imprudent. As Collins (2001) noted of effective change leaders in business, they are not gunslingers who bet the future of their organizations and employees on a whim. Rather, they take carefully calculated risks. The risk calculation of B³ Leaders is, however, more nuanced than merely assessing the risk of change. The comparison is not "change vs. perfection" or "unpopularity vs. popularity." Rather, the risk calculation compares the consequences of change—both positive and negative— to the consequences of failing to change. If the message and meaning of music are more important than a mere tune, then Bach knew that the alternative to the rage of some listeners would be the slow death of the essential ideas embedded in the musical message. Marsalis could have doubtlessly enjoyed more creature comforts leading a show band in Las Vegas than pushing the boundaries of music and engaging students in the poorest neighborhoods of New York City. Schneider perhaps leaves some people scratching their head over Amazonian bird calls in a concert, but if she failed to take that risk, where else would the message be heard?

Consider in a new light the most important change you want to make in your classroom, school, district, province, state, or nation. Then ask a new series of questions to assess the relative risks of change:

What are the consequences if I try and fail?

What are the consequences if I succeed?

What are the consequences if I never try?

In the answers to these questions, you will find the risk calculus of B^3 Leaders. As Dean Robert Allan Hill (2009, p. 83) wisely concludes, "Leaders have to lead, they don't have to succeed."

Making Connections

The compositions of Ludwig van Beethoven influence at least four eras of music: Baroque, Classical, Romantic, and "modern"—an era that began early in the 20th century and that begs for more nuanced description. Thanks to a combination of his revolutionary spirit and auditory impairments, Beethoven can arguably be placed squarely in the center of the 21st-century music as well. While many people can hum a few bars of the famous Fifth Symphony—DA DA DA DUM!— or recall the Ninth Symphony with Schiller's beautiful poetry about the brotherhood of all humankind and daughters of Elysium, it is less well known that Beethoven's teachers, peers, and students enjoyed an interplay among the arts, mathematics, literacy, and philosophy that could serve as models for contemporary leadership studies (Sachs,

2010). His words and music included themes that challenged the tra-ditional authority of emperors, monarchs, and dictators. The Ninth Symphony is a distinctly political work, challenging musical conven-tion with its occasional dissonance and political convention with its overt democratic themes. While Howard Gardner (1993) may have popularized the Theory of Multiple Intelligences, the genesis of the theory can be found centuries earlier.

Beethoven's relevance to leadership lies in the complex interrela-tionship between different disciplines. Just as Gardner (1999), in *The Disciplined Mind*, finds connections between Darwin and Mozart, Beethoven and Bach routinely connected the worlds of arts, science, and philosophy in ways that none of these disciplines alone could express. Noel Tichy, prolific leadership author and professor at the University of Michigan, has made the persuasive case that effective leaders are, above all, great teachers (Tichy and Cohen, 2002). Though education has learned much from modern studies of pedagogy, one of the teaching truths that endures through the centuries is that great teachers are able to express ideas in a variety of different ways to reach a variety of different students.

Music students know that one can find parallel harmonic struc-tures in the 12-bar blues of Blind Lemon Jefferson and the fugues of Johann Sebastian Bach. What is less evident is that just as Bach and Beethoven integrated complex political and philosophical themes in music, blues artists of the 19th and 20th century brought social jus-tice and human relationships into the musical equation. The rhetor-ical cadences of the most influential of the leaders have a direct parallel to the musical cadences of the era. Consider the music of Mar-tin Luther King, Jr. (1963):

> I have a dream that one day every valley shall be exalted, every hill and mountain shall be made low, the rough places will be made plain, and the crooked places will be made straight, and the glory of the Lord shall be revealed, and all flesh shall see it together.
>
> This is our hope. This is the faith that I go back to the South with. With this faith we will be able to hew out of the

mountain of despair a stone of hope. With this faith we will be able to transform the jangling discords of our nation into a beautiful symphony of brotherhood. With this faith we will be able to work together, to pray together, to struggle together, to go to jail together, to stand up for freedom together, knowing that we will be free one day.

This will be the day when all of God's children will be able to sing with a new meaning, "My country, 'tis of thee, sweet land of liberty, of thee I sing. Land where my fathers died, land of the pilgrim's pride, from every mountainside, let freedom ring."

And if America is to be a great nation this must become true. So let freedom ring from the prodigious hilltops of New Hampshire. Let freedom ring from the mighty mountains of New York. Let freedom ring from the heightening Alleghenies of Pennsylvania!

Let freedom ring from the snowcapped Rockies of Colorado!

Let freedom ring from the curvaceous slopes of California!

But not only that; let freedom ring from Stone Mountain of Georgia!

Let freedom ring from Lookout Mountain of Tennessee!

Let freedom ring from every hill and molehill of Mississippi. From every mountainside, let freedom ring.

And when this happens, when we allow freedom to ring, when we let it ring from every village and every hamlet, from every state and every city, we will be able to speed up that day when all of God's children, black men and white men, Jews and Gentiles, Protestants and Catholics, will be able to join hands and sing in the words of the old Negro spiritual, "Free at last! free at last! thank God Almighty, we are free at last!"

Dr. King makes explicit connections between biblical allusions that his audience surely recognized and the travails of the Civil Rights Movement.

Listen to the music of Abraham Lincoln (1865):

With malice toward none, with charity for all, with firm-
ness in the right as God gives us to see the right, let us strive
on to finish the work we are in, to bind up the nation's
wounds, to care for him who shall have borne the battle and
for his widow and his orphan, to do all which may achieve
and cherish a just and lasting peace among ourselves and with
all nations.

Like King, Lincoln knew that his audience would hear his message on
multiple levels, including not only the explicit message regarding the
present conflict—the Civil War and, a century later, the Civil Rights
Movement—but the implicit message that the cause for which both
men ultimately died was rooted in the poetry and philosophy of
ancient days. Similarly, the blues continue to resonate with a global
audience because the music and themes are universal, just as the leadership themes of Buddha, Jefferson, Gandhi, Lincoln, and King offer
meaning across many generations.

How do B³ educational leaders make connections? First, they
ensure that their stakeholders know that nothing important is merely
an educational issue, but rather the critical educational challenges fac-
ing communities are essentially health and safety issues. If a water
supply were contaminated, people would protest. If a crack house
moved into a house next door to a city council member, politicians
would be enraged. But if literacy performance is inadequate—particularly for students for whom public expectations have long been mea-
ger—then there is barely a peep of protest. B³ Leaders do not,
therefore, conduct crusades for a 4 percent increase in state test scores.
They do, however, campaign with passion and purpose for saving the
lives of children. As surely as tainted water and drug-infested neighborhoods threaten the lives and safety of our children, the multigen-
erational costs of school failure far exceed the investment necessary to
intervene effectively (Alliance for Excellent Education, 2010). B³ Leaders do not have educational initiatives; they have moral imperatives.
B³ Leaders do not announce strategic plans for incremental gains; they
proclaim, with the certain vigor of Winston Churchill, that victory,
not compromise, is the only objective. B³ Leaders, in sum, do not

make the case for change based upon a single set of data, though surely their case is supported by evidence. They make the case for change because they engage the hearts and minds of stakeholders who think not only of the present but of future generations. They elicit sacrifice not because it is popular but because it is necessary. They connect the present reality of challenge to the future hope of success and, in doing so, supplant despair and cynicism with hope and a willingness to take risks. They do not, of course, enjoy a "happily ever after" story, as the deaths of King and Lincoln attest. Churchill, who took office as Britain's prime minister when the very survival of England was threatened by the Nazis, led the nation to victory and, within months of that victory, was soundly defeated at the polls. I do not claim that B³ Leaders are popular nor that they survive, but only that they serve a purpose higher than themselves and inspire others to do the same.

Communication Obvious and Subtle

Within the daily challenges of every effective leader, there can be found the complexity of Bach, the experimentation of Beethoven, and the meaning and feeling of the blues. Artists of all three genres of music understand that there is a combination of science and structure on the one hand, and creativity and spirit on the other. Bach's compositions simultaneously offer mathematical perfection and deep inspiration. Some of the most majestic fugues ever composed are variations on only a few notes. The blues can tell a thousand stories within a remarkably similar chord and rhythm structure—12 or 16 bars, using the tonic (basic) chord, followed by the fourth, fifth, seventh, and a return to the tonic. Beethoven's sonatas and symphonies always include an exposition of a theme, variations, and return to the theme. While the structure in all of these examples seems repetitive, the listener can express only awestruck wonder at the creativity of these masters. In other words, the communication of a theme can be obvious—Beethoven's exposition, Bach's four notes, or a blues tune—but the communication of that theme can have multiple layers of nuance and variation. There is no contradiction between the directness of the message and the expression of that message with multiple layers of nuance and complexity appropriate for a variety of audiences and stakeholders.

Composing a leadership symphony requires consideration of research and systems, but in the end it is also the combination of structure and creativity. Most importantly, composers, whatever their genius, reach their greatest heights through the complementary efforts of others, from musicians to instrument makers to audience members. The more grand the symphony, the more dependent the leader will be on the diversity of skills of others.

Educational leaders must communicate the same message in many different ways. While the theme may involve the need to improve student literacy, the variations might include a variation for parents about the opportunities for future generations, another variation for senior citizens and business leaders about the positive impact on the economic vitality of the community, another variation for school system employees about the impact of literacy improvements on student population growth and job opportunities, and yet another variation for all stakeholders about the social justice imperative of literacy and an informed citizenry.

Adding Value

The fourth and final argument of this chapter is that B³ Leaders add value. Poker is a zero-sum game. You win, I lose. I win, you lose. At least in a game of poker played at home, there is no cut for the casino nor is there is a conveniently available representative of the Internal Revenue Service to appropriate a portion of the pot. In simple mathematical terms, the equation looks like this:

$$D = -Y$$

Or D, Doug's gains, are equal to $-Y$, your losses. I make 10 dollars, you lose 10 dollars. This is the classic zero-sum game in which the sum of my gains and your losses always equals zero. And when you have unwisely drawn to an inside straight and I have patiently bet on a lowly pair of two's, then this equation is one of life's great pleasures.

Unfortunately, if we multiplied both sides of the equation by -1, then we would have the very unfortunate result:

$$-D = Y$$

Or Doug's losses are equal to your gains. Your inside straight strategy succeeded, and I am left withdrawing my dwindling retirement plan assets to pay my gambling debts. In a game of poker, this is fine—or more precisely, the first equation is fine and the second one is completely unacceptable. But when it comes to allocating leadership time and attention, the equation becomes more problematic. If we are stuck in the zero-sum game hypothesis, then any resources, time, or energy devoted to one leadership objective are presumed to subvert all others. B[3] Leaders challenge that hypothesis. Leadership time and attention need not be a zero-sum game, and time devoted by leaders or students to music and other creative endeavors does not diminish other areas of focus, but enhances them.

How can educational leaders challenge the zero-sum game hypothesis and add value? First, they must assess the evidence. For example, one of the most consistent sources of dissatisfaction among teachers is the lack of time to do their jobs effectively (Ingersoll & Perda, 2009). While this discontent is undoubtedly rooted in fact—too many curriculum requirements and too little time—the conclusion need not be that effective instructional initiatives are impossible. Rather, the conclusion must be that the effective instructional initiatives must have leverage—one gram of effort results in a kilogram of impact. The increased use of nonfiction writing, for example, has been shown to have a significant and positive impact on science, math, social studies, and reading comprehension (Reeves, 2010b, 2010c, 2011). B[3] Leaders reject the notion that "we don't have time for writing" and supplant it with a strategy that uses nonfiction writing to engage students and improve achievement in multiple subjects. Similarly, policymakers and senior leaders who confront constraints on resources and time do not reject innovation out of hand, but assess in a systematic way the degree to which current and past initiatives are actually implemented and the extent to which they influence student achievement (Reeves, 2010a, 2011). Their B³ leadership adds value not only by what they do but by what they choose not to do.

Music for the Next Generation of Leaders

Paeans to the value of the arts are like politicians kissing babies. These embraces represent the exigencies of election campaigns. But after a while, babies become less cute and arts programs become less endearing. In the real world—after elections are completed and budgets are decided—the true priorities of systems emerge. It is not a coincidence that both babies and the arts are left far behind when it comes to the reality of budgetary priorities. Even people who don't like changing diapers know that today's smelly baby will be tomorrow's taxpayer, funding the Social Security payments of the reluctant diaper changer. Similarly, people who conflate music with Muzak nevertheless have a vested interest in the arts not only on aesthetic grounds but because societies that commit resources, time, attention, and energy to the arts serve their citizens better than societies that, in pursuit of rationality, do not. Above all, our collective future depends upon leaders who do more than execute strategies and manage tasks but who heed the lessons of Bach, Beethoven, and the blues.

References

Alliance for Excellent Education. (2010, June 9). The economic benefits of reducing the dropout rate in the nation's largest metropolitan areas. Retrieved from http://www.all4ed.org/publication_material/EconMSA

Collins, J. (2001). *Good to great: Why some companies make the leap . . . and others don't.* New York: HarperCollins.

Congreve, W. (1697). *The mourning bride,* act 1, scene 1. Retrieved from http://www.quotationspage.com/quote/1486.html

Gardner, H. (1993). *Frames of mind: The theory of multiple intelligences* (2nd ed.). New York, NY: Basic Books.

Gardner, H. (1999). *The disciplined mind: What all students should understand.* New York, NY: Simon & Schuster.

Greenberg, R. (Speaker). (1995). *Bach and the high Baroque.* [Audio recording]. Chantilly, VA: The Teaching Company.

Greenberg, R. (Speaker). (1998). *How to listen to and understand great music.* [Audio recording]. Chantilly, VA: The Teaching Company.

Hill, R. A. (2009). *Renewal: Thought, word, and deed.* Lanham, MD: Hamilton Books.

Hobbs, T. (1651). *Leviathan,* part I, chapter 13. Retrieved from http://www.rjgeib.com/thoughts/nature/hobbes-quotes.html

Ingersoll, R., & Perda, D. (2009). *How high is teacher turnover and is it a problem?* Philadelphia, PA: Consortium for Policy Research in Education, University of Pennsylvania.

King, M. L. (1963, August 28). I have a dream. Retrieved from http://www.usconstitution.net/dream.html

Lincoln. A. (1865, March 4). Second inaugural address. Retrieved from http://www.bartleby.com/124/pres32.html

Reeves, D. B. (2010a). The board's role in innovation. *American School Board Journal, 197*(1), 30–32.

Reeves, D. B. (2010b). Focusing on leadership essentials. *American School Board Journal, 197*(7), 39, 41.

Reeves, D. B. (2010c). The write way. *American School Board Journal, 197*(11), 46–47.

Reeves, D. B. (2011). Getting ready for the common core. *American School Board Journal, 198*(3), 23.

Sachs, H. (2010). *The Ninth: Beethoven and the world in 1824.* New York, NY: Random House.

Sacks, O. (2007). *Musicophilia: Tales of music and the brain* (Rev. ed.). New York, NY: Vantage Books.

Tichy, N. M., & Cohen, E. B. (2002). The *leadership engine: How winning companies build leaders at every level.* New York, NY: HarperBusiness.

CHAPTER SEVEN

Activating School Improvement

STEPHEN WHITE

Schools know how to change...What schools do not know how to do is to improve, to engage in sustained and continuous progress toward a performance goal over time.

—RICHARD ELMORE

IN A RECENT DISCUSSION ABOUT SCHOOL IMPROVEMENT, a senior leader noted: "You should see our school improvement process. I think you'll find it focused and right on target with the components you are describing." She was right to the degree her template directed schools to complete a comprehensive needs assessment, articulate SMART (specific, measurable, achievable, relevant, and timely) goals, describe action steps with some specificity, and assign responsibility for monitoring. The conversation revealed how easy it is to equate a form, a template, a document with school improvement, rather than improvement of practices or achievement. Richard Elmore aptly differentiates change from improvement and challenges the profession to activate and sustain real improvements. School improvement plans often resemble a scrapbook that tells the school's story rather than a road map that improves practice or lifts achievement (White & Smith, 2010).

This chapter attempts to clarify the issue by defining school improvement in its simplest terms and by identifying actions school leaders and improvement teams can take to change the paradigm from compliance to commitment. We begin with a simple definition of school improvement.

School Improvement Defined

School improvement is the collective effort of a school community to systematically alter teaching and learning practices to improve student achievement.

School improvement is not collaborative because multiple and diverse stakeholders participate, but because of collective efforts and agreements reached to make best practices common. It is not systematic when the result is only a more efficient compliance with external requirements, but becomes systematic when internal capacity is built so next year's improvement effort is more effective than last year's. The theory of action to "activate" school improvement is guided by two principles. The first is evidence-based management (EBM).

Evidence-Based Management

Dr. Douglas Reeves (2008) often speaks of the tendency of educators to engage in fact-free debates where personal preferences, traditions, and opinions trump evidence and rational discussions. In medicine, EBM assumes a level of expertise and professional judgment by practitioners, and it assumes that the unique values and preferences of patients (think teachers, parents, and students in schools) will influence decisions. Evidence-based management systematically introduces best practices and research into the process, reducing the likelihood of Dr. Reeve's fact-free debates (Sackett et al., 1996). The medical profession considers all aspects of the interaction between patient and physician as important evidence (data) to inform decision making. The application to school improvement is obvious: Recognize that all factors of teaching, leading, and learning impact student achievement and develop key metrics that predict improved performance and practice. Evidence-based educational practice is the antidote to fact-free debates and is a foundational principle for activating school improvement. The second principle is the explicit use of contingency planning to ensure results.

Contingency Planning for Results

The 2010 Chilean mine disaster in Copiapó that resulted in a 69-day rescue effort is widely recognized as the gold standard for mine rescues (pun unavoidable); high-tech intervention; and effective, coordinated planning. Behind these accomplishments was a detailed and extensive series of contingency plans that reflected a relentless commitment to success. In fact, the rescue shaft used at Copiapó was actually plan B. The commitment to extract the 33 miners by any means possible included extensive contingency planning, without which the "miracle" rescue would have been delayed for weeks if not months. The implication for school improvement for this principle is also evident: Determine the goal target and articulate a series of milestones and contingencies to ensure success. While most school improvement plans are annual, the best employ alternate contingency paths to achieve their goal. Committed schools will manage issues and identify potential risks to their success, while a compliance mentality assumes that the plan once written may or may not succeed and accepts either outcome. Activation of school improvement means teams are more serious about success than they are comfortable with a lack of it.

A theory of action has four components: (1) intention, (2) form and convention, (3) results and causal factors, and (4) context (Allwood, 1995). Our intent is to achieve a paradigm shift from compliance to commitment. The form and convention is The Leadership and Learning Center's proven improvement cycle, PIM™ (Planning, Implementation, and Monitoring), and the foundation for managing results, causal factors, and context is based on EBM and contingency planning. Let's begin by examining school improvement in its organizational context.

Window of Opportunity

Because schools are remarkably stable organizations, with clearly defined operating procedures (calendars, purchasing, budgeting, textbook adoptions), the opportunity to develop clearly defined improvement procedures is always present, albeit rarely developed. Such stability is rarely considered as a means to manage large-scale improvements or changes (Beckhard & Harris, 1987), but if schools can accomplish uniformity around materials, calendars, and purchasing, surely we can do the same around delivery of instruction, feedback systems, and celebrations. We should be able to reduce variability to make best practice common practice throughout the school.

Stability in school improvement provides the platform on which opportunities for change are presented, debated, and initiated. While priorities in curricular emphasis and the allocation of resources may be debated, few debate the importance of collaborative school improvement. Virtually every school system has negotiated a defined school improvement or shared-decision-making policy that spells out explicitly the roles, responsibilities, and membership of school improvement teams. No other mechanism has been established for the purpose of attempting something new or different, and school improvement is deeply engrained not only in the United States but also in Australia, the United Kingdom, Canada, Singapore, and the Netherlands. Consensus exists that schools are the unit scale (more than districts or classrooms) where changes are tested and refined.

The final window of opportunity is a collaborative work culture. Much has been written about the power of effective teamwork (DuFour, DuFour, & Eaker, 2008; Garmston & Wellman, 1999; Schmoker, 2006; Surowiecki, 2004). Collaborative processes such as Data Teams and professional learning communities (PLCs) represent an emerging and collaborative work culture supported by contractual time provided during the school day that was not at all the case 15 years ago. School improvement is fundamentally collaborative and invites dialogue, feedback, and support systems. A window of opportunity exists to reduce variability in what matters, test and refine desired changes, and create a collaborative culture through school improvement. The context is ideal for managing the substantive changes Elmore, in the quote that begins this chapter, challenges us to pursue.

Planning, Implementation, and Monitoring to Activate School Improvement

The PIM™ process was designed by The Leadership and Learning Center (2005) in response to urban, rural, and suburban district needs to interpret what is working well, what is not, and why, in schools across the continent. Exhibit 7.1 depicts this continuous improvement cycle.

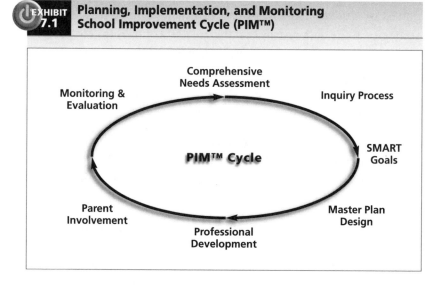

EXHIBIT 7.1   Planning, Implementation, and Monitoring School Improvement Cycle (PIM™)

Planning

Planning is characterized by a comprehensive needs assessment, a process of inquiry that generates hypotheses for action, and delineation of SMART goals. To be comprehensive, the needs assessment must gather data about more than just student achievement. Readers will recognize the alignment with the theory of action around evidence, and the most comprehensive needs assessments gather data about leadership practices and about teaching practices. Routine teaching behaviors and leadership expectations to post standards or hold student-led parent conferences all impact student achievement, and some of these factors will have a greater impact on achievement than others. A comprehensive needs assessment uses data from multiple achievement measures such as formative short-cycle assessments as well as state or provincial high-stakes assessments, leading to a process of inquiry.

Inquiry is advanced when educators triangulate the needs assessment data and analyze the degree to which practices promote achievement gains or close achievement gaps. For example, many teams may gather data about student attendance and tardies, use of scoring guides or student self-assessment protocols, and specific teaching strategies. If the data reveals that the greatest contribution to achievement was the absence of tardies, then the school improvement plan might target a reduction in tardies as a major improvement strategy. Inquiry sets the stage for hypothesis development, with the following hypothesis emerging from our example:

> IF all classroom teachers would begin class at the bell, THEN student tardies and discipline referrals would decrease while credit completion and student achievement would increase school-wide for all grades.

The "IF" statement is the genesis of an action step strategy, while the "THEN" statement is the genesis of a SMART goal. Neither is complete, but the inquiry process is designed to "tee up" SMART goals and to ensure that all goals are driven by evidence.

Much has been written about SMART goals, but John Hattie (2009) found that goal quality was a key element in predicting successful achievement. Hattie's research revealed that challenging goals where both teachers and students had to alter their routines and practices to achieve them were much more successful than less rigorous goal statements. SMART goals need to be specific about student groups. Many readers may wonder, "Isn't it wiser to have a goal for all the students, such as to reduce tardies by 5 percent, than to address just students with chronic tardies (e.g., one or more each week)?" The answer is "No," simply because the more specific goal helps all teachers pay attention (focus) to the students in need (chronic tardies). For those who are rarely tardy, the strategy is apt to help all students, even though teachers will only monitor changes for those with tardies that have been problematic. Note how this approach limits the collection of unnecessary data while encouraging focus, focus, focus.

Measurable SMART goals are achieved by establishing a baseline and using a metric that all observers can quantify or count. "Achievable" refers to the trajectory needed to close achievement gaps. If the goal is to increase by 20 percent the number of students enrolled in Advanced Placement classes, the SMART goal would set the growth target to ensure gaps among student groups would be closed within a three- to five-year period. Any longer is not closing gaps. Relevant SMART goals are related to data produced in the comprehensive needs assessment, and timely SMART goals merely mean that a fixed time is set when the measure will be taken and the achievement of the goal will be celebrated or analyzed for needed changes or modification for the next cycle.

Implementation

Implementation with fidelity is always the goal, but our research has revealed that most plans assume a school-wide application. However, there are a few critical components necessary to implement with fidelity, without which needed improvements are rarely sustained. Implementation in PIM™ refers to action step strategies, professional development required to build capacity among faculty, and the degree to which parents are engaged in the process.

Strategies should clearly describe who will do what, when, and why to guide and ensure deep implementation—a simple formula, but one that requires very explicit planning and delineation of protocols and priorities over a thoughtful time frame. The second component of quality implementation is professional development, an area that is often omitted or underestimated in terms of the coaching, feedback, and refinement needed to achieve mastery. This area is a key to building capacity. By addressing realistic needs for professional development, schools often recognize unseen limitations in their own resources and adjust by limiting goals and supporting them extensively.

We know from the work of Joyce and Showers (2002) that parent engagement is a major factor in improving student performance over time. Our model examines three attributes of parent engagement: access to school resources and individuals, communication that is timely and convenient for parents (native language, online, etc.), and parent training and educational opportunities to better support their students (technology, standards, report cards, parent portal, complaint resolution, etc.).

Monitoring

Understanding and support for this element has grown since the PIM™ process was first put in place in 2004, in part because of changing expectations at state and federal levels and an acknowledgment that more frequent, formative assessments were necessary to intervene efficiently. Monitoring within PIM™ means both student achievement and teacher practices are monitored to improve achievement and build capacity. Schools that monitor only student achievement do themselves a disservice and will struggle to activate the kinds of gains that would otherwise be possible simply because the interaction between teaching practices and student achievement will reveal what is working and what is not. The final element of monitoring is to include an evaluation of the effectiveness of the improvement plan. Did the school achieve its goals, and why or why not? What was most successful and needs to be scaled up and replicated? What needs to be discarded? To activate school improvement, practitioners need to be able to answer these questions at a minimum.

The sequence depicted in Exhibit 7.1 begins by gathering evidence holistically about contributing factors, including conditions for learning, time, materials, fidelity of implementation, and student achievement. It then invites improvement teams to reflect and engage in inquiry that yields meaningful hypotheses for action that guides development of SMART goals. The implementation plan is precise, targeted, focused, and supported with professional development and parental engagement, and the monitoring process is both formative and summative, with evaluation questions that identify lessons learned and guide formation of the next improvement plan. PIM™ works because it is practical and transparent and activates school improvement.

Distributed Leadership

Distributed leadership is like apple pie: Who could be against it? School improvement lends itself to distributed leadership simply because the work of building capacity or changing practices sufficiently to actually improve student achievement requires explicit ongoing monitoring, coaching, and a readiness to make smart midcourse adjustments when necessary. Leaders who become familiar with what it really takes to improve schools begin to recognize that there is no way the leadership team will have the time or expertise to coach, mentor, or support teachers or teams in effecting the needed change.

Most teachers I know are not interested in being in the spotlight or receiving praise before their colleagues. If they want to be recognized at all, it is for their competence and dedication, and most of all, they will embrace any opportunity to make a difference for kids. So, rather than praise them publicly, why not invite them to serve as the champion to activate a major school improvement strategy? Without requiring additional compensation or violating union rules, principals and improvement teams can recruit the right person to monitor, communicate, and coordinate efforts on a topic he is passionate about. When the champion is selected for something he is already passionate about with expertise, success is all but guaranteed, but when people are selected because it is "their turn" or because they are the department chair, the commitment is apt to be lackluster. As leaders, you know who the champions are on your staff. Still, most school improvement plans identify administrators as those responsible for major action steps, and when plans are devised under that premise, none of us should be surprised that they are rarely implemented with fidelity. The simple change of assigning responsibility to champions shifts the paradigm toward commitment and provides an opportunity to develop potential leaders while distributing leadership opportunities.

Distributing leadership in this way will yield early dividends, and the research is compelling to support it. Casciaro and Lobo (2005) discovered that the most effective individuals are often not in positions of leadership at all, but rather congenial, competent colleagues who are committed to the organization and its mission. They refer to the conundrum many face in the workforce when "competent jerks" and "lovable fools" are tolerated equally, when what is needed is competent, networked, committed individuals who lead without a title because they believe in the work. Fullan (2001, p. 136) suggests that in a culture of complexity, "our only hope is that many individuals working in concert can become as complex as the society they live in." Whether "collaborative leadership" (Reeves, 2006, p. 51), "coalition of leaders" (Fullan, 2005, p. 69), or "dispersed leadership" (DuFour et al., 2008, p. 331), the work of school improvement requires the collective effort of many hands. When this happens, school improvement is activated, as practitioners build the capacity of the organization to work together, plan together, and improve student learning together.

Just Improvement

We have seen improvement plans for a single school 256 pages long, and a similar district plan with 259 distinct objectives, examples of failed efforts before they began. Improvement plans should be limited to planned improvements in practice that our hypotheses suggest will improve achievement and nothing else. If a school adopted a six-trait writing trait initiative five years ago, it need not describe that program again in the improvement plan. Many activities become part of the school culture as unspoken, routine expectations, while other innovations become policy. For example, a teacher handbook at a school may describe a nonnegotiable teaching cycle first introduced in school improvement four years earlier, but now it is accepted as a universal expectation for all teachers every year. To include well-established practices or routines in the improvement plan pushes us back to the scrapbook function of the plan, and it shouts to stakeholders that the improvement plan is about everything, rather than about improving. If teachers meet twice monthly in their PLC or Data Teams, there is no need to include this activity in the improvement plan because it is not a current improvement, just as the teaching cycle is not a current plan for improvement but a best practice that is well established at the school. Only include changes where current practices will actually be improved in the coming cycle.

Readers may be asking, "Is it really that simple?" Consider the writing initiative referenced earlier. Although introduced several years before and consistently implemented, the practice has not yet reached a degree of fidelity across all classrooms. In that case, schools should include language about what is being done in the writing initiative to sustain it and extend it to new departments or grades. That change is an improvement that continues to be necessary. Contrast that with the reference to the nonnegotiable teaching cycle, which is established and no longer a change or an improvement. Practitioners need to hold themselves to the standard that only practices that will be explicitly improved will be included in the plan. An important benefit of addressing improvement only is that it focuses us on providing evidence of exactly what we are doing, rather than assuming we have addressed an improvement need that has been met.

The final benefit of an improvement-only approach is that the document then serves as a "dashboard" for the entire school to reference. Short, focused plans are not unlike the National Football League coach's game plan as he monitors from the sidelines. Basic blocking and tackling are expected to continue at a high level but need not be in the game plan.

A colleague tells the story about a superintendent who insisted that each educator bring her school improvement plan to every meeting, within and outside of individual schools. The expectation didn't cost much, but it communicated volumes: "What you're carrying is valuable and important, like a driver's license. Use it, learn from it, and glean ideas for it wherever your work takes you. Use it to redirect colleagues to our area of focus, and use it to recommend changes with your own plan." The cost was little, the potential benefit great. Note how this simple practice affirms the theory of action around EBM.

Soft Accountability

School improvement also often allows leaders to use a soft approach to accountability, without sanctions or high stakes. Leaders can guide teams to display data; engage grade-level and department leaders; increase the degree of transparency; and celebrate the granular, incremental gains that are predictive of larger long-term improvements and successes. Five actions by principals and teacher leaders can have a profound impact on school improvement:

- Routinely request hypotheses for action to accompany each faculty request
- Probe questions to data displays
- Schedule routine updates from PLCs at monthly school faculty meetings
- Close each meeting with a synthesis and description of next steps
- Monitor ideas borrowed, ideas given away

The first action sets up an expectation that teachers who submit an idea or request additional resources or time articulate the benefit they envision will accrue as a result of their idea. This ensures a theory of action accompanies every improvement effort and the hypothesis lends itself to a measurable target as a goal or an objective.

Data displays provide transparency that advances accountability, but unless leaders probe, many data displays tend to become wall paper or simply another bulletin board. Consider the impact when a principal invites the teacher to merely explain how he or she is using the data display to modify instruction or when the same principal points out the outlier gains made by specific students. Simply probing for meaning communicates that the principal is interested in the teacher's work while respecting the purpose and meaning of the data displayed.

Routine updates from individual Data Teams or PLCs is a very effective use of soft accountability because it alerts the teams in advance that they will be expected to go before their peers and explain their process, results, and insights. The fourth soft accountability activator is to synthesize each meeting, an activity the principal may choose to do periodically, but stronger still if invited teacher leaders are asked to synthesize. The result is greater attention to the detail and work of the faculty meeting and insights into professional practice.

The final measure of soft accountability is to communicate how important and professional the work occurring within the school walls is to improvement. Rather than relying on journals or even chapters in books like this, principals who invite teachers to share their best ideas or to borrow ideas from colleagues communicate a deep respect for their professional expertise. Proactive attention to the details of teaching and learning focuses efforts to improve schools one process and one classroom at a time. Soft accountability increases the capacity of teachers and leaders to be effective players in the accountability arena by

> being proactive and open about school performance data, and by being able to hold their own in the contentious debate about the uses and misuses of achievement data in an era of high-stakes testing. (Fullan, 2001, pp. 127–128)

High Efficacy

Efficacy in school improvement is the awareness that one has the capacity to make a difference in the lives of others and the capacity to act on that knowledge. Highly effective groups believe in their collective capacity to produce results and persevere through both internal and external difficulties to achieve them. Teacher efficacy is a function of the quality of relationships they enjoy with their students (Reames & Spencer, 1998), as schools with high teacher efficacy tend to have similar policies to empower students and adults. Principals in these schools invite teachers to participate in decision making and engage in the school's most important work. Four steps are recommended to improve individual and group efficacy: (1) limit the number of SMART goals, (2) use clear goals as a daily guide, (3) engage in meaning-making, and (4) recognize the difference between compliance and commitment.

The PIM™ research revealed that schools with fewer goals actually saw greater achievement gains than other schools (White & Smith, 2010, p. 69). Schools that reduce the number of goals appreciate the fact that even the most highly skilled group of people can only make so many decisions, learn and apply (well) only so many new skills, and sustain only so many initiatives before the feeling of being overwhelmed sets in and begins to erode both individual and group efficacy.

Amabile and Kramer (2007) describe how a stronger sense of self-worth and self-efficacy results when people understand organizational goals and how they, as individuals, can contribute to their attainment. School-wide goals generate specific classroom goals for teachers, connecting school improvement to instruction. Subsequently, teachers who help students translate classroom goals into student goals broaden the level of ownership in learning and overall efficacy of teachers and learners.

Meaning-making is everyone's responsibility. We know that "individual efficacy influences group efficacy, and both influence a sense of identity for the individual practitioner and the group" (Garmston & Wellman, 1999, p. 163). Leaders who facilitate identification of school-wide challenges and school-wide solutions will contribute to a healthy sense of self-efficacy whereby teachers are likely to expend more energy in their work, persevere longer, set more challenging goals, and continue in the face of failure.

Peter Senge (2000) describes the difference between commitment and compliance as *wanting* something versus *accepting* something. The committed person wants to attain a vision (for instance, to create a PLC) and because of that desire brings a certain energy and excitement to the task. Conversely, the compliant person accepts the vision, goes along with it, and may sincerely try to contribute, but he doesn't bring the same level of vigor and passion. Recall our theory of action and the need for contingency planning. The committed team will do everything possible to ensure the goal is achieved, while the compliant team hopes the goal will be realized.

Final Thoughts

The greatest sustainable gains in student achievement occur when excellent teaching becomes common teaching (Marzano, 2007; Reeves, 2008; Hattie, 2009; Farr, 2010). Gains are advanced further when teams of teachers and schools of teachers implement best practices with fidelity (Hargreaves & Shirley, 2009; White & Smith, 2010; Pang, 2006; Dembo & Gibson, 1985). School improvement is the only structure for translating best practices into common ones.

We defined school improvement and described how it represents an extraordinary platform for reform and innovation, identified principles guiding our theory of action, and provided five activators of school improvement to shift the paradigm from compliance to commitment.

PIM™ was presented as a proven process for a complete and thorough improvement design consistent with research and best practices. Distributed leadership was advanced as a means to identify future leaders and champions who can ensure that best intentions are realized in achieved goals. Activating school improvement by addressing only changes in practice or strategies will focus school teams, limit distractions, and shift the paradigm from compliance to commitment. Soft accountability was discussed and five discrete practices offered that school leaders can engage in to motivate, empower, focus, and hold staff accountable, all of which support cost-effectiveness in terms of time, effort, and political capital. Finally, school improvement was described as the lever to increase efficacy for teachers, staff, and students.

Leaders who cultivate these practices will activate the power of school improvement and ensure that when changes are made, schools are actually improved.

References

Allwood, J. (1995). Theory of action. In J. Verschueren, J. O. Östman, & J. Blommaert (Eds.), *Handbook of pragmatics*. Goteborg, Germany: John Benjamins.

Amabile, T., & Kramer, S. (2007) Inner work life: Understanding the subtext of business performance. *Harvard Business Review, 85*(5), 72–83.

Beckhard, R., & Harris, R. T. (1987). *Organizational Transitions: Managing Complex Change*. Boston, MA: Addison-Wesley.

Casciaro, T., & Lobo, M. S. (2005). Competent jerks, lovable fools, and the formation of social networks. *Harvard Business Review, 83*(6), 92–99.

Dembo, M., & Gibson, S. (1985). Teachers' sense of efficacy: An important factor in school improvement. *The Elementary School Journal, 86*(2), 173–184.

DuFour, R., DuFour, R., & Eaker, R. (2008). *Revisiting professional learning communities at work: New insights for improving schools*. Bloomington, IN: Solution Tree.

Farr, S. (2010). *Teaching as leadership*. San Francisco, CA: Jossey-Bass.

Fullan, M. (2001). *Leading in a culture of change*. San Francisco, CA: Jossey-Bass.

Fullan, M. (2005). *Leadership & sustainability: System thinkers in action*. Thousand Oaks, CA: Corwin.

Garmston, R. J., & Wellman, B. M. (1999). *The adaptive school: A sourcebook for developing collaborative groups*. Norwood, MA: Christopher-Gordon.

Hargreaves, A., & Shirley, D. (2009). *The fourth way: The inspiring future for educational change*. Thousand Oaks, CA: Corwin Press, p. 88.

Hattie, J. (2009). *Visible learning: A synthesis of over 800 meta-analyses relating to achievement*. New York, NY: Routledge.

Joyce, B., & Showers, B. (2002). *Student achievement through staff development* (3rd ed.). Alexandria, VA: ASCD.

Leadership and Learning Center, The. (2005). Planning, implementation, and monitoring framework (PIM). Englewood, CO: Author.

Marzano, R. (2007). *The art and science of teaching.* Alexandria, VA: ASCD.

Pang, N. S.-K. (2006). Schools as learning organizations. In J. C. Lee & M. Williams (Eds.), *School improvement: International perspectives* (ch. 5, p. 81). New York, NY: Nova Science.

Reames, E., & Spencer, W. (1998, April). *Teacher efficacy and commitment: Relationships to middle school culture.* Paper presented at the American Educational Research Association Annual Meeting, San Diego.

Reeves, D. B. (2006). *The learning leader: How to focus school improvement for better results.* Alexandria, VA: ASCD.

Reeves, D. B. (2008). *Reframing teacher leadership to improve your school.* Alexandria, VA: ASCD.

Sackett, D. L., Roseberg, W. M., Gray, J. A., Muir, H., Brian, R., & Richardson, W. S. (1996). Evidence-based medicine: What it is and what it isn't. *British Medical Journal, 312,* 71–72.

Schmoker, M. (2006). *Results now: How we can achieve unprecedented improvements in teaching and learning.* Alexandria, VA: ASCD.

Senge, P. M. (2000). *Schools that learn: A fifth discipline handbook.* New York, NY: Doubleday.

Surowiecki, J. (2004). *The wisdom of crowds: Why the many are smarter than the few and how collective wisdom shapes business, economies, societies and nation.* New York, NY: Doubleday.

White, S., & Smith, R. (2010). *School improvement for the next generation.* Bloomington, IN: Solution Tree.

CHAPTER EIGHT

Data-Based Leadership: A Proven Process for Data-Driven Decision Making

STEPHEN VENTURA

DATA-BASED LEADERSHIP is the best place to start to assess the challenges that today's educational leaders face. Data helps to identify a school's current reality in terms of student achievement, urgent needs, instructional adjustments, and targeted professional development.

The use of data substantiates that certain strategies *do* have specific effects on student achievement. When leaders properly collect and organize data, they make better decisions about leadership, teaching, and learning. The process of collecting, organizing, and analyzing data is a valuable skill that permits educators to create an action plan, complete with strategies, goals, and indicators that lead to increased levels of achievement. Moreover, we use data to improve leadership effectiveness, efficacy, and deeper inquiry to enhance overall school practice.

There is growing research indicating that data-based leadership can result in a variety of educational improvements. For many, data collection and analysis has become a source of frustration because of the perceived additional labor required to conduct this analysis. The use of data for today's educational leaders is not a choice but a necessity. Therefore, data analysis can be overwhelming if it is not done collaboratively. It is imperative for school leaders to identify structures and methods that involve teachers and other staff members. Perfect leadership is an illusion, as no leader can effectively lead everything, but a team can accomplish most anything.

This chapter identifies key strategies to improve the educational leadership of superintendents, directors, and principals. Many of these processes may be applied to examine discipline, attendance, and other nonacademic data, and they have the power to cause a shift in thinking and accountability. "This is the single best way to help educators and administrators move from 'drowning in data' to using information to make better instructional decisions. Data-driven decision making gives professionals respect, reinforcement, and feedback—the keys for improved impact on student learning" (Reeves, 2008/09).

How to Use This Chapter

A large portion of this chapter's information represents the "reality-based" experience of the author. Given the need to improve quality education in our schools, a new opportunity presents itself for principals and superintendents to assert themselves as educational leaders. This chapter features rich examples of data-based leadership. The practical applications described will assist leaders in quickly organizing data, analyzing it, and making the very best decisions about improving their own professional practice and those that are within their sphere of influence. Leaders must be able to demonstrate to teachers how to effectively use data on a consistent and regular basis. Data-based leadership paves the way for better inquiry and decision making. If we truly believe that school personnel should engage in ongoing data analysis from multiple sources to provide a comprehensive picture of a school's strengths and challenges, then leaders must demonstrate how this is accomplished. Once these processes are finalized, teachers and leaders can collectively develop a plan to prioritize and address those challenges.

Leadership Allocation and Focus

The shift in leadership focus has never been more evident within the last 25 years. I can remember being taught the four Bs of administration—buses, budgets, buildings, and bonds. It wasn't very long ago that these issues dominated the attention of most building and district leaders. A majority of time was spent on maintaining or improving the organizational structure, construction, and other nonacademic management functions. Even today, it is easy to conclude that many leaders spend a majority of their time on noninstructional or non-educational issues.

With the recent laser-like focus on improving schools and demonstrating the acquisition of federal growth targets, many building and district-level leaders have learned to shift their focus from "plant" management to instructional management. Additionally, this focus has provided more opportunity for leaders to assess their district's status, provide attention to developing and implementing plans, and develop mutually agreed upon methods to achieve desired educational outcomes. Educational leadership must be data driven. That means that planning, programs, and instructional strategies are selected based on where specific improvement is needed.

Effective schools research reveals that the most powerful variable in school improvement is strong instructional leadership. As you will see, the use of data can provide the foundational framework to enhance and cultivate sound instructional decision making.

Data-Based Leadership and Perception Data

Perception data from the school or district community can be enlightening because they help educators pay attention to the opinions and ideas of the school community. Leaders need to recognize the many different members of the school community and realize that how they value the school's services impacts students profoundly. Bernhardt (2004, p. 20) states "Analyses of demographics, perceptions, student learning, and school processes provide a powerful picture that will help us understand the school's impact on student achievement."

Perception data can be collected in a variety of formats. In the case study discussed below, a questionnaire was developed to determine teacher perceptions about student learning.

Case Study—Perception Data

During my time as an administrator, I conducted a perception survey for middle school teachers. At the time the survey was administered, faculty morale was low for a number of reasons:

1. The school achievement scores had remained stagnant for several years.

2. The school was experiencing record high levels of student failures.

3. The school was experiencing record low levels of student engagement.

In this demoralizing environment, teachers were having difficulty connecting their own adult teaching behaviors to student achievement. Additionally, their frustration was more outcome based than cause based.

During one of our curriculum meetings, I distributed a survey to be completed by the teachers. The purpose of the survey was to have teachers *predict* how their students might respond to the same survey. The survey consisted of 30 statements with a level of agreement ranging from "Strongly Disagree" to "Strongly Agree." Once the survey was completed, I determined the average response for each statement. Remember, the teachers responded to the survey *as if their students were actually responding.*

As you can see in Exhibit 8.1, 36 teachers responded to the survey with an average response of 3.2, based on a five-point scale.

To get the most unbiased teacher responses, I did not reveal to teachers that students would actually take the same survey. I was interested in comparing actual student responses to teacher predictions so the benefit of perception data could truly inform the current learning environment. Sometimes educators are afraid that data analysis might produce results they do not want to see because it might expose a lack of ability or skill. Data-based leadership can help replace hunches and hypotheses with facts that identify root causes of problems, and not just the symptoms. It is important to communicate that perception

EXHIBIT 8.1   Teacher Survey Results

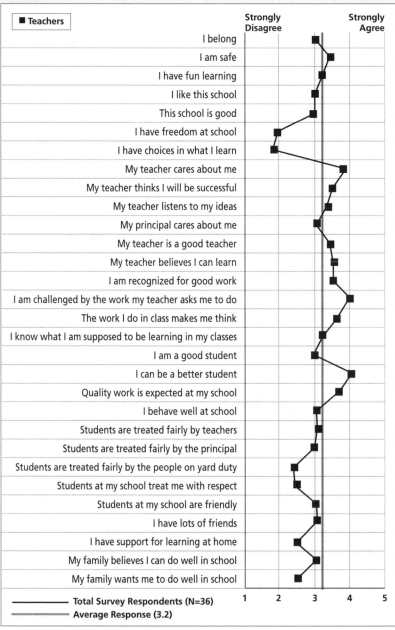

Note: Adapted from Bernhardt (2004).

data is not a white-glove test used to "beat up" other educators. We simply want to assess needs and target resources to address those needs.

The same survey was then administered to more than 700 middle school students. Before sharing those results with teachers, I conducted some pre-analysis and discovered that three statements showed the largest difference between teacher predictions and student responses:

1. My family wants me to do well in school.

2. I have support for learning at home.

3. I am challenged by the work my teachers ask me to do.

I asked the teachers how they thought their predictions would compare to student responses. The teachers felt that they had done a good job of predicting student responses and perceptions about school climate. After all, these were the students teachers worked with day in and day out.

After I created a comparison matrix, I shared the results with the middle school staff.

Exhibit 8.2 illustrates the comparison between teacher predictions and student responses.

Leadership Implications of Perception Data

As you can see, the discrepancy between teacher predictions and student responses is large. As leaders, what might we conclude about these surprising results? Could teacher perceptions about students' families influence their teaching? Are assignments engaging, relevant, and meaningful?

Data-based leadership provides multiple opportunities to focus on improvement, not blame. Teachers soon realized that missing assignments were not always caused by parental complacency and apathy. In fact, teachers discovered that many students go home to parents who monitor homework completion and many students go home to chaos. Parents who want their children to succeed in school

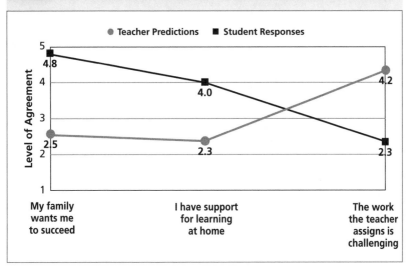

Comparison between Teacher Predictions and Student Responses

(Graph: Level of Agreement, with Teacher Predictions and Student Responses)

- My family wants me to succeed — 2.5, 4.8
- I have support for learning at home — 2.3, 4.0
- The work the teacher assigns is challenging — 4.2, 2.3

and parents who help their children with homework and other assignments represent two entirely different situations. To see a decrease in student failures, the teachers and administrators understood that if some students were to finish assignments, those assignments would have to be completed before, during, or after school.

What about rigor and assignments? Many students indicated that the work they were asked to complete was not challenging. Teachers concluded that student motivation and boredom could have contributed to this particular response.

To encourage students to become self-motivated, independent learners, teachers implemented the following strategies:

- Provide frequent, early, positive feedback that supports students' beliefs that they can do well.

- Ensure opportunities for students' success by assigning tasks that are neither too easy nor too difficult.

- Help students find personal meaning and value in the material.

• Create an atmosphere that is open and positive.

• Help students feel that they are valued members of a learning community.

The teachers also incorporated research that stressed the use of better everyday teaching practices to counter student apathy rather than special efforts to attack motivation directly (Ericksen, 1978). This strategy worked well on a number of different levels because the focus was on cause, or adult teaching behaviors, a much easier element to improve than going after individual levels of student motivation. Teachers also helped students to set achievable goals for themselves so they could help determine their own levels of rigor.

Feedback from teachers about perception survey results and strategies were mostly encouraging. The students began responding positively to those classrooms that were well organized and taught by teachers who had an interest in students and what they learned. Additionally, those teacher activities that promoted learning also enhanced students' motivation.

Lessons Learned

The collaborative process that followed the dissemination of survey results allowed teachers to explore personal positions on important questions about student perceptions. Focusing on perception data toward educational improvement enables practitioners to collaboratively and powerfully explore ways to improve their craft. This focus enables them to *use* data, rather than *be used by* data.

Data-Based Leadership and Inferences

Not only is inference making central to student reading comprehension, it is also central to leadership decisions. Making inferences means choosing the most likely explanation about student performance data or other data trends and patterns. When leaders analyze process data, demographic data, student learning data, or perception data they must be able to draw conclusions or judgments based on that data. Making informed predictions about the outcomes of potential actions supports the decision-making process. Making inferences and predictions about student performance data leads teachers to think deeply about student needs. Over time and with practice, both teachers and leaders can make inferences with more validity. "Teachers use test results in order to make inferences about their students' cognitive status. Once those score-based inferences have been made, the teacher then reaches instructional decisions (at least in part) on those inferences. Educational assessment revolves around inference making" (Popham, 2003, p. 60).

Exhibit 8.3 features three years of fifth-grade English Language Arts summative assessment results by category:

- Word analysis

- Reading comprehension

- Literary response

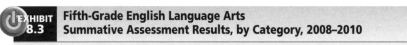

EXHIBIT 8.3   Fifth-Grade English Language Arts Summative Assessment Results, by Category, 2008–2010

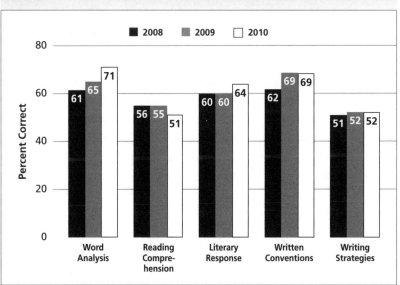

• Written conventions

• Writing strategies

What might you infer based on the data provided in Exhibit 8.3? Which subtest has experienced the highest rate of growth over the past three years? Which subtest has steadily declined, and which subtest has remained the same? Our ability to collect and organize data must help identify student-prioritized needs and appropriate instructional strategies. Instructional leadership can be elusive unless leaders can properly infer, act, and implement.

Take a look at the writing strategies subtest category. The percentage correct has remained virtually the same for the past three years. First, we could infer that *declining scores are the same with different students from different years.* Second, we could infer that there is a need to study adult teaching behaviors and writing instruction. Third, we could infer that similar test results with different students means that the differential is cause based.

Making inferences and predictions about student performance data leads teachers to think deeply about student needs. Again, over time and with practice, teachers can make inferences with more validity.

Data-Based Leadership and Prioritized Needs

When leaders can identify obstacles, such as low writing scores, and make inferences about those obstacles, they can then work with teachers to create a list of prioritized student needs. The question is, based on these priorities, how should we begin to align and plan instruction?

The chart in Exhibit 8.4 demonstrates a simple process for identifying an obstacle, three inferences, and a prioritized need. Once needs are identified, we can discover those best practices and effective teaching strategies that can be emphasized for a specific teaching/learning cycle.

Another example of determining prioritized needs, using longitudinal test results and cohort test results, is shown in Exhibit 8.5. The exhibit illustrates district writing scores by grade level for three years. It reveals growth for each grade level, some more dramatic than others.

EXHIBIT 8.4   Sample Identification Process for Obstacles, Inferences, and Needs

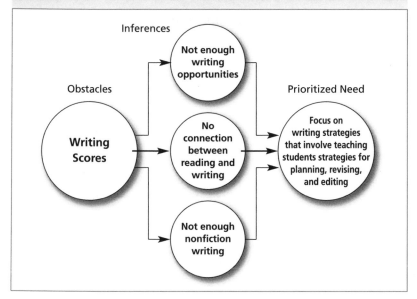

If we study the same scores by cohort, the data set reveals other areas of concern (Exhibit 8.6). What might you conclude based on two to three years of cohort data? What happens to writing scores in fourth grade? Can we use this data to prioritize our needs? Which grade level may need additional technical support with writing instruction?

From this data, teachers learned that it would be more beneficial to add more writing to their instruction, including strategies to increase literacy in other content areas, like mathematics and science. The correlation between increased writing opportunities and standardized tests is strong:

- Entrance and exit slips/tickets
- Cornell notes
- Summaries (various forms)
- Combination notes

These samples appear in the book *Writing Matters in Every Classroom* (Peery, 2009).

EXHIBIT 8.5 Sample Process for Determining Prioritized Needs: Grade by Grade, 2008–2010

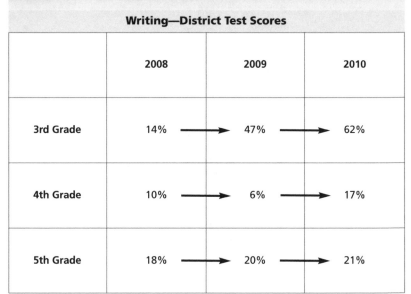

Writing—District Test Scores

	2008	2009	2010
3rd Grade	14% →	47% →	62%
4th Grade	10% →	6% →	17%
5th Grade	18% →	20% →	21%

EXHIBIT 8.6 Sample Process for Determining Prioritized Needs: Across Grades, 2008–2010

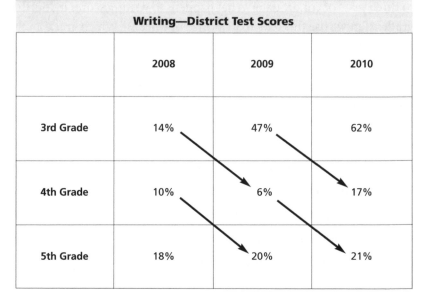

Writing—District Test Scores

	2008	2009	2010
3rd Grade	14%	47%	62%
4th Grade	10%	6%	17%
5th Grade	18%	20%	21%

Exhibits 8.7, 8.8, and 8.9 illustrate additional writing strategies.

 Student Example of Entrance Slip, Middle School Math

Adding and subtracting positive and negative numbers is not that hard, but now that we are doing the multiplying and dividing I'm getting confused. What I would like to learn in class today are some "hints" and things I can say to myself when I'm doing the work so that I make sure I use the right sign.

 Student Example of Exit Slip, High School Chemistry

Today we talked about acids and bases. All the time in this class, I learn about how everyday substances are formed chemically— what they are made of, etc. So today I found out that things we have around the house are either acids or bases. Vinegar is an acid. Ammonia is a base.

EXHIBIT 8.9 **Example of Combination Notes**

Key Ideas	Notes and Visuals to Help Me Remember
A positive number represents a quantity greater than zero.	Quantity = amount − − − 0 + + +
A negative number represents a quantity less than zero.	− − − 0 + + +
The absolute value is the numerical value of a number regardless of its sign. It's the distance of the number from zero on the number line.	The absolute value of 3 and −3 is 3. It doesn't matter whether it's + or −, it's still 3. (negative side) −3 −2 −1 0 1 2 3 (positive side)
Summary:	All numbers have absolute value that is neither positive nor negative. On the number line, though, numbers are either positive or negative depending on where they are relative to zero.

Another way of connecting inferences, prioritized needs, and strategies is to differentiate each category by student performance group. Exhibit 8.10 categorizes four different student groups based on pre-assessment scores designed to determine student prerequisite skills before instruction:

1. Students who are already proficient

2. Students who are close to proficiency

3. Students who are far from proficiency

4. Students who are not likely to be proficient between the pre- and post-assessment

This last example demonstrates the power of purposeful inference making, prioritized needs, and the selection of instructional strategies, all based on data. Leaders must recognize differences among learners,

EXHIBIT 8.10 **Differentiation by Student Performance Group**

Inferences	Prioritized Needs	Strategies
Proficient students Understand the descriptive vocabulary	Describe how changes in the descriptive words used would impact the reader—*push students to the evaluation level of thinking*	Comparison matrix—Work in pairs during center activity time using literature circle books
Students close to proficiency Have read a lot of other narratives	Did not identify/understand all of the descriptive words—vocabulary usage problems	Non-linguistic representations—Pairs working within the classroom
Students far from proficiency Lack of vocabulary impacted understanding	Did not list all descriptive words for character or setting—reported confusion when questioned	Non-linguistic representations—Small group during guided reading
Students not likely Poor decoding skills	Students reported that they had a hard time reading all of the words in the passage—group below grade level in reading	Decoded for fluency strategies—guided reading group

how they learn, learning preferences, and individual interests (Anderson, 2007). Data-based leadership is the best way to work with teachers and other leaders to take an abundance of student data and use this information to improve educational practice. Additionally, the application of inquiry is useful in improving overall school practice.

The relationship between inference making, prioritizing needs, and instructional strategies can lead to universal student achievement, but the leader must be able to skillfully teach, implement, and sustain these practices (Exhibit 8.11).

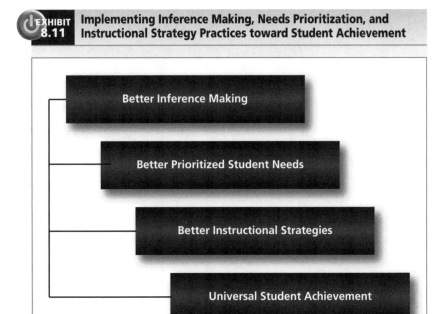

EXHIBIT 8.11 Implementing Inference Making, Needs Prioritization, and Instructional Strategy Practices toward Student Achievement

Now more than ever, school and district leaders must be able to effectively monitor and adjust those strategies which can improve student achievement. However, some of the best teaching and leadership strategies wind up in the graveyard of good intentions and interventions, never to be seen again. Why? Because there is no consistent method to provide feedback on the effect of the strategy. These indicators are critically important when we look to replicate practices that are not only personally and professionally rewarding, they have an immediate and positive effect on student learning outcomes.

Data-based leadership isn't just about collecting and sharing data. The data we collect must be thoughtfully analyzed by all stakeholders so we can collectively agree on those practices and programs that are worth our investment. Time is the most precious commodity in all of education. With more clarity and focus, we reduce clutter, allowing us the time to go deeper with learning progressions that achieve curricular gains.

Conclusion

The purpose of this chapter is to provide leaders with the quantitative and qualitative techniques that are needed to engage in the process of school improvement planning through the use of data. Data-based leadership does not have to be a source of stress and fatigue. In fact, using data can help build capacity among all stakeholders so that student achievement data is used to improve instruction. Remember, leaders must help teachers understand that they *cannot focus on everything*. Use your student data to identify specific skills and knowledge from the standards that students need to learn well and deeply. Then, help teachers think about what they can *stop* doing in order to really focus instruction on those essential learnings.

References

Anderson, K. M. (2007). Tips for teaching: Differentiating instruction to include all students. *Preventing School Failure, 51*(3), 49–54.

Bernhardt, V. (2004). *Data analysis for comprehensive schoolwide improvement* (2nd ed.). Larchmont, NY: Eye on Education.

Ericksen, S. C. (1978). The lecture. (Memo to the Faculty No. 60). Ann Arbor, MI: Center for Research on Teaching and Learning, University of Michigan.

Peery, A. (2009). *Writing matters in every classroom*. Englewood, CO: Lead + Learn Press.

Popham, W. J. (2003). *Test better, teach better: The instructional role of assessment*. Alexandria, VA: ASCD.

Reeves, D. (2008/09). Looking deeper into the data. *Educational Leadership, 66*(4), 88–89.

SECTION 3

LEADERS FOCUSING ON

PROCESSES

CHAPTER NINE

Leaders Developing Learning Systems

BRIAN A. MCNULTY

SINCE THIS IS A BOOK ABOUT LEADERSHIP AND CHANGE, it seems appropriate to start with a simple leadership maxim: If you want different and better outcomes, lead differently. In other words, do not expect outcomes to change if you do not change your own leadership practices. The most powerful leaders lead by publicly learning themselves and then by encouraging individual and collective learning across the whole organization.

Introduction to Learning Systems

Given that the primary purpose of schools is teaching and learning, it is reasonable to assume that schools and districts are good examples of learning systems or learning organizations. Unfortunately, this is not the case in most schools or districts. As Hayes Jacobs (2010, pp. 60–61) points out, "The overwhelming majority of our schools run on the same length of the school year and same daily schedule, with the same rigid grouping of students, and the same faculty organizations, and fundamentally the same type of buildings as in the late 1890s."

When you compare what goes on in most schools and districts with the definition of learning organizations, these gaps are even more evident. "A learning organization is one that regularly (and often informally) incorporates new knowledge, works efficiently, readily adapts to change, detects and corrects errors, and continually improves" (Seashore, 2009, p. 134).

While one could make the case that schools and districts often work to incorporate new knowledge, often this new knowledge is poorly implemented and therefore short lived. As Elmore (2004, p. 107) has noted, "schools are accustomed to changing—promiscuously and routinely—without producing any improvement." Whereas learning organizations readily adapt to change, schools look remarkably like they did 100 years ago. And whereas learning organizations identify and correct errors and continually improve, this type of continuous improvement is all too rare in schools and districts. Although many schools and districts are "in school improvement," most do not systemically put practices in place to make continuous improvement a reality.

As a starting point, then, leaders need to lead differently by creating conditions that improve their own learning as well as the learning of those they work with. More effective leaders inquire more deeply into the effectiveness of their own actions, and also into the actions of those that they work with. The ability to "collaboratively inquire" in a systematic way is critical if schools and districts are to make continuous progress. Interestingly, then, the two most important factors associated with developing more effective inquiry are (David, 2008/09):

• Leadership, and ...

• Norms that support collaboration and more effective data use

"Learning about improvement occurs in the growth and *development of common understandings about why things happen the way they do*" (Elmore, 2004, p. 56; emphasis added).

To assess whether your school or district understands why things happen the way they do, answer the following questions:

1. Are you making measurable progress as a building or district?
   • How do you know this?

- What evidence do you have?
- Do you know why you are making progress?
- What specific adult actions caused these outcomes?

2. If you are not making measurable progress, do you know why?
    - What is not working?
        - Which specific actions, strategies, or programs are not working? Do you know why?
        - Do you know what to do to change this?

Your answers should identify what the adults in the system have done (or not done) differently and what specific "adult actions" have been implemented (or not implemented) that "caused" the outcomes you have (i.e., what specific teaching and leadership actions have the adults taken, or not taken, that resulted in these outcomes). If you know what specific adult actions were taken to get better outcomes, do you know how to replicate them? Have you been able to replicate them?

I will come back to the specific topic of learning organizations later in this chapter, but here I focus on specific leadership actions that, if implemented well, support the development of collaborative inquiry and continuous improvement and learning at every level of the system.

Singer and songwriter John Hiatt says in his song "Buffalo River Home," "there's only two things in life ... but I forget what they are!" I am hopeful, however, that most people can remember at least three things, especially three things that are critical to school and district success. These three critical leadership actions are:

1. Developing Data Teams and leaders at all levels of the system

2. Focusing on instruction as the primary work

3. Learn as a system, through implementing, monitoring, and inquiring

Each action is discussed in detail below.

Developing Data Teams and Leaders at Every Level of the System

Making systemic improvement requires the development of instructional leadership across the entire district. The first step in developing broad-based instructional leadership involves creating and supporting data-based teams that are focused on instructional improvement at every level of the system.

It is through the use of these teams at the classroom, school, and district levels that you can assess and provide feedback and support in a timely fashion to move the instructional improvements forward on a building and district-wide basis. While the formation of these teams is important, it is what the teams *do* that matters most. By this I mean data, analysis, and inquiry are all important, but only if they lead to taking action.

Without an effectively functioning team at each level of the system (classroom, school, and district) there is no opportunity to collectively assess progress, make ongoing corrections, and then provide appropriate feedback and support across the entire system. To make continuous system-wide progress you need to engage in a process that shares responsibility and accountability widely across every classroom, school, and district.

To address this, we recommend the development of Data Teams at three different levels:

- A District-level Data Team (DDT)
- A Building-level Data Team (BDT)
- Teacher-based Instructional Data Teams (IDTs)

The purpose of the each Data Team is to improve instructional practice and student learning. The teams model inquiry through the examination of formative, summative, and monitoring data that focuses on both the implementation of the shared research-based instructional practices and the effectiveness of each teacher-based instructional data team (IDT).

Like the other teams, the primary purpose of the District Data Team (DDT) is to strengthen instruction in every classroom and every school. It achieves this by systematically examining the implementation and effectiveness of the district-level improvement strategies (i.e., specific, powerful instructional practices and IDTs) along with examining the effectiveness of each of the building-level Data Teams (BDTs). The DDT becomes the "guiding coalition" (Kotter, 1996; Fullan, 2009) that leads the improvement work of the district forward. The DDT reviews the district's data, develops the district improvement plan, ensures the provision of professional development and other supports, monitors the implementation and effectiveness of the strategies in every building, and learns how to replicate and sustain success. The team actively communicates the improvement work across the entire district.

The composition of the DDT is broader than just the central office; it includes teachers, support staff, and principals, each of whom brings a broader perspective on how well the work is really being implemented.

While many buildings have some form of building leadership team, the single purpose of the Building Data Team (BDT) is to focus on the quality of instruction and its impact on student performance. The BDT is constantly examining grade, subject, and course performance data in relation to the implementation of the shared instructional practices and the effectiveness of the each of the teacher-based Instructional Data Teams (IDTs) as well as any other interventions being used by the building.

The membership of the BDTs includes the principal; representatives from each grade level or department (depending on the size); and other staff members who serve in leadership positions, such as instructional coaches, special education teachers, English language learner teachers, and other support staff.

The third level of teams are the teacher-based IDTs. These teams are smaller groups of teachers who collaborate to improve instruction and accelerate student learning. These IDTs focus on academic achievement and are driven by common academic standards. They also examine student data generated from common formative assessments. The principal is essential in the development of the teacher teams, however they are not an ongoing member of the IDTs.

The IDTs use a formal six-step protocol to carry out their work, as follows:

1. Collect and chart data from the common formative assessment.
2. Identify strengths and needs based on student work.
3. Establish SMART (specific, measurable, achievable, relevant, and timely) goals.
4. Select instructional strategies and commit to classroom follow-through.
5. Determine results indicators.
6. Monitor and evaluate results.

Each of the three teams has a specific purpose and functions of their own, but they also have a "reciprocal" relationship to one another, so that their success is tied to one another (see Elmore, 2004). The teams operate under the premise that "we are not successful (as a team) if you are not successful as an individual or a team." Our job is to make you successful.

Having teams at all three levels is essential to operating as a successful system. Without a BDT, it is difficult to develop or sustain effective IDTs across the whole school. The same holds true at the district level: Without a DDT, it is difficult to evaluate the progress of each school, identify and replicate successful practices within and across schools, or generate and provide the necessary supports that are needed to have effective schools across the whole district. Of all three levels of teams (district, building, and classroom), however, the most powerful teams are the IDTs, which examine and act on student and teacher learning in an ongoing way. Therefore, one of the highest priorities of the school and district-level teams is to structure and facilitate effective teams at the classroom level.

If you are to be successful at reaching broad-based consensus on the problems and the strategies for improvement and at accurately assessing your progress, it is essential that you create broad-based ownership of all of these problems and solutions. The creation of these teams provides the opportunity for input, examination, and learning at each level of the school system. The teams offer deeper and broader leadership opportunities for individuals from across the system to own both the problems and the solutions.

Murphy and Meyers (2008) found that making systemic improvements district-wide requires the development of effective teams at all levels. They conclude that the key to continuous improvement is getting the best performance from everyone in the district by changing the culture of the classroom, school, and district through the development and use of effective teams at each level.

While teams are often not the most efficient way to work, they are particularly well suited to addressing complex issues such as student and systems learning. As Ancona, Malone, Orlikowski, and Senge (2007) found, no single person has the

- intellectual capacity,
- imaginative power,
- operational ability, and
- interpersonal skills

to move this kind of complex work forward by himself.

Similarly, Leithwood, Day, Sammons, Harris, and Hopkins (2007) found that school leadership was more effective and had a greater influence on staff and students' outcomes when it was widely distributed across the school. Most recently, Louis, Leithwood, Wahlstrom, and Anderson (2010, p. 19) found that "Collective leadership has a stronger influence on student achievement than individual leadership." It also makes sense that if you want the whole district to make progress, then you need to develop many leaders working collaboratively across the district rather than only relying on people who have positional authority (Fullan 2008; Kotter, 1996).

What do we know about the effectiveness of such teams? The good news is that ample evidence supports the effectiveness of both school- and teacher-based Data Teams (Darling-Hammond, 2010; Supovitz, 2006; Reeves, 2007; Weinbaum & Supovitz, 2010; DuFour, DuFour, & Eaker, 2008), and now there is strong evidence emerging on the effectiveness of teams at the district level (Knapp, Copland, Honig, Plecki, & Portin, 2010; Bottoms & Fry, 2009; Honig, Copland, Rainey, Lorton, & Newton, 2010). What we have learned is that teams can be highly effective in helping individuals and organizations examine their strategies and progress more deeply, and gain consensus on what might be the most powerful next steps.

So if teams *can* be successful, what is the specific work that they need to undertake? If the goal is to make continuous improvement across the whole district, then the primary responsibilities of each team must be to monitor two factors: the level of implementation of research-based instructional practices and the effectiveness of each IDT. Then, on the basis of their monitoring data, each team needs to identify the learning needs of individuals and teams and ensure the provision of differentiated professional development and supports necessary for their learning.

In our own four-year research project at The Leadership and Learning Center (see McNulty and Besser, 2011), we found that most teams struggle with providing this level of individualized support. This is a new and challenging role for most teams. When individuals and teams are making progress, everything is fine. However, when individuals (student or adults) or teams are not making progress, it becomes the responsibility of the teams (at the classroom, school, and district levels) to analyze why and to make recommendations for more effective interventions and supports for students and adults. As mentioned earlier, the team structure creates opportunities to examine multiple and deeper perspectives on what is happening and why. Effective teams also have a more realistic and grounded perspective in terms of making recommendations for specific instructional practices, supports, and interventions to continue to move the work forward more expeditiously.

Teams Continuously Using Data to Guide Decision Making

Data is feedback to the system. Without data being collected at every level of the system, decisions are based on suppositions, impressions, or blind guesses. Learning systems use data paired with inquiry to help guide their decision making and to assess the effectiveness of their actions.

At each level of the system, the teams (at the classroom, building, and district levels) use data to assess two factors:

1. The effectiveness of implementation

2. The impact of the strategies that they have chosen

Let's examine each of these separately.

The Effectiveness of Implementation

Anyone who has ever worked in a school or district intuitively knows that we have a problem with implementing change initiatives well. This problem is so prevalent that this has come to be labeled "the implementation gap" (McNulty & Besser, 2011). The lack of follow-through is a problem not just for teachers but also for administrators at every level of the system (McNulty & Besser, 2011; Wiliam, 2007; Hattie, 2009; Duke, 2007; Elmore, 2004). The problem of implementation is endemic to the entire education system.

Doug Reeves (2006, 2008, 2010) has presented data on the critical importance of deep implementation for a number of years. Most recently he found that "half hearted implementation was actually worse than minimal or no implementation" (Reeves, 2010, p. 36). His studies further reveal that unless you can implement at the 90 percent level, you should not expect to get the outcomes that are promised in the research literature. It is probably fair to say that currently most schools and districts do not meet this 90 percent implementation standard.

Interestingly, however, this lack of follow-through is usually not related to people's lack of knowledge, but rather to a lack of execution. Because we do not implement well, we do not get good results. Then, we typically blame the lack of results on the intervention strategies rather than the real culprit, our own lack of deep implementation.

So when talking about data, the first step that teams need to take is to collect and examine data on the degree or level of implementation of their improvement strategies. The teams must be able to answer the question "How well are we implementing?"

While most educators have become familiar with looking at student performance data, most schools and districts have not examined implementation data, that is, the measure of adult implementation (or lack thereof) that contributed to these outcomes. The first question we should always ask is, "Are the adults using the practice(s)?" Before you ever begin to assess the "impact of the strategies" (student outcomes) you have to assess how well you have implemented the strategies. This topic is discussed in greater detail later in the section on monitoring, but it is important to understand here that you must have some methodology for collecting data on the degree of implementation.

The Impact of the Strategies

The second area for data collection needs to focus on the impact that the strategies are having on student learning. While the ultimate outcome will usually be measured by the state assessment, most districts, buildings, and classrooms need more formative assessment measures of student progress. This process begins at the classroom level with the IDTs developing their own common formative assessments. These teams also need to develop a way to compile and report this data to the BDT. While some districts may have benchmark or quarterly assessments, others do not. Regardless, there must be some way to measure, compile, and report student progress data to the BDT and DDT. When teachers focus on and use more powerful research-based instructional practices, the outcome is usually evident immediately in student work. This kind of progress should be relatively easy to document.

Only when you have data on both the level of implementation and its impact on student learning can teams make intelligent decisions regarding their own work.

Focusing on Instruction as the Primary Work

The second area of focus is instruction. If we are to make any gains in performance across the district, it will be as a result of effectively using more powerful instructional practices. This means that instruction must become the highest priority for everyone in the district, from the superintendent to the classroom teacher. Everyone must devote more time and energy to learning about and using more powerful teaching practices. Part of this priority is addressed by participating in the teacher-based IDTs, but superintendents, central office staff, and principals must also make a personal and public commitment to spending more time learning about and focusing on high-quality instruction. They must lead the learning in instruction. The superintendent should set the example that everyone has more to learn about instruction. Furthermore, the superintendent must emphasize the expectations that "everyone involved is working on their practice, [and] everyone is obliged to be knowledgeable about the common task of instructional improvement" (City, Elmore, Fiarman, & Teitel, 2009, pp. 4–5).

All teaching is not created equal. If we've learned nothing else from the research in the last 20 years it is that the difference between highly effective teachers and less effective teachers is not what they know, but what they do in classrooms. The reality is that more effective teachers regularly use more effective teaching practices. To get better outcomes for all students, you need to strengthen the quality of instruction in every classroom.

This effort requires learning and leadership at every level of the system, hence the use of teams at each level. The primary work of the teams is to focus on increasing the quality of instruction in every classroom of the district. This is addressed through the two primary strategies:

1. Learning to appropriately and effectively use specific research-based teaching practices

2. Using IDTs

I have referred to this approach as top-down and bottom-up learning (McNulty & Besser, 2011). What we and others have found is that collectively learning to use more effective, research-based practices while simultaneously learning as a part of an IDT strengthens teacher learning by strengthening the connection between specific teacher actions and student performance. Focusing on one without the other is insufficient. Jacobson (2010) recently raised the question of whether it is possible to work on both coherent instructional improvements and professional learning communities simultaneously. If not, he argues neither is strong enough to result in continuous improvement.

We believe that it is not only possible but also preferable to work on both top-down and bottom-up learning. These are discussed below.

Top Down:
Creating a Focus on Learning Specific Teaching Practices

To get better student outcomes, teachers need to use more powerful teaching practices. Given this reality there are three overriding questions the classroom, building, and district teams needs to be able to answer:

- What specific teaching or instructional practices should we all learn together?
- How well can we implement and learn the practices?
- Do the instructional practices make a difference in student learning?

Recently there has been strong consensus on what effective teaching looks like (for example, see Darling-Hammond et al., 2008; Wahlstrom & Seashore Louis, 2008). In addition several meta-analytic studies have identified specific instructional strategies that have a profound effect on students and their learning (see Marzano, Pickering, & Pollock, 2001; Hattie, 2009).

This research has been extremely helpful in developing consensus among educators on what more powerful instruction looks like. However, there are still concerns over how to support teachers in appropriately and effectively using these practices. It is not enough to just learn about the practices if we do not know how and when to use them appropriately.

If we are to encourage people to use new practices, then we also need to support them in learning these new practices. This may include traditional approaches like training and professional development, but if we really want people to change their practices, we need to meet them where they are and provide them with individualized supports so that they can be successful. Weinbaum and Supovitz (2010, p. 69) found that once you are clear about what practices you want people to learn, you "must consider the level of complexity that the change presents to school staff. More complex changes will demand a higher level of both engagement and support."

Reeves (2010) concludes that successful learning of new effective teaching practices is a result of "deliberate practice." He identifies the components of deliberate practice as

- a focused task that is

- practiced over time and

- receives immediate feedback through accurate self-assessment, coaching, or modeling.

Educators often underestimate the amount of time, or number of trials, that it takes to effectively learn a new skill. Darling-Hammond, Wei, Andree, Richardson, and Orphanos (2009) found that traditional professional development does not have a noticeable impact on either instruction or student learning because it does not provide teachers with enough intensity or duration to support their use of the new practices.

According to different studies (see Joyce & Showers, 2002), it takes between 20 and 50 trials (depending on the complexity of the skill) before learners feel relatively confident in using a new practice. This means you have to provide people with extended opportunities for practice, paired with feedback, if you really expect them to effectively use new practices.

Bottom Up: Learning Through Data-Based Teams

If we choose to focus only on learning specific instructional practices over time, the outcomes will be limited and take too much time to result in district-wide improvement. So, along with teachers individually learning to implement new and more effective strategies, there must also be ongoing, powerful, collective learning through the use of IDTs at the classroom level.

Instructional Data Teams are small, grade-level, department, course, or like-content teams that examine work generated from a common formative assessment. They generally use academic priority standards or Power Standards (Ainsworth, 2003) as a starting point. Instructional Data Teams optimally meet weekly, but at a minimum every two to three weeks, and use an explicit data-driven protocol for every meeting. In the meeting teachers disaggregate data, analyze student performance, set incremental goals, engage in dialogue, commit to using explicit instructional practices, and create a plan to monitor student learning and teacher instruction. Teacher leaders usually facilitate the IDTs. The team leader and team members monitor the effectiveness of the collaboration and the results along with the school principal and BDT.

Learn as a System, Through Implementing, Monitoring, and Inquiring

For Reeves (2010, 2006), monitoring means focusing on the "adult actions." In other words, are the adults following through on their use of the practices? He found that districts and schools that scored high in monitoring, evaluation, and inquiry had gains that were two to fives times greater than schools and districts that scored lower on these dimensions.

As stated earlier, the single biggest gap that we see in schools and districts is the lack of monitoring and feedback. Because in most cases we do not collect data on our implementation effectiveness, we do not really know how well we are implementing. Therefore, it is extremely difficult for us to know whether we are making progress with our implementation. All too often we are quick to judge that something did not work when the reality is, we never really implemented the practice deeply or well.

The process of monitoring requires that we have some way of collecting data on the level and quality of our implementation. Schools and districts need to be able to answer the question, "How well we are implementing the instructional strategies and the Data Teams process?" Both the DDT and the BDT need to develop specific monitoring tools or rubrics to collect data on the level of implementation of these two strategies.

It is critical, however, to remember that *the primary purpose of monitoring is to provide feedback* to the staff on how well they are implementing the strategies. Fullan (2008) warns us that negative monitoring does not work. It is important to understand that the purpose of monitoring is not to punish people for their lack of follow-through, but rather to provide feedback and to assess how well our support (e.g., training, coaching, modeling) is working.

Monitoring should help us determine where our implementation is being successful and where we need more support. The challenge for the BDT and DDT is to interpret the data and decide which specific supports have been effective or ineffective and which supports to try now in order to move the work forward.

The monitoring data becomes an important barometer in terms of assessing our "reciprocal accountability." By this we mean if individuals or teams are struggling with their implementation, can they, and do they, seek support and suggestions from the other teams? Each person and each team is responsible for the success of each other person and team. If the grade-level, department, or course teams are not successful, what actions has the BDT taken to support them? If the BDT needs help, what support has the DDT provided? What is critical to understand is that individuals and teams need differential kinds and levels of support if they are to implement new practices well, and this only happens if we collect and use the monitoring data well.

Inquiry and Learning

Twenty years ago Peter Senge (1990) brought the concept of learning organizations into the mainstream. He proposed that a learning organization is a group of people working together to collectively enhance their capacities to create results that matter to them. He outlined five disciplines as part of learning organizations; the one that is most important for our purposes is "team learning."

It seems ironic that educators need to consciously work at becoming learning organizations—isn't that what schools are supposed to be? However, for the most part, teaching is still an isolated profession and most classrooms, schools, and districts do not learn well individually or collectively. While there are clearly many successful teachers, administrators, and teams in many districts, "there is no tradition or organization that supports carefully supervised learning of this kind" in most classrooms, schools, and districts (Levin, 2008, pp. 80–81).

Elmore (2004) makes the point that improving instruction requires continuous and collective learning on the part of every person in the district. He challenges all of us when he states "The existing institutional structure of public education does one thing very well: it creates a normative environment that values idiosyncratic, isolated, and individualistic learning at the expense of collective learning. The existing system does not value continuous learning as a collective good and does not make this learning the individual and social responsibility of every member of the system. *Leaders must create environments* in which individuals expect to have their personal ideas and practices subjected to the scrutiny of their colleagues. Privacy of practice produces isolation; isolation is the enemy of improvement" (p. 67; emphasis added).

As stated earlier, leaders play an especially important role in personally leading, creating, and demonstrating changes in norms, expectations, and structures that cause people to think and carry out their work in different and more reflective ways. Supovitz (2006) found that district leaders play a particularly critical role here. He concludes that the "*district's capacity to promote and support ambitious instruction hinges on the leader's abilities both to learn themselves and help oth-*

ers to learn new ideas. In other words, leaders' beliefs about learning predicated the way they conceived of and structured learning opportunities within their own organizations" (pp. 9–10; emphasis added).

If we really hope to improve the quality of instruction and educational outcomes for all students, leaders must be willing to publicly learn themselves, and also put structures and processes in place that encourage and set expectations for others to learn.

By collaboratively using teams to:

- learn from data;

- focus goals and strategies;

- improve instruction;

- identify successes and challenges of implementation; and

- monitor, provide feedback, and support,

the DDT, BDT, and IDTs can develop a deeper sense of how to facilitate learning at every level.

As Fullan (2008) says, "Learning is the work" of the teams and the district. Put another way, Data Teams at each level of the system create the structures whereby "organizational learning is the engine of sustainability" (Supovitz, 2006, p. 160). Developing teams that are responsible to each other creates a more robust accountability system whereby each level of the system is responsible for the success the other levels.

Darling-Hammond (2010, p. 271) sees this shift in accountability as a new paradigm for both schools and districts. "In this new paradigm the design of the school district office should also evolve from a set of silos that rarely interact with one another to a team structure.... This means they must continuously evaluate how schools are doing, seeking to learn from successful schools and to support improvement in struggling schools by ensuring that these schools secure strong leadership and excellent teachers, and are supported in adopting successful program strategies. Districts will need to become learning organizations themselves—developing their capacity to investigate and learn from innovation in order to leverage productive strategies and develop their capacity to support successful change."

A similar paradigm shift must occur simultaneously at the building and classroom levels through the establishment of a BDT and
IDTs, which also learn from their own work. The BDT should review
the ongoing progress of every student in the building, the effectiveness
of the instructional strategies being used by teachers, and the effectiveness of each IDT. If teams are making observable progress, the BDT
should learn from this and share this learning with other teams in the
school. If other teams are not making progress, the BDT should intervene and provide differential supports. If the strategies being used by
IDTs are not effective, then the BDT must take similar action. This
may involve providing more supports to individual teachers or IDTs
or developing tiered interventions for specific students, or groups of
students. If the BDT is not successful in its efforts, then it must solicit
the support of the DDT. Every team is responsible for the success of
each other. This may require additional professional development,
coaching, or direct leadership by the principal or central office staff.
The point here is that all of the teams and team members must take
responsibility and accountability to act if staff or students are not
making progress.

In all of these cases there is a reciprocal accountability (Elmore.
2004) between the teams. It is not acceptable for one team to let
another team not make progress on improvement. Multiple studies
have shown that using teams to distribute leadership throughout the
systems not only develops leadership at all levels but also improves
instruction and student achievement (Chrispeels & Gonzales, 2009).
The likelihood of significantly improving classroom practices is limited if we cannot develop broader and deeper leadership capacity
across each school and the entire district.

Schools and districts that make continuous progress create systems, structures, and supports where there is an active inquiry process
and follow-up actions that are grounded in data, analysis, reflection,
and learning. Reeves (2006) found that schools that were rated higher
in their degree of "inquiry" performed three times better than their
counterparts. He concludes, "If you believe that adults make a difference in student achievement, you are right. If you believe that adults

are helpless bystanders while demographic characteristics work their inexorable will on the academic lives of students, you are right" (p. 72). The defining difference is whether the adults took personal responsibility for student achievement. The development of Data Teams at each level of the system supports the development of personal responsibility paired with collective accountability.

Leaders Make It Happen

After teachers, both principals and superintendents make the most difference in student achievement (Hallinger & Heck, 1996; Mangin, 2007; Marzano, Waters, & McNulty, 2005; Marzano & Waters, 2008; Robinson, 2007; Robinson, Lloyd, & Rowe, 2008). More recent research identifies specific actions that both principals and superintendents can take to positively impact student achievement. In particular the research highlights the need for leaders to model learning and to create capacity across the organizations to learn.

Principal Research

A recent comprehensive review of the literature on principal leadership by McNulty and Besser (2011) reiterates that the principal is second only to the classroom teacher as an influence on student achievement. Several recent meta-analytic studies have identified specific principal leadership actions that are positively associated with student achievement (see Marzano, Waters, & McNulty, 2005; Robinson, 2007; Robinson et al., 2008).

Robinson and her colleagues (2007, 2008) identified five key principal leadership practices that positively impact student achievement, along with effect sizes for each:

1. Establishing goals and expectations

2. Strategic resourcing

3. Planning, coordinating, and evaluating teaching and the curriculum

4. Promoting and participating in teacher learning and development

5. Ensuring an orderly and supportive environment

Interestingly, of all the factors associated with principal leadership and student achievement, the one with the highest effect size (ES 0.84) was "promoting and participating in teacher learning and development." This finding provides strong empirical support for principals being actively involved as the "lead learners" in their schools. The researchers found that principals must not only promote but also participate in learning alongside their own staff.

In turn, the principal must lead the learning in instruction, and for our purposes this means that he or she must actively lead the learning of the two instructional improvement strategies (research-based instructional practices and the IDTs). Principals need to know, or learn, what the instructional practices and Data Teams look like when they are being implemented well. They will need to be able to provide guidance to both the BDT and the IDTs.

There are two important points to be made here: The principal must lead and be a part of the professional learning in school, and the principal needs to ensure the development and effective implementation of the IDTs, by making sure teachers are actively engaged in the Data Teams process, challenge low expectations, and follow up in their classrooms using more powerful and effective teaching practices.

In addition to the leadership responsibilities identified by Robinson and her colleagues (2008), several other recent studies have focused on defining the specific components that make up instructional leadership. These studies also have important ramifications for principals. What these studies found is that the most important part of instructional leadership in terms of student achievement is the principal's use of data. Fullan (2008, p. 31) found that "the effect sizes of principals promoting and participating directly with teachers in the formal and informal learning of the use of data to influence appropriate instructional activities, was more than twice as powerful as any other leadership dimension." It appears that part of the reason is that "active engagement with data of various kinds seems to prompt a more focused, improvement oriented conversation" (Portin et al., 2009, p. 62). When principals use and apply data to inform their instructional feedback to teachers, it resulted in higher levels of teacher collective efficacy and greater gains in student achievement (Filbin, 2008).

These findings have important implications for where and how principals spend their time, and they echo the critical nature of the principal's leadership role in both the BDT and the IDTs. Schools that are successful at improving instruction and developing "accountable cultures" have principals who lead through the use of data (Portin et al., 2009; Filbin, 2008; Fullan 2008).

Superintendent Research

Recently, more research has been published on the role of the superintendent and central office and their impact on student achievement. These studies conclude that without effective leadership at both the building and district levels, continuous progress is unlikely to occur (Louis et al., 2010; Robinson et al., 2008; Leithwood et al., 2007; Leithwood & Jantzi, 2008; MacIver & Farley-Ripple, 2008; Marzano et al., 2005; Marzano & Waters, 2008).

Marzano and Waters (2008) found that there was a statistically significant correlation of almost 10 percentile point gains between superintendent leadership and student achievement. It is interesting to note that the overall effect size for gains in student performance for superintendents was almost identical to the effect size for principals (see Marzano, Waters, & McNulty, 2005). The comparable effect size is surprising given the fact that superintendents are further removed from having a direct influence on teachers, the classroom, and students.

In reviewing the most recent research on district leadership, there appears to be fairly strong consensus on what effective districts do to improve student academic outcomes. In their review of the research, Leithwood and Jantzi (2008) identified eight organizational conditions characterizing effective districts. The following is an adaptation of that research review by McNulty and Besser (2011) and includes:

1. A district's focus on student achievement and the *quality of instructional practices*, including the use of effective research-based instructional practices (Togneri & Anderson, 2003; Simmons, 2006; Supovitz, 2006; Leithwood & Jantzi, 2008; MacIver & Farley-Ripple, 2008; Marzano & Waters, 2008; Fullan, 2010; Harris & Chrispeels, 2009)

2. The development of *instructional leadership* at the district, school, and classroom levels, including training for central office staff, principals, and teachers on high-quality instruction and the leadership of improvement (Togneri & Anderson, 2003; Leithwood & Jantzi, 2008; MacIver & Farley-Ripple, 2008; Fullan, 2010; Harris & Chrispeels, 2009)

3. Training, capacity building, support, and expectations in the *effective use of data* across the district in decision making and assessing student learning and progress; emphasis on the role of principal promoting and participating in the formal and informal use of data (Togneri & Anderson, 2003; Marsh et al., 2005; Leithwood & Jantzi, 2008; Amanda, Park, & Kennedy, 2008; MacIver & Farley-Ripple, 2008; Fullan, 2010; Harris & Chrispeels, 2009; Filbin, 2008; Fullan, 2008)

4. *Collaborative goal setting in establishing a limited number of focused, nonnegotiable district goals* for achievement and instruction that are stable over an extended period of time; creating understanding and support for the district goals from school boards, community partners, and all school staff (Leithwood & Jantzi, 2008; Marzano & Waters, 2008; Fullan, 2010)

5. *Monitoring* the implementation of the strategies, evaluating the results, *and creating feedback* loops to all staff on

progress in achievement and instructional goals (MacIver &
Farley-Ripple, 2008; Marzano & Waters, 2008)

6. Ongoing, targeted, and differentiated *professional
   development*, and the phasing in of improvement efforts
   over time (Leithwood & Jantzi, 2008; Harris & Chrispeels,
   2009; Darling-Hammond et al., 2009)

7. *Distributing leadership* with an emphasis on the
   development of teams and professional communities
   (Leithwood & Jantzi, 2008; Harris & Chrispeels, 2009;
   Hattie, 2009; Darling-Hammond et al., 2009)

8. *Allocating and aligning resources* to support the goals for
   achievement and instruction, including district-sponsored
   professional development (Togneri & Anderson, 2003;
   Leithwood & Jantzi, 2008; Marzano & Waters, 2008;
   MacIver & Farley-Ripple, 2008)

While each district condition is correlated to student achievement, the largest effect size and the strongest statistical relationship is
with the district's expressed concern for student achievement and the
quality of instruction (Leithwood & Jantzi, 2008; MacIver & Farley-
Ripple, 2008). The most consistent finding across all of the research
studies is the importance of districts maintaining a strong focus on
improving instruction (Bottoms & Fry, 2009).

In reviewing this list, what should become clear is that the primary focus for the superintendent and the district is on improving
instruction. As identified earlier, the focus of this instructional
improvement should be on the two primary instructional improvement strategies: Data Teams at every level, and deep implementation
of the research-based instructional practices.

Many, if not most, districts are overly zealous when it comes to
establishing goals and selecting strategies. The research, however, indicates that districts should learn about their improvement efforts by
focusing on a few important aspects of instruction, and then examine
the effectiveness of the implementation of these strategies. Districts do
this by focusing on a limited number of specific goals and strategies

that can be implemented deeply and monitored and for which feedback can be provided frequently, and then tailoring their support through professional growth opportunities such as peer observations, modeling, and coaching. Once the chosen instructional practices or strategies have been implemented deeply, other instructional practices can be phased in over time.

By targeting the work of the schools and the district, the DDT, the BDT, and the IDTs can focus on the two primary improvement strategies, and then, it is hoped, learn from their implementation of this focused work. By focusing the work of the teams on continuous learning, you create a new paradigm for schools and districts.

Darling-Hammond (2010, p. 271) says "In this new paradigm the design of the school district office should also evolve from a set of silos that rarely interact with one another to a team structure. . . . This means they must continuously evaluate how schools are doing, seeking to learn from successful schools and to support improvement in struggling schools. . . . Districts will need to become learning organizations themselves—developing their capacity to investigate and learn from innovation in order to leverage productive strategies and develop their capacity to support successful change."

Both the superintendent and central office staff must reconceptualize the focus of their work, as well as how they carry out this work in a more collaborative way that helps everyone to continuously learn from what is working and why, and what is not working and why. Creating a focused improvement agenda is the right first step, but if teachers, schools, and districts cannot learn from their implementation, they will not achieve continuous improvement.

In a recent article Tom Hoerr (2010) raised the question that if "value-added" is good for students and teachers, shouldn't it also be good for administrators? If so, what would be the value that administrators could add? He goes on to address the question by asking what principals (and superintendents and central office staff) can contribute to teacher learning and growth. If we want all teachers to perform better each year, shouldn't administrators be held accountable for contributing to the growth of teachers and principals?

In a true learning organization, wouldn't everyone be held accountable to contribute to the learning of others? The concept of reciprocal accountability (Elmore, 2004), mentioned throughout this chapter, dictates that the entire school system be designed in such a way that all of the adults are responsible for developing the capacity and performance of each other.

Conclusion

Schlechty (2009) makes the point that developing professional learning communities within the current bureaucratic system will doom them to failure. The only way that professional learning communities will be successful is by embedding them in broader-based learning organizations. What I have attempted to provide here is the beginning of a framework of what it would take to move schools and districts in the direction of becoming learning organizations.

For a more comprehensive description of the framework, please refer to McNulty and Besser (2011).

References

Ainsworth, L. (2003). *Power standards*. Englewood, CO: Lead + Learn Press.

Amanda, D., Park, V., & Kennedy, B. (2008). *Acting on data: How urban high schools use data to improve instruction*. Los Angeles, CA: Center on Educational Governance, Rossier School of Education, University of Southern California.

Ancona, D., Malone, T. W., Orlikowski, W. J., & Senge, P. M. (2007). In praise of the incomplete leader. *Harvard Business Review* (Feb. 1), 92–103.

Bottoms, G., & Fry, B. (2009). *The district leadership challenge: Empowering principals to improve teaching and learning*. Atlanta, GA: Southern Regional Educational Board.

Chrispeels, J. H., & Gonzales, M. (2009). The challenge of systemic change in complex educational systems. In A. Harris and J. Hageman Chrispeels, *Improving schools and educational systems*. New York, NY: Routledge.

City, E. A., Elmore, R. E., Fiarman, S. E., & Teitel, L. (2009). *Instructional rounds in education: A network approach to improving teaching and learning*. Cambridge, MA: Harvard Education Press.

Darling-Hammond, L. (2010). *The flat world and education: How America's commitment to equity will determine our future*. New York, NY: Teacher College Press.

Darling-Hammond, L., Barron, B., Pearson, P. D., Schoenfeld, A. H., Stage, E. K., Zimmerman, T. D., & Tilson, J. L. (2008). *Powerful learning: What we know about teaching for understanding*. San Francisco, CA: Jossey-Bass.

Darling-Hammond, L., Wei, R. C., Andree, A., Richardson, N., & Orphanos, S. (2009). *Professional learning in the learning profession: A status report on teacher development in the US and abroad*. Oxford, OH: National Staff Development Council.

David, J. L. (2008/09). What the research says about . . . collaborative inquiry. *Educational Leadership, 66*(4), 87–88.

DuFour, R., DuFour, R., & Eaker, R. (2008). *Revisiting professional learning communities at work: New insights for improving schools*. Bloomington, IN: Solution Tree.

Duke, D. (2007). Turning schools around: What are we learning about the process, and those who do it. *Education Week 26*(24), 35–37.

Elmore, R. F. (2004). *School reform from the inside out: Policy, practice, and performance*. Cambridge, MA: Harvard Education Press.

Filbin, J, F. (2008). *Examining the effects of changes in pedagogical precision, principal data use, and student achievement on collective efficacy* (Unpublished doctoral dissertation). University of Denver.

Fullan, M. (2008). *The six secrets of change: What the best leaders do to help their organizations survive and thrive*. San Francisco, CA: Jossey-Bass.

Fullan, M. (2009). Have theory, will travel: A theory of action for system change. In A. Hargreaves & M. Fullan (Eds.), *Change wars*. Bloomington, IN: Solution Tree.

Fullan, M. (2010). *All systems go: The change imperative for whole system reform*. Thousand Oaks, CA: Corwin.

Hallinger, P., & Heck, R. (1996). Reassessing the principal's role in school effectiveness: A review of empirical research, 1980–1995. *Educational Administration Quarterly, 32*(1), 5–44.

Harris, A., & Chrispeels, J. H. (2009). *Improving schools and educational systems: International perspectives.* New York, NY: Routledge.

Hattie, J. (2009). *Visible learning: A synthesis of over 800 meta-analyses relating to achievement.* New York, NY: Routledge.

Hayes Jacobs, H. (Ed.). (2010). *Curriculum 21: Essential education for a changing world.* Alexandria, VA: ASCD

Hoerr, T. R. (2010). Values worth adding. *Educational Leadership, 68*(4), 89–90.

Honig, M. I., Copland, M. A., Rainey, L., Lorton, J. A., & Newton, M. (2010). *Central office transformation for district-wide teaching and learning improvement.* Seattle, WA: Center for the Study of Teaching and Policy, University of Washington, and the Wallace Foundation.

Jacobson D. (2010). Coherent instructional improvement and PLCs: Is it possible to do both? *Phi Delta Kappan, 91*(6), 38–45.

Joyce, B., & Showers, B. (2002). *Student achievement through staff development* (3rd ed.). Alexandria, VA: ASCD.

Knapp, M. K., Copland, M. A., Honig, M. I., Plecki, M. L., & Portin, B. S. (2010). *Learning-focused leadership and leadership support: Meaning and practice in urban systems.* Seattle, WA: Center for the Study of Teaching and Policy, University of Washington, and the Wallace Foundation.

Kotter, J. P. (1996). *Leading change.* Boston, MA: Harvard Business School Press.

Leithwood, K., Day, C., Sammons, P., Harris, A., & Hopkins, D. (2007). *Seven strong claims about successful schools leadership.* Nottingham, England: National College of School Leadership.

Leithwood, K., & Jantzi, D. (2008). Linking leadership to student learning: The contributions of leader efficacy. *Educational Administration Quarterly, 44*(4), 496–528.

Levin, B. (2008). *How to change 5000 schools: A practical and positive approach for leading change at every level.* Cambridge, MA: Harvard Education Press.

Louis, K. S., Leithwood, K., Wahlstrom, K. L., & Anderson, S. E. (2010). *Learning from leadership: Investigating the links to improved student learning.* St. Paul, MN: Center for Applied Research and Educational Improvement, University of Minnesota; Ontario, Canada: Ontario Institute for Studies in Education, University of Toronto.

MacIver, M. A., & Farley-Ripple, E. (2008). *Bringing the district back in: The role of the central office in instruction and achievement.* Alexandria, VA: Educational Research Services.

Mangin, M. M. (2007). Facilitating elementary principals' support for instructional teacher leadership. *Educational Administration Quarterly, 43*(3), 319–357.

Marsh, J. A., Kerr, K. A., Ikemoto, G. S., Darilek, H., Suttorp, M., & Zimmer, R. W. (2005). *The role of districts in fostering instructional improvement: Lessons from three urban districts partnered with the Institute for Learning.* Santa Monica, CA: RAND.

Marzano, R. J., Pickering, D., & Pollock, J. (2001). *Classroom instruction that works.* Alexandria, VA: ASCD.

Marzano, R. J., & Waters, T. (2008). *District leadership that works: Striking the right balance.* Bloomington, IN: Solution Tree.

Marzano, R. J., Waters, J. T., & McNulty, B. A. (2005). *What works in school leadership: Research to results.* Alexandria, VA: ASCD.

McNulty, B., & Besser, L. (2011). *Leaders make it happen: An administrator's guide to Data Teams.* Englewood, CO: Lead + Learn Press.

Murphy, J., & Meyers, C. V. (2008). *Turning around failing schools: Leadership lessons from the organizational sciences.* Thousand Oaks, CA: Corwin.

Pfeffer J., & Sutton, R. (2000). *The knowing-doing gap: How smart companies turn knowledge into action.* Boston, MA: Harvard Business School Press.

Portin, B. S., Knapp, M. S., Dareff, S., Russell, F. A., Samuelson, C., & Yea, T. H. (2009). *Leadership for learning improvement in urban schools.* Seattle, WA: Center for the Study of Teaching and Policy, University of Washington.

Reeves, D. B. (2006). *The learning leader: How to focus school improvement for results.* Alexandria, VA: ASCD.

Reeves, D. B. (Ed.). (2007). *Ahead of the curve.* Bloomington, IN: Solution Tree.

Reeves, D. B. (2008). *Reframing teacher leadership to improve your school.* Alexandria, VA: ASCD.

Reeves, D. B. (2010). *Transforming professional development into student results.* Alexandria, VA: ASCD.

Robinson, V. M. J. (2007). *School leadership and student outcomes: Identifying what works and why* (No. 41). Wimallee, Australia: Australian Council of Educational Leadership.

Robinson, V. M. J., Lloyd, C. A., &. Rowe, K. J. (2008). The impact of leadership on student outcomes: An analysis of the differential effects of leadership types. *Educational Administration Quarterly, 44*(5), 635–674.

Schlechty, P. C. (2009). *Leading for learning: How to transform schools into learning organizations.* San Francisco, CA. Jossey-Bass.

Seashore, K. R. (2009). Leadership and change in schools: Personal reflections over the last 30 years. *Journal of Educational Change, 10,* 129–140.

Senge, P. (1990). *The fifth discipline.* New York, NY: Random House.

Simmons, J. (2006). *Breaking through: Transforming urban schools.* Amsterdam, NY: Teacher College Press.

Supovitz, J. A. (2006). *The case for district-based reform: Leading, building, and sustaining school improvement.* Cambridge, MA: Harvard Education Press.

Togneri, W., & Anderson, S. E. (2003). *Beyond islands of excellence: What districts can do to improve instruction and achievement in all schools—a leadership brief* (Stock No. 303369). Washington, DC: Learning First Alliance.

Wahlstrom, K. L., & Seashore Louis, K. S. (2008). How teachers experience principal leadership: The roles of professional community, trust, efficacy, and shared responsibility. *Educational Administration Quarterly, 44*(4), 458–495.

Weinbaum, E. H., & Supovitz, J. A. (2010). Planning ahead: Make program implementation more predictable. *Phi Delta Kappan, 91*(7), 68–70.

Wiliam, D. (2007). *Content then process: Teacher learning communities in the service of formative assessment.* In D. B. Reeves (Ed.), *Ahead of the curve.* Bloomington, IN: Solution Tree.

CHAPTER TEN

Change Readiness:
A Practical Process
for School Leaders

MIKE WASTA

A new superintendent is hired for a small urban district. The board of education is very clear: "Student performance in the district is unacceptable. Action must be taken to improve the situation, and results need to be seen quickly." The superintendent is well prepared for the challenge. She has recently received her doctorate in education from a prestigious institution while serving as assistant superintendent in a larger urban district. She quickly studies the situation in her new district and determines the critical areas of curriculum, assessment, structure, instruction, and leadership that need to be addressed. She presents her conclusions to the board along with her plan of action to dramatically and quickly make the changes that will improve student performance. Her plan is bold, but well supported by research and experience. The board is very pleased and encourages the superintendent to proceed. With this vote of confidence the superintendent moves quickly to begin implementation of her plan. Although the teachers and administrators unions express reservations (they have been down this road before), the superintendent quickly dismisses their concerns and moves forward. She meets with parents who, although not fully understanding the details of her plan, are swept up by her enthusiasm. The superintendent realizes that all of her leaders may not have all of the skills they need to implement the dramatic changes she has in mind but remains confident that she will be able to bring them along or remove them.

As the changes in how teachers and leaders will work, how schools are structured, and what the new expectations for students will be are implemented, there is a rewarding degree of support and compliance and a minimal amount of resistance by all concerned. The superintendent is encouraged and convinced that with hard work on the part of all, success is in the future.

As the months pass and the initial "glow" begins to wane, issues start to emerge. The leaders are struggling to implement dramatically different leadership roles they have never experienced. They are less confident and some have committed high-profile gaffes. The teachers are trying to implement the changes, but the training is often insufficient, and they are beginning to realize that their workload is substantially increasing. The unions representing both leaders and teachers are beginning to field more and more complaints from their members. As parents begin to fully understand the dramatic changes in grading practices, curriculum, and schedules, a number begin to yearn for the comfort of familiar practices. The superintendent is not particularly surprised by these issues. She realizes change is difficult and works longer and harder to calm the waters, confident that with time all will be well.

As the months pass and turn into years, the disgruntled members of various groups begin to express their concerns and increasing frustration to local politicians and board of education members. At first these concerns are passed off as the typical angst associated with any change. However, as they continue and even grow, the policymakers become increasingly anxious.

At board of education meetings questions arise more frequently about the superintendent's plan. The three new board members in particular who did not participate in the hiring of the superintendent begin to question the dramatic changes. The superintendent responds to these challenges by presenting evidence that the changes, although dramatic, are starting to result in improved student performance.

The situation reaches a climax when the superintendent recommends that a number of veteran leaders in the school district be removed from their positions because they have demonstrated over a period of time that they are either unwilling or unable to implement the new practices. This action serves as a lightning rod for all of the parties that have struggled with and been anxious about the changes. Board of education meetings become tense and confrontational as members of these parties appear at each meeting to express their frustration and anger. Although maintaining a unified defense of the changes and the superintendent in public, in private the board of education is beginning to fracture over the issues. The fracture bursts into the public domain when the board votes to not extend the superintendent's contract by a 5–4 count.

Over the ensuing year as a new superintendent is installed, the changes are unofficially deconstructed and gradually fall into disuse. No official statement is ever made to abandon the changes; they just fade away, and within two years the district looks much like it did before the previous superintendent arrived.

THE PRECEDING STORY IS, unfortunately, all too common. At the district or school level there are powerful cultural and political forces at play to maintain the status quo, even if the status quo means that students are not receiving the quality of education they deserve and that could be delivered if the adults running the system were willing to make the known and necessary changes in the way they interact and work. Why is it that, even in the face of an increasing body of knowledge about what works in schools to improve outcomes for students, it is so difficult to form a consensus for action?

This is a complex social issue that requires a complex set of answers. Those looking for single-factor answers continue to be disappointed. And those who recognize the complexity of the situation and attempt to implement the array of changes necessary are also often frustrated or overwhelmed by the entrenched responses of those affected, even those who would appear to benefit.

So what is to be done? It is understandable at this point that some would abandon hope and conclude that real, sustained, dramatic change in the way schools work is impossible. Based upon the track record of changes attempted and failed, this is not an irrational position.

But there is hope. Substantial change can occur to improve student outcomes in a more than serendipitous manner; it does not have to occur only when the stars align and the right combination of players happens to be in the right place at the right time. For isn't that what successful changes resemble? Isn't that why, when a few individuals change, things begin to unravel? Sustained change cannot be personality based. Sustained change in a complex social situation such as a public school must involve large numbers of people.

Far too often the unsuccessful changes we have witnessed have been tied to a charismatic individual who literally overwhelms opposition in the short term. This may be effective and desirable in the beginning, but if large numbers of people across the spectrum do not agree to change their behavior, such changes are eventually doomed to fail.

The following quote from Senge (1999) sums up one of the frequent problems associated with change attempts in the public schools:

The fundamental flaw in most innovators' strategies is that they focus on their innovations, on what they are trying to do—rather than on understanding how the larger culture, structures and norms will react to their efforts.

Are We Ready for Change?

Because so many change initiatives in education follow a pattern similar to that described at the beginning of this chapter, it may be helpful to consider an alternative course. In this alternative course the change agent or catalyst would slow the process down. He would take Senge's words to heart and stop to consider the effect of his proposed change on the culture into which it is being introduced. This is a difficult approach to take for most change leaders and innovators. They are frequently hired to bring about a dramatic change from the status quo. In addition they usually believe passionately in the ideas they are advocating. Finally, the policymakers or administrators who hired them are frequently impatient for the situation to "turn around." All of these conditions conspire to force a change to be developed and implemented long before the development work has been done to prepare the culture for the change. It should be no surprise, then, that even when the change is clearly necessary to an outside observer the culture conspires to inhibit or stop the change. If the change agent or catalyst takes a moment or two to consider the complexities of the culture into which the change is being introduced, perhaps he may stop to strategize on how to prepare the culture for the proposed change. Exhibit 10.1 conveys some of the complexities present in any school or district and some of the stakeholders and their possible interactions.

As we consider the complexities of the situation it is understandable why some leaders throw their hands up and take a blunt force approach. But they do so at their own peril. While it is true that a blunt force approach will often flatten the opposition present in many of the stakeholder groups, particularly if it is delivered with a high degree of passion and urgency, it is a fundamental mistake to think

Complex Forces at Work

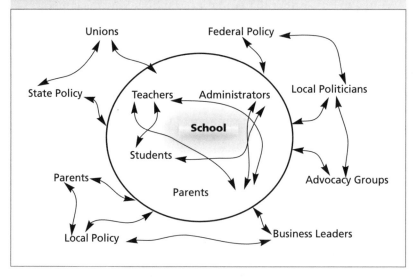

that the opposition has ceased to exist. Like our example of the new superintendent, the forces involved may be muted at the outset, but if their issues are not addressed they will come back to seriously impact the change initiative. It is because of this fact—that at the outset this blunt force approach appears to be successful in bringing about significant change—that it is so frequently repeated. However, sustained change is often elusive when using this approach. Of course if the change agent or catalyst is in the drive-by mode, she is often long gone by the time the changes are dismantled.

A more considered, long-term approach to a change that has a greater chance of being absorbed into the existing culture and being sustained as a fixture in the revised culture might begin with a thoughtful consideration of the readiness of the culture for the proposed change.

It is at this point that the change agents bemoan the fact that this kind of delay in getting to the issue is a waste of time. Often passionate and energetic arguments are mounted that it is obvious to even the most casual observer that dramatic change is needed in the school or district and that there is no point in delay. Perhaps the words of Michael Fullan (2007) will serve as a caution:

Not every situation is alterable, especially at certain periods of time.

Non-implementable programs and reforms probably do more harm than good when they are attempted.

The characteristics of the change, the makeup of the local district, the character of individual schools and teachers and the existence and form of external relationships interact to produce conditions for change or no change.

If the foregoing has cooled the ardor of the change leader just a bit, it is perfectly reasonable for her to ask, just what are we going to do?

The suggestion here is that the leader and her inner circle stop and take the time to assess the conditions present in the culture in question and the readiness of the various stakeholder groups to undertake the change in mind. This process can begin by asking a series of questions such as the following:

1. What skills will the people charged with implementing the change need? Do they already possess these skills? If not, how will they acquire them?

2. How much training will be needed? Where will we get the training? How much will it cost? Where will we get the funding?

3. How are parents (and here you can insert any stakeholder group affected by the change) likely to feel about the change?

4. If we start to receive some push back, what is the board of education likely to do?

5. How will we approach the teachers union so that it does not just react negatively?

6. How can we develop the political support we will need to see this change through?

7. Am I, as the change catalyst, prepared to stay here for the several years it is likely to take to embed this change in the culture?

8. How are we going to develop a plan that will allow us to deal with the issues we cannot possibly anticipate beforehand?

9. Are there skills that I, as the change catalyst, need to acquire before I attempt this change?

These are just a few of the questions we should be asking ourselves *before* we begin to initiate the change. By asking these questions now, and by being brutally honest in our answers, we can develop a plan that will increase the chances of our change being meaningful and sustained.

The Change Readiness Assessment

The Change Readiness Assessment is a formal mechanism for answering these questions and more before embarking on a change initiative. By completing this assessment, a great deal of time can be saved later in the process, and this assessment becomes an initial step in the change process itself that will inform the initiative and usually improve it.

The Change Readiness Assessment serves three basic purposes:

• It allows the change leader to determine the initial reaction of each stakeholder group to the proposed change and the likely degree of support or opposition.

• It allows the change leader to determine the capabilities of the system and those charged with implementing the proposed change.

• It can be the first step in a reciprocal process between the change leader and the stakeholders in building a shared understanding of the need for the change and the plan to achieve the change.

Conducting the Assessment

Step One

In order to start the process the change leader needs to describe the current situation and create a compelling vision of an alternative state. This is frequently done by most change leaders. However, at this point it is recommended that the plan to achieve this new, improved state be broad in scope and limited in detail. Although it may sound counterintuitive to many, this is a critical point. If the change leader is to respect the culture and people in it, he must demonstrate that respect by enlisting their support in crafting the new future. When a change leader (particularly one new to the system) comes in with all of the details of a change plan developed, there is no room for stakeholder input. Stakeholders immediately start to feel that this change is "being done to them." The change leader must start with the idea that the changes to be made, if they are to be sustained, must eventually be strongly supported by large numbers of members of each stakeholder group. Overlooking this point has resulted in many of the failures like the one described at the beginning of the chapter. The change leader's real mission is not to force stakeholder members to change; it is to convince stakeholders that they want to change and that they will work through this painful process because they have become equally passionate about the benefits.

So at this early stage the plan presented by the change leader is broad and compelling but short on details. The change leader readily and frequently acknowledges that the details need to be crafted by members of the stakeholder groups whose knowledge and experience will only make the plan better. An example from a school illustrates the point:

> *A new principal has been hired to serve at a failing high school. He and his leadership team study the current situa-*

tion (which is dismal) and review the literature on making dramatic changes at this level. They determine that changing the school from a typical 9–12, departmentalized structure to a series of small learning communities with highly engaging themes is the best way to proceed. However, rather than this small team working out all of the details involved in such a dramatic change, the leader and his team decide to conduct a Change Readiness Assessment to determine the readiness of this school to make this change.

Step Two

The change leader and his team next identify all of the stakeholder groups that will be affected by the proposed change. Continuing the high school example introduced above, this group would probably include the following:

Teachers; Building administrators; District leaders (including the superintendent); Board of education; Parents; Students; Unions; Political leaders; Support staff

As time goes on more stakeholder groups may be identified and will be added to the list.

Step Three

A focus group composed of members of each identified group will be invited to a meeting to discuss the proposed plan. At the meeting the change leader and her team present the evidence they have gathered about the current situation and the vision and plan they are proposing. Because this is the first time many members of the focus group are hearing the proposal, the presentation must emphasize the unacceptable current condition and present a compelling vision of what is possible. A combination of data and personal consequences for the students is often compelling at this point. The plan to move from what is to what could be is described in the level of detail discussed in step one above. It is made clear to all participants that the details are limited purposely to encourage participation by as many as possible in informing and crafting the complete plan.

Participants are encouraged to ask questions, make suggestions, and express opinions. Through the course of the meeting the leader and her team are looking for answers to a series of questions that are designed to solicit the position of participants on the following domains (based upon the research of Charles C. Reigeluth):

1. Their previous experience with change

2. The need for change

3. Their willingness to change

4. Their faith in the leadership to bring about the change

5. The change plan itself

6. The skill level of those charged with implementing the change

Although each situation will be unique, some examples of starter questions regarding each domain are presented in Exhibit 10.2.

It is strongly suggested that detailed minutes of the meeting be kept by a recorder. Taping of the meeting would be helpful, but only if the group is comfortable with the idea.

Immediately after the meeting, the leader and her team review the minutes or tape and rate the group's response in each domain area on the Change Readiness Continuum (Exhibit 10.3).

After gathering information concerning each stakeholder group's readiness to change, place each group's rating on the continuum for each domain using the Change Readiness Continuum Rubric (Exhibit 10.4).

Of course these are approximate judgments about each group on each domain. If the leadership team is uncertain about a group's response, it can seek additional information through follow-up interviews, reviews of official documents, or direct observations.

After a focus group has been conducted with each stakeholder group, the scores on each domain for each group can be entered into the Stakeholder Change Readiness Matrix (Exhibit 10.5).

EXHIBIT 10.2   **Suggested Change Readiness Focus Group Starter Questions**

History

What past or current change efforts can you recall?
What did you think about each?
How comfortable are you with change in general?

Need for Change

Is there a need for improvement in your schools?
What are you most dissatisfied with?
What changes would you like to see?

Willingness to Change

Would your group be willing to make changes in the way you do business
    to accomplish the change needed?
Could you give some examples of changes you would be willing to make?
Would you make these changes even if you were likely to experience a
    period of difficulty or were uncomfortable for a period of time?
Would these changes be temporary or permanent?
Do you think other stakeholders would be willing to make changes even if
    they were difficult and would make them uncomfortable at first?

Faith in Leadership

Do you think the current leadership has the ability to successfully
    accomplish the proposed change? Why or why not?

Change Plan

Do you think the plan that has been described has the potential to achieve
    the goal(s)? Why or why not?
What do you think are the strong points of the plan? The weaknesses?
What would you change in the plan to improve it?

Skills Necessary to Implement

Do you think your group has the knowledge/skills necessary to implement
    the change plan?
If not, do you think your group would be willing to acquire the necessary
    knowledge/skills?
How long do you think that would take?
Do you think there are some members of the group who, even if willing,
    would be unable to acquire the necessary knowledge/skills?

EXHIBIT 10.3 **Change Readiness Continuum**

Stakeholder Group

History

Ready   Intermediate   Not Ready

|--|

10   9   8   7   6   5   4   3   2   1

Need for Change

Ready   Intermediate   Not Ready

|--|

10   9   8   7   6   5   4   3   2   1

Willingness to Change

Ready   Intermediate   Not Ready

|--|

10   9   8   7   6   5   4   3   2   1

Faith in Leadership

Ready   Intermediate   Not Ready

|--|

10   9   8   7   6   5   4   3   2   1

Change Plan

Ready   Intermediate   Not Ready

|--|

10   9   8   7   6   5   4   3   2   1

Skills Necessary to Change

Ready   Intermediate   Not Ready

|--|

10   9   8   7   6   5   4   3   2   1

Change Readiness Continuum Rubric

Domain	Ready	Intermediate	Not Ready
History	Previous changes viewed as positive and generally successful.	No experience with previous change. Previous change viewed as insignificant impact on group.	Previous change viewed as generally unsuccessful. Negative experience.
Need for Change	Recognition that present conditions unacceptable. Recognition that change is required at this time if progress is to be made.	Realize that things could be better but not completely dissatisfied with things as they are.	Present condition is not viewed as so negative or troublesome that this change is required. May see need for others to change but not self.
Willingness to Change	Willing to make difficult choices (personal and group) to bring about change. Willing to accept that change will be difficult with a lengthy period of discomfort possible.	Will change if the change does not require a significant inconvenience to group.	Sees no need to change. Resistant to doing anything significantly different that may create discomfort for group.
Faith in Leadership	Believe that the current leaders have the ability to accomplish the change.	Don't have strong opinions toward leadership either positive or negative due to past experience or lack of knowledge.	Negative toward current leaders capabilities and/or motives in general. Don't believe leaders can accomplish the change.
Change Plan	Possess a good understanding of the vision for the future associated with the change plan. Believe that the change plan, as presented, has the potential to achieve the goal(s).	Do not have a clear understanding of the vision for the future associated with the change plan. Have doubts about major components of the change plan as the right approach to achieve the goal(s).	Do not agree with the vision of the future after the change. Do not believe the change plan, as presented, is necessary or has the potential to achieve the goal(s).
Skills Necessary to Implement	Believe the group represented or responsible has the knowledge and/or skills necessary to implement the plan.	Believe the group represented or responsible has some of the knowledge and/or skills necessary to implement the plan and believe that many of those who do not will be able to acquire the knowledge and/or skills.	Have serious doubts that the group represented or responsible has the knowledge and/or skills necessary to successfully implement the plan and doubt that most members of the group can acquire the knowledge/skills.

EXHIBIT 10.5 — Stakeholder Change Readiness Matrix

Domain → Stakeholder Group ↓	History	Need for Change	Willingness to Change	Faith in Leadership	Change Plan	Skills Necessary to Implement
Teachers						
Building Administrators						
Superintendent						
Senior District Leadership						
Board of Education						
Parents						
Students						
Unions						
Political Leaders						
Support Staff						

Step Four

At this point the leader and his team have a comprehensive picture of the readiness of each stakeholder group to proceed with the proposed change. In addition, he has gathered a significant amount of material from each stakeholder group concerning the proposal that can make it more customized to the particular set of circumstances.

Armed with this information, the leader and his team must make some critical decisions.

1. Do we proceed as planned?
2. Do we significantly modify the plan in response to what we have learned?
3. Do we postpone the proposed change until conditions are more favorable?
4. Do we develop a new plan in response to the issues addressed in the assessment?

Returning to our high school example:

If the assessment revealed that in spite of the demands of some, the board of education as a whole was strongly opposed to the plan, what would be the chances of success?

If the teachers union pointed out that most of the actions proposed in the plan would violate sections of their contract and they were unwilling to negotiate a change, would the plan have a chance to succeed?

If the parents, in spite of the poor performance of students, were strongly opposed to the narrowing of their children's education, would the plan have a chance to succeed?

Having identified issues such as these may mean that time needs to be spent on changing attitudes and beliefs before moving to implementation. Failure to do so may compromise the ultimate ability to implement and sustain the change. Understandably, to a passionate change leader it may be difficult to accept this delay; however, history appears to be teaching us that the long-term rewards justify the patience.

Systemic change will be a difficult process under the best of conditions. If conditions are less than optimal, systemic change will be all the more difficult. It seems likely that there are some conditions under which systemic change should not be undertaken or at the very least, attention must be directed to changing those conditions before a systemic change effort should be undertaken. Readiness is defined simply as the preconditions necessary for a good chance of success in a systemic change effort. (Reigeluth, 1995)

To those eager to begin implementation, a thorough evaluation of the readiness of the stakeholders involved to make the change may take as little as three months. This seems like a small price to pay to greatly enhance the probability of success.

By taking the time to assess the readiness of the system stakeholders to change, the change catalyst and his team can combine aspects of the technical issues involved with the process of change. This attention to the process of change is frequently the missing ingredient in systemic change initiatives. The straightforward, dynamic process described above which we call a Change Readiness Assessment is a relatively simple mechanism, that when implemented properly, forces the catalyst to attend to both of these indispensable aspects of any systemic change.

References

Fullan, M. (2007). *The new meaning of educational change.* New York, NY: Teachers College Press.

Reigeluth, C. M. (1995). A conversation on guidelines for the process of facilitating systemic change in education. *Systems Practice, 8*(3), 315–328.

Senge, P. (1999). *The dance of change.* New York, NY: Doubleday.

CHAPTER ELEVEN

A Framework to Support Successful Leadership

CONNIE KAMM

Scenario 1

It is nearly 7:30 p.m. and Maria, an elementary school principal in a large, urban K–8 school, is still in her office, once again going over the data from district assessments. Maria had hoped to see gains in reading and math at all levels. The school intervention focused on vocabulary development seemed to be going well with many teachers implementing the vocabulary strategies in their classrooms. Instead of the expected assessment gains, however, Maria sees that students have not shown growth in any grade level, in either math or reading. In sixth-grade math and seventh-grade reading, the percentage of students at proficient and above has actually declined from the previous assessment. With this performance Maria worries about the future opportunities for the students in her school who do not have the skills to be successful as they move to middle school and beyond. In addition, Maria knows that she will be embarrassed in front of her peers at the next day's district-wide principals meeting. She will be asked to explain her school's lack of growth on these academic indicators. She is also dreading the school faculty meeting where this data will further threaten the already low morale of her staff. She has no idea what to do next.

MANY SCHOOL LEADERS identify with Maria's circumstance. To be an educator today can be a daunting task, often filled with frustration and uncertainty. Educators are experiencing demanding and transparent accountability reporting whereby the results of achievement tests are publicly posted and school leaders are often severely criticized. Without question, it is the responsibility of educational leaders to ensure the academic success of the students in their schools; however, as in Maria's case, many school leaders have not been supported with the guidance, structures, processes, and training necessary to stimulate continued learning success in their schools, and they are unclear about what to do. As Karen Seashore (2009, p. 132) wisely points out, "Change is not just about implementing top-down mandates. It also involves empowerment, effective professional development, and deep collaboration." This empowerment applies not only to teachers but to leaders as well.

In this complex and pressure-filled era of accountability and reform, districts are wise to remember that educational leadership has a significant impact on student learning (Marzano, Waters, & McNulty, 2005; Augustine et al., 2009; Wahlstrom et al., 2010). If student achievement is to improve, educational leaders must be provided with systems of support that aid them in inspiring and guiding continuous school and district improvement. Implementing a Comprehensive Accountability Framework ensures this support for system-wide leadership that is shared and instructionally focused.

Leadership Impacts Student Achievement

In *Improving School Leadership: The Promise of Cohesive Leadership Systems*, Augustine and colleagues (2009) state that nearly 60 percent of a school's impact on student achievement is attributable to principal and teacher effectiveness, with principals accounting for 25 percent and teachers 33 percent of a school's total impact on achievement. In another stellar research project, Wahlstrom and colleagues note that educational leadership impacts student achievement primarily through the leaders' influence on teachers' motivation and working conditions (Wahlstrom, Louis, Leithwood, & Anderson, 2010). This large-scale, six-year study included educators from nine states, 43 school districts, and 180 schools and relied on data collected from thousands of educators through surveys, by interviews, and in classroom observations. Wahlstrom and colleagues (p. 9) state:

> In developing a starting point for this six-year study, we claimed, based on a preliminary review of research, that leadership is second only to classroom instruction as an influence on student learning, After six additional years of research, we are even more confident about this claim. To date we have not found a single case of a school improving its student achievement record in the absence of talented leadership.

Talented educational leadership today emphasizes the instructional responsibility of the leader. According to Richard Elmore (2006), the purpose of leadership is the improvement of instructional practice and performance, regardless of role. In *Visible Learning: A Synthesis of over 800 Meta-analyses Relating to Achievement,* John Hattie (2009, p. 83) states that the major focus of instructional leaders is "on creating a learning climate free of disruption, a system of clear teaching objectives, and high teacher expectations for teachers and students." From the research that Hattie synthesizes, he concludes that leaders "who promote challenging goals, and then establish safe environments for teachers to critique, question, and support other teachers to reach these goals together" have the largest effect on student outcomes (p. 83). Hattie examines specific actions of instructional leaders that have the greatest impact on improving student performance (pp. 83–84):

- Promoting and participating in teacher learning and development
- Planning, coordinating, and evaluating teaching and the

curriculum through classroom visits and providing formative and summative feedback

- Aligning resource selection and allocation to priority teaching goals
- Ensuring a supportive environment where teaching and learning time are protected from outside interruptions
- Establishing an orderly environment both inside and outside the classroom

In "The Impact of Leadership on Student Outcomes: An Analysis of the Differential Effects of Leadership Types," Robinson, Lloyd, and Rowe (2008, p. 636) state, "the more leaders focus their relationships, their work, and their learning on the core business of teaching and learning, the greater their influence on student outcomes."

Most school districts recognize the positive impact of effective leadership on student growth, and many school districts are also aware of the characteristics and practices of effective instructional leaders. Districts often flounder, however, with what to do to support the growth and effectiveness of their leaders. To provide guidance for school and district administrators, many districts turn to evaluation protocols that list qualities embodied by outstanding educational leaders. One of the most widely referenced sources for educational leadership policy standards in the United States are the Interstate School Leaders Licensure Consortium standards adopted by the National Policy Board for Educational Administration (Council of Chief State School Officers, 2008). These thoughtfully written standards state that an educational leader promotes the success of every student by (p. 18)

1. Facilitating the development, articulation, implementation, and stewardship of a vision of learning that is shared and supported by all stakeholders

2. Advocating, nurturing, and sustaining a school culture and instructional program conducive to student learning and staff professional growth

3. Ensuring management of the organization, operation, and resources for a safe, efficient, and effective learning environment

4. Collaborating with faculty and community members, responding to diverse community interests and needs, and mobilizing community resources

5. Acting with integrity and fairness and in an ethical manner

6. Understanding, responding to, and influencing the political, social, economic, legal, and cultural context

Although these standards, with their accompanying functions, are meant to be viewed at a policy level, districts often use them to dictate what a leader needs to be and do without a system of support to make these words a reality in leadership behaviors. In order to truly ensure the leadership growth required to transform schools into flourishing learning communities where both students and educators thrive, it is imperative that leadership be viewed as a whole system commitment and not just the responsibility of individual leaders operating in isolation. Consider another scenario focused on a high school principal from a district that has implemented a Comprehensive Accountability Framework.

Scenario 2

Jeff is a high school principal in a large district where 86 percent of the students receive free and reduced lunch. For the first time in years, his school is making great academic gains. In fact, this year the school made adequate yearly progress goals in all areas, and Jeff is elated.

It is 5:45 p.m., and he is glowing about a meeting that he observed earlier that day with the four-member biology team. Jeff explains that the team was analyzing student results from a common post-assessment and challenging their own teaching methods based on these results. One teacher who had a higher percentage of students scoring proficient and advanced described how he had used the study guide to engage his students actively in teaching one another in a dynamic, hands-on approach. His colleagues asked questions and contributed additional insights about the study guide methodology as they worked to adapt the approach to implement in their own classrooms.

Jeff points out that prior to the district-wide implementation of Data Teams (grade-level, content-specific teams) the teachers were not working together to analyze results of common assessments. And they were definitely not using assessments to inform their instruction. Instead, each teacher was planning lessons, testing students, and assigning grades. There was very little conversation about the quality of instruction or about implementing the same instructional strategies. There were some examples of exemplary teaching and deep student learning, but those teachers were isolated.

When asked more about the Data Teams structure, Jeff clarifies that all content-area teachers in each department are part of a Data Team. Implementing Data Teams in each school is a district-wide initiative. The district has not only supplied the training but also required all schools to focus on deep Data Teams implementation. The district has brought in teachers to build standards-aligned curriculum documents to support the Data Teams work and has provided time every week for teachers to meet in Data Teams with their content-area or grade-level colleagues at each of the district's schools. Principals received additional training on how to support the Data Teams work. In addition, the number of district meetings that principals are expected to attend has been significantly minimized in order to provide time for the principals to meet with Data Teams in their schools.

In response to further probing, Jeff explains that the larger context for the Data Teams initiative is supported by a Comprehensive Accountability Framework that has been developed by a design team representing all of the stakeholder groups in the district. This Comprehensive Accountability Framework has been approved by the governing board and written into board policy. It clearly states that Data Teams are the core of accountability for learning. As a result, all of the educators in the district can feel confident that this Data Teams practice is not likely to disappear with the next change in superintendent. Jeff states:

> The teachers feel like the entire district is committed to the Data Teams process and that this initiative is here to stay. They also feel like they are being respected as professionals. For the first time in my very long career, I can honestly say that we are a team of professionals deeply engaged in an inquiry process concentrated on student learning. And the students are responding positively to this thriving learning culture as well. I feel confident that through more engaging instruction, we are doing a much better job of connecting students with the skills they need to be successful in their next stages of learning. Through our Comprehensive Accountability Framework, I know that the district backs me in our work at the school, and that makes a great difference to me as a principal.

Unfortunately, unlike Jeff, many educational leaders cannot boast of a staff of professionals committed to collaborating with one another in a culture that promotes inquiry-based teaching and learning. And unlike Jeff, many educational leaders do not credit district-wide support for the success of school-implemented initiatives.

Wahlstrom and colleagues (2010, p. 15) found that "school districts are able to influence teaching and learning, in part, through the contributions they make to positive feelings of efficacy on the part of school principals." In addition, they found that "district efforts had the greatest impact [on a principal's sense of efficacy] when they focused on developing the professional capacity of principals and teachers, and on creating supportive organizational conditions" (p. 16). A Comprehensive Accountability Framework supports educational leaders by outlining district-wide procedures and practices that promote collaboration, stimulate professional growth, and unite all stakeholders in a district toward the accomplishment of one vision—optimal student learning.

Overview of a Comprehensive Accountability Framework

A Comprehensive Accountability Framework includes several research-grounded components (see Exhibit 11.1) that are captured in a written document and involve all system-wide stakeholders in a mutual and dynamic exchange of ideas and concerns. This reciprocal interaction is intrinsic to an accountability framework. Richard Elmore (2002, p. 5) links this concept of reciprocity to accountability:

> For every increment of performance I demand from you, I have an equal responsibility to provide you with the capacity to meet that expectation. Likewise, for every investment you make in my skill and knowledge, I have a reciprocal responsibility to demonstrate some new increment in performance. This is the principle of "reciprocity of accountability for capacity." It is the glue that, in the final analysis, will hold accountability systems together.

EXHIBIT 11.1 A Comprehensive Accountability Framework: Transforming Teaching, Leading, and Learning

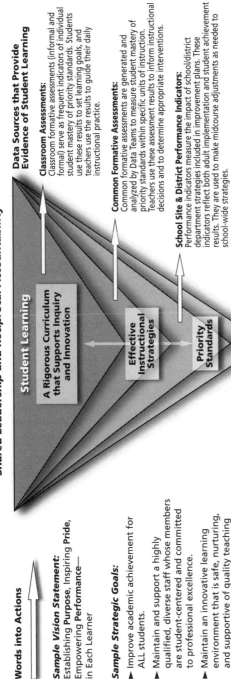

Shared Leadership and Reciprocal Accountability

Words into Actions

Sample Vision Statement:
Establishing Purpose, Inspiring Pride, Empowering Performance—in Each Learner

Sample Strategic Goals:

▶ Improve academic achievement for ALL students.

▶ Maintain and support a highly qualified, diverse staff whose members are student-centered and committed to professional excellence.

▶ Maintain an innovative learning environment that is safe, nurturing, and supportive of quality teaching and learning.

▶ Foster strong partnerships with parents and the community.

Student Learning

A Rigorous Curriculum that Supports Inquiry and Innovation

Effective Instructional Strategies ↔ Priority Standards

Data Sources that Provide Evidence of Student Learning

Classroom Assessments:
Classroom formative assessments (informal and formal) serve as frequent indicators of individual student mastery of priority standards. Students use these results to set learning goals, and teachers use the results to guide their daily instructional practice.

Common Formative Assessments:
Common formative assessments are generated and analyzed by Data Teams to measure student mastery of priority standards within specific units of instruction. Teachers use these assessment results to inform instructional decisions and to determine appropriate interventions.

School Site & District Performance Indicators:
Performance indicators measure the impact of school/district department strategies included in improvement plans. These indicators reflect both adult implementation and student achievement results. They are used to make midcourse adjustments as needed to school-wide strategies.

System-Wide Performance Indicators:
State or provincial assessments and other large-scale indicators measure the district's progress toward the achievement of system-wide strategic goals.

PRIMARY COMPONENTS INCLUDED IN THE FRAMEWORK

Improvement Plans	Data Teams	Evaluation System	Rigorous Curriculum	Professional Development	Communication Protocols	Reward and Support Plan
Robust school and district improvement templates and guidelines are provided in the Framework. These guidelines are grounded in the categories from The Leadership and Learning Center's research-based Planning, Implementation and Monitoring™ Rubric.	Data Teams are collaborative teacher-based teams that are described in the Framework. They design and implement scaffolded units of instruction; they also generate and analyze common formative assessments aligned with these units of instruction in order to determine student mastery of standards.	Precise procedures for dynamic, multidimensional teaching and leadership evaluation systems are described in the Framework. These systems include performance continuums, professional growth plans, and coaching protocols.	The Framework describes the dimensions of a rigorous curriculum which is anchored on prioritized standards. The curriculum includes formal and informal assessments, suggests effective research-based strategies, develops units of study that follow logical learning progression, and embeds differentiated learning experiences.	The Framework provides guidance for deeply embedded professional development practices that include theoretical knowledge, modeling, practice, feedback, reteaching and coaching.	The Framework guides specifically outlined procedures for frequent and effective communication (internal and external) focused on school and district progress.	The Framework provides specific criteria and protocols for recognizing and guiding the effective implementation of strategies to ensure the achievement of goals.

Elmore's principle of reciprocity is woven into a Comprehensive Accountability Framework through the processes that stimulate engagement between stakeholders, the practices that foster mutual support, and the structures that build leadership capacity.

This principle of reciprocity is apparent in the words of educational leader John Van Pelt, the superintendent of District 41 in Lake Villa, Illinois. District 41 successfully implemented its Comprehensive Accountability Framework in 2008. The district has continued to enjoy academic growth and professional success through this work. Van Pelt (personal communication, December 30, 2010) explains:

> Our Comprehensive Accountability Plan aligns planning, implementation, and reporting into a single process where teaching and learning remain the focus. This makes sense to staff. It is our mission. If we don't get this done the rest doesn't matter. Leadership is about keeping the focus on classrooms, developing and supporting the staff, and increasing learning and achievement. Our Comprehensive Accountability Plan helps get this accomplished.

Like Van Pelt, Olwen Herron, the chief academic officer in Fort Bend Independent School District in Sugar Land, Texas, has firsthand experience with the development and implementation of a Comprehensive Accountability Framework. Fort Bend is also demonstrating impressive academic growth. Herron (personal communication, January 3, 2010) focuses on the connectivity inherent in the district's Comprehensive Accountability Framework:

> A comprehensive accountability system provides a framework for collecting and analyzing data at all levels of the organization in order to make sound instructional decisions. With the systemic perspective created in the framework, all continuous improvement processes become aligned and implemented to high levels due to continuous monitoring of results and the connection between results and practices. The framework becomes a structure for holding it all together as we seek to continuously improve!

In both District 41 and Fort Bend Independent School District, their Comprehensive Accountability Frameworks have unified the districts' schools, leading to a common focus and greater academic success. These districts can both be described as "tightly coupled" in their focus on student learning, whereby each district and its schools work together, unified under a single vision and common goals. In *Getting Serious about School Reform: Three Critical Commitments*, Robert Marzano (2008, p. 2) notes that the historical structure of schools "might be characterized as 'loosely coupled'—individual schools within a district and individual teachers within a school operate in total autonomy and isolation." Marzano states that "until districts and schools become 'tightly coupled' regarding student achievement, they cannot be thought of as serious about school reform" (p. 2). A Comprehensive Accountability Framework fosters a sense of reciprocal accountability and ensures that districts and schools align their focus, providing all district leaders with a supportive system that facilitates learning success for all.

Designing a Comprehensive Accountability Framework

In each district, the composition of a Comprehensive Accountability Framework is led by a design team, a district-wide group of stakeholders composed of school board members, community leaders, parents, administrators, and teachers (including union leaders). This diverse representation ensures multiple viewpoints, legitimizes the work, secures a level of readiness and a sense of shared responsibility, and stimulates momentum for change.

To begin its task, the design team initially determines guiding principles through which it will continually filter the framework. The following principles and definitions are samples of those often selected by design teams:

- **Sustainability:** The Comprehensive Accountability Framework is designed to consistently guide the district even as changes occur in personnel and policy.

- **Respect for diversity:** The Comprehensive Accountability Framework includes multiple measures of student achievement, some of which apply to all schools, some of which apply to individual schools, and some of which apply to central office departments.

- **Feedback for continuous improvement:** The Comprehensive Accountability Framework includes indicators that emphasize student achievement and requires the use of results to make informed decisions about areas for improvement and new initiatives.

- **Connectivity:** The Comprehensive Accountability Framework ensures that schools and central office departments share information with one another about their improvement efforts and the impact of their strategies.

- **Fairness:** The Comprehensive Accountability Framework is structured so that everyone knows the "rules of the game" and that all schools and departments have the opportunity to play by the same rules.

These guiding principles establish the level of rigor to which the design team holds itself in creating its framework.

Although each district design team customizes the framework that it will use as its guide for system-wide improvement, the following components are most often addressed:

1. System-wide vision and strategic goal statements

2. Multiple indicators of student learning

3. Robust school and district improvement protocols and templates grounded in The Leadership and Learning Center's Planning, Implementation, and Monitoring research

4. Thorough Data Team guidelines and protocols ensuring district-wide implementation and support

5. Evaluation protocols for educators that are supportive, are based on clear standards, and include professional growth plans

6. Clearly stated requirements for research-based professional development practices

7. Vital internal and external district and school communication requirements

8. Specific guidelines for resource management that support the achievement of strategic goals

9. Meaningful reward and support structures that uphold the framework

10. Precise timelines that pace the implementation of the components contained in the accountability framework (see Exhibit 11.1)

For the purposes of this discussion on the impact of a Comprehensive Accountability Framework to provide support for system-wide leadership that is shared and instructionally focused, the following sections primarily concentrate on the first four components of the framework: system-wide vision and strategic goals, indicators of student learning, improvement plan guidelines and templates, and the Data Teams process.

System-Wide Vision and Strategic Goals

To begin the cycle of continuous improvement, it is essential that everyone in the organization share a system-wide vision and strategic goals. When determining a vision, it is important to have a statement that is succinct and meaningful. Long vision descriptions that members of the organization cannot remember or connect with do not elicit action. Clear visions and strategic goals unite people helping to direct, align, and inspire action. In *Leading Change*, John Kotter (1996, p. 7) points out that, "Without an appropriate vision, a transformation effort can easily dissolve into a list of confusing, incompatible, and time-consuming projects that go in the wrong direction or nowhere at all."

John Hunter, the assistant superintendent of Valley Central School District in Montgomery, New York, attests to the power of a Comprehensive Accountability Framework/Plan to operationalize a vision. Valley Central developed and successfully implemented its Comprehensive Accountability Plan in 2007. Hunter (personal communication, December 29, 2010) states,

> Just about everything you read about leadership speaks to having a clear vision or expectations for your organization or school. Vision statements have been written for years but are useless unless action is taken to implement whatever the vision states. The Comprehensive Accountability Plan provides a framework that enables teachers, administrators, and board of education members to identify the goals that support their vision and to establish specific action plans to accomplish their goals.

Strategic goals are general, long-term targets that express what an organization wants to achieve in alignment with its vision. Strategic goals are the end toward which all effort is directed, and they provide unifying targets toward which all plans are designed and actions are measured. In a Comprehensive Accountability Framework, system-wide indicators are selected that measure the district's progress toward reaching the strategic goals. In turn, goals, strategies, and indicators included in school and central office department improvement plans are designed to align with district-wide strategic goals and indicators, creating a circular relationship and thus a continuum of improvement.

Not only does this alignment demonstrate a district's commitment for improvement, but it also supports educational leaders in their efforts to unify the members of their staff toward a common focus. In the final report for *Learning from Leadership*, Louis, Leithwood, Wahlstrom, and Anderson (2010) show that school leaders who believe themselves to be working collaboratively toward clear, common goals with district personnel, other principals, and teachers in their schools are more confident in their leadership.

Indicators of Student Learning

The words in vision statements focused on improved student learning are put into action through a rigorous curriculum that is anchored in prioritized standards; well-designed units of instruction with appropriate learning progressions; research-based, differentiated instructional strategies; and formal and informal assessments. Collecting, analyzing, and acting on these assessment results are at the heart of a Comprehensive Accountability Framework. It is through evidence of student learning that educational organizations determine whether they are moving toward the accomplishment of their strategic goals for improved student achievement. In addition, analyzing data about student learning helps educators to openly evaluate the efficacy of their teaching and leadership practices so that they can make the necessary adjustments. In order to maximize the effectiveness of this analysis, leaders must establish a culture of trust.

In a case study conducted by Park and Datnow (2009, p. 483) on "exploring the connections among system and school-level leadership practices and activities that supported data-driven decision making," the researchers point out that successful school systems in their study examined data about their effectiveness in a nonevaluative manner. This approach allowed data about school and district effectiveness to be discussed openly in a setting of trust and support. Instead of placing blame, educators in this setting looked for solutions and embraced their opportunity for continuous improvement. This constructive and open approach to viewing data is foundational to a Comprehensive Accountability Framework.

Murry Schekman is the assistant superintendent for Secondary Education for the Pajaro Valley Unified School District in Watsonville, California. Schekman (personal communication, December 29, 2010) focuses on the impressive and effective district-wide response to data:

> A Comprehensive Accountability Framework has School
> Site Councils reviewing data, faculty meetings reviewing
> data and sharing best instructional practices, and our
> support staff fully understanding their role with regard

to student learning, including the secretaries and custo-
dial staff, as another example. It is all about leadership to
be able to take so many stakeholders to that place where
student learning is dissected and then followed up with
resources and effective instruction because ultimately,
everything that we do in a school district is focused on
student learning.

As Schekman aptly points out, an accountability framework supports the analysis of data system-wide. This comprehensive focus on
studying the evidence of student learning can be organized in categories moving from system-wide data to the most granular student
classroom assessment results. The four main categories of data are
system-wide performance indicators, school and central office performance indicators, Data Team common formative assessments, and
classroom assessments (see Exhibit 11.2).

- **System-wide performance indicators:** These indicators are
  selected by the design team for each strategic goal.
  Improving the results of these measures is the responsibility
  of everyone in the system. In *Accountability in Action*,
  Douglas Reeves (2004, p. 115) defines these system-wide
  indicators as "measures of educational performance that are
  used by every building in the system. They represent the core
  values of stakeholders, those 'non-negotiables' that must be
  measured and considered at every grade level in every
  school."

- **School and central office performance indicators:** These
  performance indicators measure the impact of implemented
  strategies at each school site and within district departments. Both adult actions and student results are measured
  by these performance indicators. At schools, the indicators
  may include the results of school-wide or Data Team
  assessments as well as the percentage of teachers who are
  implementing a determined strategy with fidelity. In district
  departments, the indicators may include data collected

Building Data-Rich Cultures

A Systems Approach to Aligning Standards and Indicators in Districts, Schools, and Classrooms

School systems collect and analyze data on a variety of levels, from general to specific, from comprehensive state tests to individual classroom assessments. Educators must align and focus this influx of data so that all stakeholders can use the information from key data indicators to make sound instructional decisions that positively impact individual student learning.

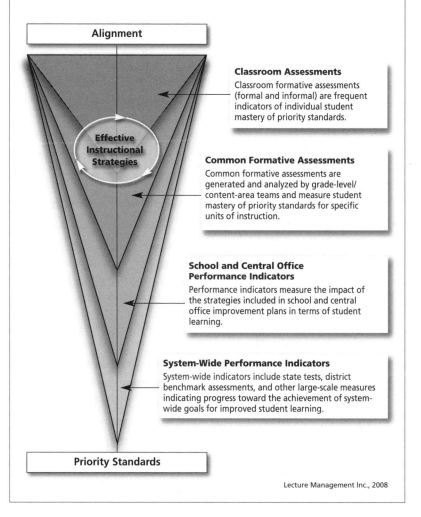

Alignment

Effective Instructional Strategies

Classroom Assessments

Classroom formative assessments (formal and informal) are frequent indicators of individual student mastery of priority standards.

Common Formative Assessments

Common formative assessments are generated and analyzed by grade-level/content-area teams and measure student mastery of priority standards for specific units of instruction.

School and Central Office Performance Indicators

Performance indicators measure the impact of the strategies included in school and central office improvement plans in terms of student learning.

System-Wide Performance Indicators

System-wide indicators include state tests, district benchmark assessments, and other large-scale measures indicating progress toward the achievement of system-wide goals for improved student learning.

Priority Standards

Lecture Management Inc., 2008

about the timeliness of completed work orders or the on-time and safe delivery of students to school. These indicators are viewed frequently in order to determine necessary midcourse corrections (Kamm, 2010, p.162).

• **Data Team common formative assessments:** Common formative assessments are generated and analyzed by Data Teams—grade-level and content-area teams of teachers—to measure student mastery of priority standards within specific units of instruction. The results of these assessments are viewed collaboratively by the Data Teams and are used to guide the implementation of effective instructional strategies that ensure learning for all students (Kamm, 2010, p. 163).

• **Classroom assessments:** Classroom formative assessments (informal and formal) are generated by teachers and serve as frequent indicators of individual student mastery of priority standards. The results of these indicators are used to inform instruction and to guide students as they set personal goals for deeper learning (Kamm, 2010, p. 163).

Hope Stuart, the principal of Berea Elementary School in Montgomery, New York, has enjoyed the benefits of being a leader in a district with a well-established accountability system focused on the effective analysis of data at all levels. Stuart (personal communication, January 1, 2011) shares her observations of the impact of data to inform the decision of the teacher leaders in her school:

Now that our teachers at Berea Elementary School are using deliberate data, they are able to monitor learning on a daily basis in order to make necessary adjustments and plan for future instruction in a timely manner. Our deliberate data endeavors have minimized the length of time it takes to obtain data and have maximized our teachers' ability to analyze learning and adjust instruction. The essence of a Comprehensive Accountability Framework inspires all stakeholders to become instructional leaders. This inspiration fosters a self-sustaining focus on academic excellence that nurtures lifelong learning in our teachers, which ensures all our students reap the rewards of this cyclical process.

Improvement Plan Guidelines and Templates

Current research on educational leadership has moved away from a focus on individual leaders occupying specific roles to an emphasis on sharing leadership practices, expertise, and action (Elmore, 2002; Harris, 2007). A Comprehensive Accountability Framework supports shared leadership by emphasizing the importance of purposeful collaboration focused on complete implementation and frequent monitoring of research-based strategies by every member of the staff.

Within the structure of a Comprehensive Accountability Framework, improvement plans are generated, monitored, and adjusted by each school and each central office department. As Elmore aptly notes, successful school reform begins with teachers, administrators, and school staff, not with external mandates. In *School Reform from the Inside Out* (2006), he captures the intent of the continuous improvement process inherent in a Comprehensive Accountability Framework. He states that the way to school reform is in "enhancing the skills and knowledge of the people in the organization, creating a common culture of expectations around the use of those skills and knowledge, holding the various pieces of the organization together in a productive relationship with each other, and holding individuals accountable for their contributions to the collective result" (p. 59).

In a Comprehensive Accountability Framework, the development and implementation of improvement plans are grounded in the Planning, Implementation, and Monitoring (PIM™) protocol developed and researched by The Leadership and Learning Center (see Exhibit 11.3). Each accountability design team builds its improvement templates and writes guidelines based on the PIM™ research and specific to its state or provincial requirements. The guidelines that accompany the improvement plan templates suggest a narrow focus on no more than a few goals and strategies. There is also an emphasis on aligning

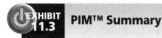

EXHIBIT 11.3   PIM™ Summary

Please note that the following category descriptions only provide a general overview of the much more specific PIM™ rubric created by The Leadership and Learning Center.

Planning

Comprehensive Needs Analysis—A systematic and comprehensive analysis of the school's instructional and organizational effectiveness (strengths and weaknesses) provides the foundation for the school improvement plan.

Inquiry Process—Cause and effect relationships are determined and the correlation between needs and strategies is identified. The focus is on a few vital issues that will have the biggest impact on student achievement. Root causes are routinely identified and addressed.

Specific Objectives (Goals)—SMART Goals guide school improvement: Specific, Measurable, Achievable, Relevant, and Timely.

Implementation

Targeted Research-Based Strategies—All strategies are grounded in sound research, and evidence demonstrates how strategies will support improved achievement. All strategies directly impact student learning.

Parental Engagement—The plan identifies frequent (beyond traditional grading periods) empowering ways to include parents in improving student achievement. The plan also identifies and matches areas where parents might need training and education, and differentiates the provision of that training to meet the needs of parents and their children.

Master Plan Design—A limited number of action steps are indicated and clear. Timelines are purposeful, and the capacity for midcourse corrections is indicated in the plan. Action steps designate the person(s) responsible, and necessary resources are clearly delineated.

Professional Development—Critical professional development strategies are aligned with school/district objectives. Teachers and administrators focus on effective instructional strategies that impact student achievement. There is a system in place for coaching/mentoring that sustains the selected strategies.

Monitoring Plan—The plan describes explicit steps for monitoring progress towards the attainment of ALL school objectives. Multiple forms of data to be collected are clearly explained. Key people are designated who will monitor activities. A process for midcourse corrections and for reporting progress to the staff is indicated in the plan.

Monitoring Frequency—The plan includes frequent monitoring of student achievement indicated by specific timelines. The monitoring schedule (> monthly) reviews both student performance and adult teaching practices.

Evaluation—The evaluation plan compares planned results with achieved outcomes and includes a specific improvement cycle. The plan describes how results and next steps will be communicated and distributed to all stakeholders.

Monitoring

plans for improvement with the district-wide strategic goals and indicators. For example, consider the Action and Monitoring Form from a section of a middle school improvement plan (see Exhibit 11.4).

Note that the measurements of effectiveness in this Action and Monitoring Form include both adult implementation indicators that measure the depth and fidelity of implementation and student results indicators that measure student learning. Reeves (2006) reminds educators that it is essential to monitor not only student results, *effect data,* but also adult actions, *cause data*: "Only by evaluating both causes and effects … can leaders, teachers, and policymakers understand the complexities of student achievement and the efficacy of teaching and leadership practices" (p. 132).

The improvement plan guidelines and templates that are incorporated into a Comprehensive Accountability Framework and aligned with PIM™ research are designed to build a common expectation for improved practice and, as a result, enhanced student learning. Within the construct of the improvement plans there are requirements for monthly monitoring of goals and strategies. The frequent monitoring stimulates midcourse improvements when the data collected indicates the need. The guidelines for improvement also specify that research-based strategies are collaboratively selected based on the analysis of performance data and that the selected strategies are implemented by all members of the staff with fidelity. Under this structure, all members of the staff are accountable for leading the continuous improvement initiatives. The practices supported by improvement plan guidelines and templates build a culture of school and district reform "from the inside out."

In "What Do We Already Know about Educational Leadership?" Leithwood and Riehl (2005, p. 13) remind leaders that they are responsible for "mobilizing and influencing others to articulate and achieve the school's shared intentions and goals." Hall and Hord (2006, p. 193) note that leaders of effective change decrease the isolation of the staff, build its collective capacity, nurture positive relationships, and impel "the unceasing quest for increased effectiveness so that students benefit." Through the guidelines and templates embed-

EXHIBIT 11.4	**Action and Monitoring Form from a Middle School Improvement Plan**

DISTRICT-WIDE GOAL	Improve academic achievement for ALL students.
DISTRICT-WIDE PERFORMANCE INDICATOR	Percentage of students scoring proficient or above in writing on state assessments.
SCHOOL SITE OR DISTRICT DEPARTMENT SMART GOAL	The percent of students scoring proficient and above on non-fiction writing assessments will increase from 53% to 65% as measured on the district's writing assessment given in March 2010.
RESEARCH-BASED STRATEGY (Include differentiation to ensure access for targeted student populations)	Implement non-fiction writing with fidelity in each content area minimally three times per grading period. Use the district-wide writing rubric and anchor papers to guide scoring. The faculty collaboratively scores writing samples. Teachers provide specific and timely feedback to each student about their writing progress building in time for revisions and additional feedback.
	Differentiation to ensure access for targeted student populations:
	Emphasize pre-writing strategies for EL students, continuously checking for understanding, and build from oral language to print according to individual English proficiency levels.
DATA TEAM IMPLEMENTATION (Explain how Data Teams implement and measure school-wide strategies)	Each content area Data Team will build non-fiction writing experiences into units of instruction, minimally three times each quarter. Core area Data Teams will report the scores of the final non-fiction writing assessments to the principal at the end of each quarter. All Data Teams will use the district writing rubric to guide scoring.

PERFORMANCE INDICATORS AND DATA SOURCES	
ADULT IMPLEMENTATION INDICATOR (Cause Data)	**STUDENT PERFORMANCE INDICATOR (Effect Data)**
Increase the percent of teachers providing their students with quality nonfiction writing experiences, where writing is scored using a common rubric and feedback is provided to each student with multiple opportunities for students to revise and improve their work.	Increase the percent of students scoring proficient or above on quarterly non-fiction writing assessments (disaggregated by subgroups).
Data Source: Lesson plans, scores submitted to principal, and sample student work Learning Walk Observations	**Data Source:** Assessments given and scored (using district rubric) in each core class and reported to principal on district data site

ded within a Comprehensive Accountability Framework, leadership is shared and focused on continuous improvement so that student learning flourishes.

The Data Teams Process

Data Teams continue this tradition of shared leadership focused on student learning to an even more granular level. In addition to focusing on school-wide improvement goals and strategies, Data Teams concentrate on student learning within each standards-based unit of instruction. Data Teams are the epicenter of a Comprehensive Accountability Framework.

Data Teams are grade-level or content-area teams of teachers, usually from within a school, who meet frequently (at least twice monthly) to formatively analyze assessment results and to use those results to improve their instruction. These highly organized teams follow a cycle of meetings that revolve around a six-step process:

1. Collect and chart data
2. Analyze student performance strengths, errors, and misconceptions
3. Set, review, and revise incremental learning goals
4. Select and implement effective instructional strategies
5. Determine results indicators to measure student learning progress
6. Monitor and evaluate learning results

Through their actions, Data Teams build strong professional communities that inspire collaboration, ensure student learning success, and promote shared leadership. In the final report for their study *Learning from Leadership*, Louis and colleagues (2010) found that professional communities encourage teachers to become leaders. From their research, these scholars drew the following conclusions about shared leadership and student learning (Wahlstrom et al., 2010, p. 10):

• When principals and teachers share leadership, teachers'

working relationships are stronger and student achievement is higher.

• Leadership effects on student learning occur largely because leadership strengthens professional community; teachers' engagement in professional community, in turn, fosters the use of instructional practices that are associated with student achievement.

• The professional community effect may reflect the creation of a supportive school climate that encourages student effort above and beyond that provided in individual classrooms.

Within a Comprehensive Accountability Framework, Data Teams build shared leadership that in turn supports instructional leadership. John Hunter (personal communication, December 29, 2010), the assistant superintendent from Valley Central School District, writes,

"The establishment of Data Teams tied to a structure that enables them to develop specific plans to improve instruction works." Hunter goes on to say, "Data analysis, by itself, will not improve student outcomes unless action is taken upon what was learned. The Comprehensive Accountability Plan provides that structure."

Celebrating a Comprehensive Accountability Framework

In *How Leadership Influences Student Learning*, Leithwood, Louis, Anderson, and Wahlstrom (2004, p. 9) point out that:

Successful educational leaders develop their districts and schools as effective organizations that support and sustain the performance of administrators and teachers, as well as students. Specific practices typically associated with this set of basics include strengthening district and school cultures, modifying organizational structures, and building collaborative processes.

The insight offered by Leithwood and colleagues comes to fruition for districts and schools that have implemented a well-designed Comprehensive Accountability Framework. In referring to both the research of scholars and the rich experience of practitioners, it is clear that an accountability framework supports leadership as a shared practice where the continuous improvement of teaching and learning is celebrated.

A prime example of this celebration is captured in a recent e-mail from Murry Schekman, the assistant superintendent for Secondary Education in the Pajaro Valley Unified School District. Through the development and consistent, reflective implementation of a Comprehensive Accountability Framework, the school district is enjoying improved student academic performance. In his e-mail Scheckman (personal communication, September 24, 2010) expresses his excitement about the district-wide Data Fair—data displays focused on strategies and results—hosted for the district's board of education:

> Three principals shared their schools' outcomes and then we adjourned so the Board could walk around and see data boards from each school. After about 30 minutes the Board came back in session. I expected some questions, but they had none. All they could do was congratulate our staff-teachers, administrators, parents, support staff, and kids. They were moved that so many different factions in our district are part of this [accountability] process now. We're a district that historically has struggled with implementation. But we kept the course and are continuing to do so ... expanding to include more teachers in leadership positions within our Data Teams. So, it's been a glorious week, and we feel quite proud for the outcomes our kids are experiencing. Today's session was with secondary folks, and they wouldn't break for lunch because they were so engaged.

A Comprehensive Accountability Framework builds a culture of inquiry in which all members of the organization are united by a common vision realized through shared leadership, aligned goals, deliberate analysis of data, rich collaborative processes, and an unwavering commitment to continuous improvement.

References

Augustine, C. H., Gonzalez, G., Ikemoto, G. S., Russell, J., Zellman, G. L., & Constant, L. (2009). *Improving school leadership: The promise of cohesive leadership systems.* Santa Monica, CA: RAND.

Council of Chief State School Officers. (2008). Educational leadership policy standards: ISLLC 2008. Retrieved from http://www.ccsso.org/ Documents/2008/Educational_Leadership_Policy_Standards_2008.pdf

Elmore, R. F. (2002). *Bridging the gap between standards and achievement: The imperative for professional development in education.* Washington, DC: Albert Shanker Institute.

Elmore, R. F. (2006). *School reform from the inside out: Policy, practice, and performance.* Cambridge, MA: Harvard Education Press.

Hall, G. E., & Hord, S. M. (2006). *Implementing change: Patterns, principles, and potholes* (2nd ed.). Boston, MA: Pearson.

Harris, A. (2007). Distributed leadership: Conceptual confusion and empirical reticence. *International Journal of Leadership in Education 10*(3), 1–11.

Hattie, J. (2009). *Visible learning: A synthesis of over 800 meta-analyses relating to achievement.* New York, NY: Routledge.

Kamm, C. (2010). Accountability and the data teams process. In *Data Teams: The big picture* (pp. 159–174). Englewood, CO: Lead + Learn Press.

Kotter, J. P. (1996). Transforming organizations: Why firms fail. In J. P. Kotter, *Leading change* (pp. 3–16). Boston, MA: Harvard Business School Press.

Leithwood, K., Louis, K. S., Anderson, S., & Wahlstrom, K. (2004). *How leadership influences student learning. Review of research.* Retrieved from http://www.wallacefoundation.org/KnowledgeCenter/KnowledgeTopics/ CurrentAreasofFocus/EducationLeadership/Pages/HowLeadership InfluencesStudentLearning.aspx

Leithwood, K. A., & Riehl. C. (2005). What do we already know about educational leadership? In W. A. Firestone and C. Riehl (Eds.), *A new agenda for research in educational leadership* (pp. 12–27). New York, NY: Teachers College Press.

Louis, K. S., Leithwood, K., Wahlstrom, K., & Anderson, S. E. (2010). *Learning from leadership: Investigating the links to improved student learning—final report of research findings.* Retrieved from http://www.wallacefoundation.org/KnowledgeCenter/KnowledgeTopics/CurrentAreasofFocus/EducationLeadership/Documents/Learning-from-Leadership-Investigating-Links-Final-Report.pdf

Marzano, R. J. (2008). *Getting serious about school reform: Three critical commitments.* Centennial, CO: Marzano and Associates.

Marzano, R. J., Waters, T., & McNulty, B. A. (2005). *School leadership that works: From research to results.* Alexandria, VA: ASCD.

Park, V., & Datnow, A. (2009). Co-constructing distributed leadership: District and school connections in data-driven decision making. *School Leadership & Management, 29*(5), 477–494.

Reeves, D. B. (2004). *Accountability in action: A blueprint for learning organizations* (2nd ed.). Denver, CO: Advanced Learning Press.

Reeves, D. B. (2006). *The learning leader.* Alexandria, VA: ASCD.

Robinson, V. M. J., Lloyd, C. A., & Rowe, K. J. (2008). The impact of leadership on student outcomes: An analysis of the differential effects of leadership types. *Educational Administration Quarterly, 44*(5), 635–674.

Seashore, K. R. (2009). Leadership and change in schools: Personal reflections over the last 30 years. *Journal of Educational Change, 10*(2/3), 129–140.

Wahlstrom, K., Louis, K. S., Leithwood, K., & Anderson, S. E. (2010). *Learning from leadership: Investigating the links to improved student learning—executive summary of research findings.* Retrieved from http://www.cehd.umn.edu/carei/Leadership/Learning-from-Leadership_Executive-Summary_July-2010.pdf

Index

Accepting, wanting and, 146–147
Accountability, xvii, xviii, 6, 9, 29, 44, 101, 105, 194, 220, 225, 231, 237, 239; celebrating, 242–244; collective, 189; comprehensive, 228; demands for, 85; effective, 84; establishing, 191, 236; external, 82; framework for, 234; internal, 82, 84, 85; leadership and, 243; learning, 82–83; performance and, 84; plan, 70, 83; reciprocal, 83, 185, 188, 195, 226; shared, 82–84; shifting, 152, 187; soft, 144–145, 147; system for, 63
Accountability in Action (Reeves), 82, 234
Accountability Virus Infection Syndrome (AVIS), 4
Achievement, 13–14, 66, 85, 100, 101, 102, 103, 106, 108, 131, 133, 145, 146, 154, 209; expectations about, 94; impact on, 99, 134, 138, 220; improving, 25, 36, 71, 95, 123, 130, 142, 233; influences on, 112; leadership and, 220–223, 226; student, 12, 39, 48, 60, 66, 78, 94, 105, 113, 114, 134, 137, 138, 140, 141, 147, 151, 153, 165, 166 (exh.), 167, 188–193, 221, 229, 239, 242; teaching and, 69, 140
Achievement gaps, 6, 60, 67, 138,139
Action, 21, 36, 40, 84, 113; asking for, 31, 32–33; high-impact, 32, 33, 38–40; plans, xv, 14–15, 33, 151; teaching, 173, 182; theory of, 97, 109, 135, 137–138, 144, 147
Action and Monitoring Form, 239, 240 (exh.)
Administrators, 13, 70, 194; coaching by, 26; identification/promotion of, 72
Advanced Placement, 6, 139
Alliance for Excellent Education, xiii
American Recovery and Reinvestment Act (2009), 60
America's Best High Schools List (*Newsweek*), 66
Analysis, 39, 112, 174, 184, 223; critical, 101; data, 12, 15, 59, 63, 77–81, 99, 103, 138, 151, 154, 159, 184, 219, 233, 242, 244; effective, 236; word, 159
Art, 46, 131
Assessments, 12, 64, 78, 180, 201; adopting, 60; analyzing, 233; appropriate, 104; classroom, 234, 236; conducting, 209–211, 216–217; data from, 219; as feedback, 114; formative, 11, 58, 78, 105, 138, 233; high-stakes, 138; inferences and, 159; informal, 233; math, 104 (exh.); school-wide, 234; summative, 11, 159 (exh.). *See also* Common Formative Assessments
Assignment menu, 75, 76 (exh.)
Assistant principals (APs), 17, 18
Attitudes, 39, 45, 47, 108, 114, 216
Australian National Assessment Program—Language and Numeracy, 112

B3 Leaders, 123, 127, 130, 131; purpose/meaning and, 121, 128; risk/value and, 120, 121, 124
Bach, Johann Sebastian, 119, 120, 121, 122–123, 124, 125, 128
BDTs. *See* Building-level Data Teams
Beethoven, Ludwig van, 119, 120, 121, 124–125, 128

Behavior, 20, 21, 58; change in, 45, 47, 51, 204; influencing, 52, 53; leadership, 19, 52, 223; teaching, 13, 154, 158, 160
Bennis, Warren, 15
Besser, Laura, 189, 192, 195
Block scheduling, 58–59
Blues artists, 119, 120
Brophy, Jere E., 18, 19
Building a New Structure for School Leadership (Elmore), 72
Building-level Data Teams (BDTs), 174, 175, 176, 180, 184, 185, 187, 190, 194; establishment of, 188; principals and, 191

California School Leadership Academy, 7
California's Academic Performance Index, 5
Campsen, Lauren, 81
Capacity building, 73, 189, 192, 195, 228
Career interests, 69, 77, 85
CCSS. *See* Common Core State Standards
Center for Organizational Learning, 9
Center for Performance Assessment, 5
Certification Training, 5
Challenges, 40, 54, 64, 66, 72, 81, 99, 100, 187; meeting, 59, 119
Change, xiii, 6, 22, 27, 37, 47, 49, 51, 53, 106–107, 108, 128, 139, 173, 183, 216, 229, 227 (exh.); achieving, 209; actions/benefits and, 21; adapting to, 58–59, 172; casual, 109; characteristics of, 207, 208; commitment to, 123; demonstrating, 186; dramatic, 203, 205, 210; effective, 204, 239; in grading, 36, 202; impediments to, xv, 3, 21; implementing, xiv, xviii, 3, 7, 45, 52, 136, 148, 179, 202, 206, 207, 208, 210, 217; improvement and, 133, 172; leadership and, xvii, 7–9, 44, 171, 211; leading, 4, 11, 18–19; need for, 5, 209, 211; perfection vs., 123; problems with, 203, 204–205; proposed, 205, 210, 216; radical, 121–122; readiness for, xviii, 205–208; resistance to, 21; risks of, 124; secrets of, 8–9, 15; stakeholders and, 209, 217; successful, 9, 187, 194; sustained, 204, 206; willingness for, 211
Change Leadership (Wagner and Kegen), xvii
Change Readiness Assessment, xviii, 208–211, 216–217
Change Readiness Continuum, 211, 213 (exh.)
Change Readiness Continuum Rubric, 211, 213 (exh.), 214 (exh.)
Change Readiness Focus Group, starter questions for, 212 (exh.)
Chauncey, Caroline, 84
Chenoweth, Karen, 63
Childress, Stacey, 84
Christy, Chris, 61
Churchill, Winston, 127, 128
Civil Rights Movement, 126, 127
Classroom observations, 46, 221, 222